MY YEAR 2012:
CENTERS COLLAPSE

SELECTED BOOKS BY THE AUTHOR

POETRY

Dinner on the Lawn (1979, 1982)
Some Distance (1982)
River to Rivet: A Manifesto (1984)
Maxims from My Mother's Milk/Hymns to Him: A Dialogue (1985)
Along Without: A Fiction for Film in Poetry (1993)
After (1998)
Bow Down (2002)
First Words (2004)
Dark (2012)
Stay (2018)

PROSE

Letters from Hanusse (2000)
Reading Films: My International Cinema (2012)
My Year 2000: Leaving Something Behind (2017)
My Year 2001: Keeping History a Secret (2016)
My Year 2002: Love, Death, and Transfiguration (2015)
My Year 2003: Voice Without a Voice (2013)
My Year 2004: Under Our Skin (2008)
My Year 2005: Terrifying Times (2006)
My Year 2006: Serving (2009)
My Year 2007: To the Dogs (2015)
My Year 2008: In the Gap (2015)
My Year 2009: Facing the Heat (2016)
My Year 2010: Shadows (2017)
My Year 2011: No One's Home (2018)
My Year 2012: Centers Collapse (2019)

My Year 2012:

Centers Collapse

READINGS
EVENTS
MEMORIES

by
Douglas Messerli

GREEN INTEGER
KØBENHAVN & LOS ANGELES
2019

GREEN INTEGER
Edited by Per Bregne
København / Los Angeles
(323) 937-3783 / www.greeninteger.com

Distributed in the United States by
Consortium Book Sales & Distribution / Ingram Books
(800) 283-3572 / www.cbsd.com

First Green Integer Edition 2019
Copyright ©2019 by Douglas Messerli
Essays in this volume have previously appeared in
EXPORING fictions, *Green Integer Blog, Green Integer Review,
My International Cinema, Nth Position* [England], *Or, Rain Taxi,
The Supplement to the Bulletin of the Maryland Writers Council,
USTheater, Opera, and Performance, World Cinema Review*

Design: Per Bregne
Typography: Pablo Capra
Cover photographs (clockwise, from top left):
Elizabeth Bowen, Samuel Beckett, Stephen Sondheim, Tennessee Williams

LIBRARY OF CONGRESS CATALOGING-IN-PUBLICATION DATA
Douglas Messerli [1947]
My Year 2012: Centers Collapse
ISBN: 978-1-55713-445-5
p. cm – Green Integer 267
I. Title II. Series

Green Integer books are published for Douglas Messerli
Printed in Canada

Table of Contents

Standing Alone: An Introduction

THROUGHOUT THE PLAYS, films, operas, books, and events I encountered in 2012 there seemed to be an individual (or small group of individuals) who suddenly found himself without a roof over his head or, at least, in a world that seemed to suggest an apocalyptic landscape that held out little hope for the future. The figure might still be able to sing "I'm Still Here," as did the former Goldman girl, Carlotta, in Stephen Sondheim's *Follies*; or the character might stand still waiting for the impossible to arrive, as in Beckett's *Waiting for Godot*; the utterly abused and sexually transformed survivor of Pedro Almodóvar's *The Skin I Live In* was able even to return home and declare his true identity. But none of these figures had delusions any longer that things were in order. Everything around them, seemingly, had gone sour. "Something Bad is Happening," as Dr. Charlotte warned in William Finn's and James Lapine's *Falsettos*.

Children were running away from home—and with good reason, suggested Wes Anderson in his *Moonrise Kingdom*. The government was spying upon its citizens argued Clint Eastwood in his *J. Edgar*. Or the government had so failed it citizens that it hardly mattered anymore, as Russell Banks suggested in his novel *Lost Memory of Skin*. The entire world seemed to have been turned upside down. Hard workers like Willy Loman in *Death of a Salesman* ended up with nothing to show for it, having failed in their attempts to achieve the American Dream. Although people talked a lot, what they said had little meaning—an idea I explored in the several dialogue novels I taught to my students at Otis College of Art. In Richard Linklater's comical recounting of a popular East Texas undertaker, Bernie Tiede almost got away with murder.

Indeed, a number of movies I explored created imaginary landscapes that questioned the very existence of any coherent meaning. It was, after all, a time in which the United States Congress and Senate chose not to pass any major legislation. Although President Obama was reelected, he was left with the inability to pass any major elements of his agenda. And as the voting revealed, the US was a nation more divided than it had been in decades. The center, whatever one defined as being central to one's life, seemed to have collapsed. The world suddenly seemed to exist only in extremes.

There were moments of sanity, of course. Some people not only survived, but learned from their bleak experiences. One has only to watch Jafar Panahi's underground film of 2011 (shown in the US during this year), *This is Not a Film*, to realize that in such a world survival and creativity are still possible. Through some state referendums and the bravery of a few federal judges, gay marriage inched closer to becoming the law of the land. Sometimes things that might once have seemed insignificant suddenly appeared to be of great importance: a large rock was maneuvered through the Los Angeles streets to the wonder of nearly everyone to sit as a piece of art at the Los Angeles County Museum of Art. Some fictional figures simply bore with the suffering with which they were faced. And a great many figures opened their mouths to sing and laugh instead of to howl.

Yet we all knew by the end of 2012 that our once cherished institutions, the shared experiences we had so loved, the very casual intimacy with which we had previously spoken to our neighbors, was probably a thing of the past. Our sense of blissful balance had been, we now realized, just another grand illusion.

Fortunately I was personally offered love and support, as always, by a wide range of friends who came together from various viewpoints to encourage me to plod on in my nearly impossible endeavor to make sense of the first decades of the 21st century. Once more people such as Will Alexander, David and Eleanor Antin, Thérèse Bachand, Susan Bee, Charles Bernstein, Diana Daves, Rosemary DeRosa, Rebecca Goodman, Michael Govan, Dan Guerrero, Michael Heim, Roz Leader, Eric Lorberer, Deborah Meadows, Jim Morphesis, Martin Nakell, my Otis class of students, Marjorie Perloff, Nick Piombino, Pam and Charles Plymell, Toni Simon, Val Stevenson, Carol Tavris, Paul Vangelisti, and Mac Wellman helped me survive the collapsing world around me. Pablo Capra, as always, made this book readable and handsome to the eye. Howard Fox made my life possible.

Bad Day on the Seville Streets

LORENZO DA PONTE (LIBRETTO), WOLFGANG AMA-
DEUS MOZART (COMPOSER) **DON GIOVANNI** / LOS ANGE-
LES, LA OPERA AT THE DOROTHY CHANDLER PAVILION /
THE PERFORMANCE I ATTENDED WAS THE MATINEE ON
SUNDAY, SEPTEMBER 30, 2012

CERTAINLY THERE IS not much left to be said about Mozart's masterwork, *Don Giovanni*; and it seems almost pointless to attempt to write, accordingly, about the opera. But one thing struck me in this story about a very "bad" day in the life of Don Giovanni (Ildebrando D'Arcangelo) while watching the LA Opera version the other afternoon: except for a very few important scenes, this wealthy citizen of the upper class spends most of his time, like a vagabond, on the city streets. Indeed, one might almost describe the opera, metaphorically, as being like an intense Western, wherein the hero's luck has changed, as in *Bad Day at Black Rock*, where everything seems to be going against the already maimed man.

Of course, Don Giovanni is not really a hero. He begins by attempting to rape Donna Anna (Julianna Di Giacomo), who—either out of a desire to have him finish the job or to out the villain to others, we do not know which—tries to hold the man close to her, as if the victim cannot release herself from the offender. When her father, the Commendatore (Ievgen Orlov), comes to her rescue, dueling with the ruffian, Don Giovanni kills him. From that moment on Don Giovanni is doomed to remain on the streets, for the most part, on the run for his actions—while still absurdly attempting to seduce each woman he encounters along the way.

Because his life is so public, it is easy for his ex-wife, the furious Donna Elvira (Soile Isokoski), to find him. Indeed she is the very first person he encounters along his spiraling path down to hell. Donna Elvira is both a significant force against him—revealing Giovanni's horrible deeds to anyone who might listen—and a kind of comic figure, a spectre, appearing long before the Commendatore's final ghostly manifestation, that haunts him wherever he goes, as well as foils his attempts to seduce Zerlina (Roxana Constantinescu) and

her maid.

Twice during the long day on the road, however, Giovanni does return to his palatial estate, the first time to join in a drunken party he has ordered up so that he might get the men out of the way in order to bed Zerlina. Yet the sober and oafishly jealous Masetto stands in his way, while Zerlina herself—if at first all too ready to surrender to Giovanni's seductions—remains steadfast in her love for Masetto.

Again Giovanni takes to the street, this time, dressed as his servant Leporello, pretending to participate in a mad chase while really trying to save his own life. As the sun begins to sink, we still find him in a public space, in the cemetery where he encounters the

Commendatore's horrifying talking statue whom he flippantly invites to dinner.

While Giovanni is at risk for most of the day upon the streets, it is in his own home, as he sits down for a lonely dinner—even now torturing Leporello—where he is finally "captured" and brought to justice through the visitation of the Commendatore's apparition.

Hell, strangely enough (at least in the LA Opera version, based on the Lyric Opera of Chicago production), manifests itself in Giovanni's own dining room, not in the public square, suggesting that it is Giovanni's own private hell, not a spectacle of public proportions; only Leporello observes this event

Giovanni's punishment, however, has resulted

from all his *public* crimes, from his inability to remain alone but for a few moments each day. It is almost as if Giovanni will not even sleep, so determined is he to seek out and find new prey. If the final showdown occurs out of the public eye, it is only because Giovanni is most vulnerable in his own house, since public transgressions are what truly define who he is. A villainous gunslinger cannot play that role in a lonely farmhouse, just as a lascivious seducer cannot act out his identity in an empty estate. If the particular day Mozart and Da Ponte show us is the worst day of Giovanni's life, it is also—except for his murder of the Commendatore and his inability to seduce anyone—not much different from any other day; for Giovanni is a man doomed to roam Seville's public streets and squares instead of enjoying the private pleasures of a wealthy life.

LOS ANGELES, OCTOBER 4, 2012.
Reprinted from *Green Integer Review* (October 2012).

So are We All

LORENZO DA PONTE (TEXT), WOLFGANG AMADEUS MOZART (MUSIC) **COSÍ FAN TUTTE** / LOS ANGELES, LA OPERA AT THE DOROTHY CHANDLER PAVILION / THE PERFORMANCE I SAW WAS ON SUNDAY, OCTOBER 2, 2011

DESPITE THE OFTEN splendiferous musical beauty of Da Ponte's and Mozart's wise comic satire, there is something patently unfair about the major series of events. Yes, we easily conclude with Don Alfonso, "Women are like that," but so too, do we compre-hend, are men. And it is the men in this opera who truly step out of bounds in test-ing their sweethearts' faithfulness.

To be fair, the two young soldiers,

Ferrando (Saimir Pirgu in the production I saw) and Guglielmo (the handsome Ildebrando D'Arcangelo), begin the opera singing endless praises of their loves, Fiordiligi (Aleksandra Kurzak) and Dorabella (Ruxandra Donose). We immediately recognize their naiveté; and when I say *we*, I think I can speak for the whole of USA society given that the current divorce rate is 50% and rises substantially with second and third marriages. Although divorce may be caused by many things other than unfaithfulness, it appears that, in the US at least, Americans are fickle.

The young men are easily challenged. Their friend Don Alfonso (Lorenzo Regazzo), without much difficulty, convinces them to lie to their sweethearts by pretending to go off to war, and to themselves play cheats. After all, to dress up in the costumes of other men, taking on their very different personalities, and to court each other's fiancées certainly suggests that they are willing to be guilty of behavior they do not hope to find in their fiancées. Costumes are extremely important in *Così fan tutte* (and, of course, in the whole of the *commedia dell'arte* tradition, on which much of this opera is based); a slight costume change, an attached moustache, a bit of acting immediately convinces others that a familiar figure is someone else. Even women like the maid Despina can easily dupe their employers when dressed like a man (she becomes in the opera both a mesmerist doctor and a notary). In short, by donning costumes they temporarily *become* another person, and so too are these young soldiers allowing themselves in their transformations to become unfaithful seducers of the two sisters they proclaim to love.

Mozart gives his sweet heroines a great deal of reverence and fortitude to protect them. The celestial song they sing as their lovers go off to war, "Soave sia il vento" ("May the wind be gentle"), is almost enough to convince the most hard-hearted realist that these

two mean what they say. And to back it up, Fiordiligi sings the powerful "Come scogli" ("Like a rock"), pledging her love to Guglielmo.

The weaker of the two is obviously Dorabella who must be reminded consistently by her sister of the role she should play, and seems, quite early on, more distressed by being left alone than by the absence of Ferrando. Yet, despite her obvious interest in the two strange Albanians who suddenly appear in the sister's home, she also remains impervious throughout Act 1.

The Albanians, on the other hand, although declaring their love for the two beauties, seem more interested in their own prowess than in the women they are trying seduce. A great part of the humor of Da Ponte's text lies in the constant metaphors that point up their "endowments," Guglielmo, in particular, pointing to his masculine attributes in "Non siate ritrosi" ("Don't be shy").

In the production I saw this was reiterated by their attempt at suicide by arsenic poisoning, wherein their dying bodies were laid out upon a chaise longue, the two men almost on top of one another, hinting at a greater interest in their own bodies than in the two whom they describe later as "the fair sex." If nothing else, the scene suggested a long homoerotic embrace between Ferrando and Guglielmo, made even more apparent when the women come to revive them, all four crawling over and under one another.

Clearly they are not "playing fair," forcing the women to brush against and touch them—often in somewhat lewd positions. These are beautiful young people, all four of them; and like most young people, they are easily aroused.

What Mozart and Da Ponte also make clear is just how boring these wealthy sisters' lives are. Except for the excitement of sexual flirtation, there is little to do in their house, as Dorabella, in particular, makes clear. Despina serves them meals and sweets such as chocolate, they play puzzles, and, mostly, sit discussing their situations. Might it not be fun to do something else since their soldiers have gone off?

Dorabella despicably gives in, exchanging a neck-lace, containing Ferrando's picture, for a gift from the Albanian Guglielmo, but Fiordiligi runs away from her temptation, desperately trying to regain control of the situation through her conscience "Per pietà, ben mio, perdona" ("Please, my beloved, forgive"). Her brief de-cision to dress up like a soldier and run off to war to find her lover is absurdly touching, if ludicrous. There is, ob-viously, no war, and one wonders to where she might run. And if she were to find Guglielmo, how could she show him her love, dressed—like Isaac Bashevis Sing-er's Yentl—as a man? The opera, fortunately, does not take us down that path. Instead, Ferrando challenges

her again with suicide. What is a woman to do, given that she has already tried to save him as chastely as she can? Her only choice apparently is to give in.

The men, all ego, are furious with the obvious turn of events, but fortunately Don Alfonso is wise enough to insist that they accept the natures of their loved ones, without mentioning their own obvious failures and deceits. "Marry them," he advises, and so, apparently, they do, both symbolically, with the fake notary marrying Dorabella and Fiordiligi to the Albanians (each linked to the opposite of their lovers in their previous existences), and then again—at least in promise—to the miraculously returned soldiers. What does it matter, truly, who marries whom, when a simple moustache and coat can alter any personality? And, in that sense, *Così fan tutte* is neither a celebration of faithfulness or even a return to order, but a joyful tribute to sexually-inspired love.

LOS ANGELES, OCTOBER 3, 2011
Reprinted from *Green Integer Blog* (October 2011).

The Writer's Other Self

DEZSŐ KOSZTOLÁNYI **KORNÉL ESTI**, TRANSLATED
FROM THE HUNGARIAN BY BERNARD ADAMS (NEW
YORK: NEW DIRECTIONS, 2011)

THIS 1933 CLASSIC Hungarian fiction begins with the
author's comments about a supposed friend, Kornél
Esti, a boy from his childhood, who, in opposition to
the author's decorous and often unadventurous behavior, relentlessly challenged his friend to take chances,

racked up debts for which the
author was often charged—the
two apparently look alike—and
behaved generally in a way that
caused the narrator to break off
their relationship. Yet years later
the two encounter one another
again and strike up a new friendship in which together they write
a book based on Esti's fabulous

adventures, the very book the reader holds in his hands. Of course, the reader quickly recognizes Esti as a convenient "doppelgänger," which permits the author to tell stories about himself that he might not dare otherwise reveal.

Strangely, however, once the tales get underway, Esti, we perceive, is not at all the scandalously misbehaving creature that he has been depicted to be in the first chapter. The author, Dezső Kosztolányi, disappears into authorial objectivity as Esti's life is gradually revealed in the first or third person throughout. While the publisher and others quoted on the back cover refer to this book as a novel, it might be more accurately described as a series of loosely connected stories, a kind of relaxed picaresque that in portraying Esti's travels and adventures portrays Hungarian culture from a humorous perspective.

If Esti seems all-knowing and a bit of a cad in Kosztolányi's first chapter, he is soon revealed as an utter innocent, a proper and almost prudish young man. In an early tale he is forced to endure a train trip in a car with a mother and daughter, the latter of whom, a plain and simple-looking child, pretends to sleep so Esti himself will doze as well, at which point she mischievously plants a kiss upon his lips. Throughout, she makes lewd gestures, while the mother politely looks on. She is, we discover, insane, and will eventually have to be institutionalized. What is hilarious about this story, is that Esti, far from being a man-of-the-world as he has been portrayed, is both a prude and, we soon discover, a sentimentalist who becomes highly affected by the young girl's behavior. In Venice he dons a bathing suit and gradually wades into the water:

> Then in flung his body, arms outstretched, into the pearly blueness, at last to be united with it. He no longer feared anything. He knew that after this no great harm could come to him. That kiss and that journey had consecrated him for something.

The contradictory nature of this story matches the pattern of most of the works in the fiction. In the very next story, the author moves closer to a kind of satiric philosophical tale as Esti and a friend visit a town where everyone is painfully honest, going out of their way to tell the truth. The citizens of this town do not speak to one another unless they truly want to. A beggar carries a card saying: *I am not blind. I only wear dark glasses in summer.* A shoe store announces: *Crippling shoes. Corns and abscesses guaranteed. Several customers' feet amputated.* In trying to comprehend this seemingly self-destructive behavior the friend discovers that because the citizens have gone out of their way to suggest the worst, they find everything far more pleasant than they might in a city which proclaims that everything is perfect, which, of course, would be a lie.

In another tale, Esti comes into a rather large inheritance, but as an aspiring writer he dares not reveal his good fortune, fearing that it would end his career and he might lose his struggling friends. Consequently, while putting away just enough to survive for a few years, he attempts to give the rest away to strangers, slipping money into books, coats, and even—in a kind of reverse of pickpocketing—the pockets and billfolds of people on buses and trams. Ironically, he is arrested when a recipient is convinced that he has stolen something from him.

It is this kind irony that permeates the book and perhaps best characterizes the author's style. In another story, Esti attempts, while traveling through Bulgaria—speaking a language in which he knows only one or two words—to carry on a long conversation with a train conductor without the other ever suspecting that he does not comprehend the conversation. Through the use of "yes" and "no," tonal differences, head and hand movements and patient listening, he succeeds in befriending and, later, offending the conductor, bringing him even to tears. Another "yes" restores their close friendship.

While swimming in a river, Esti is nearly drowned, surviving only because a young man rushes in to pull him out. Beholden to his savior he offers to become a life-time friend. But when the boring young man moves in with him, revealing a greater interest in theater magazines and the women they portray than in serious ideas, Esti becomes disgusted with his savior and fearful that he will never be able rid himself of the pest. One night, as they pass not far from the spot from where he has been saved, the elder pushes the young man into the river.

Sought out for a contribution, Esti becomes a benefactor to a woman and her suffering family. He helps the woman get a newspaper kiosk, and places her tubercular daughter in a hospital. The more he does for the family, however, the worse off their lives become. Finally, her son dies, the daughter grows more ill, and the mother, attempting to care for them, gives up her kiosk. As the old woman tells her sad story, Esti runs away from her, begging her to stop!

Perhaps the funniest satire in the volume concerns Esti's studies in Germany, where he discovers a university president who falls peacefully asleep whenever one of the professors begins a speech, waking up precisely at each speech's conclusion. Kosztolányi takes his humor even further when, during summer break, the president becomes an insomniac, nearly dying from lack of rest.

The last tale, in which Esti can hardly cling on to an overstuffed subway, might be said to be an allegory of his life. Gradually, through pushes and pulls, he makes his way further and further into the car, finally finding a small slot in which he can sit. Disgusted by most of the humanity around him, he finds joy in the face of a poor working woman, and ultimately begins to feel some comfort in the trip only to have the conductor call out: "Terminus."

Despite the publisher's enthusiasms, I cannot describe this work as a "masterpiece"; but it is, nonetheless, an enjoyable series of ironic musings that nicely alternate between the comic and the tragic, the everyday and the bizarre.

LOS ANGELES, SEPTEMBER 28, 2011
Reprinted from *EXPLORING*fictions (September 2011).

Approaching the Real

KIRK LYNN **THE METHOD GUN,** CREATED AND PER-
FORMED BY THE RUDE MECHS / CULVER CITY, CALIFOR-
NIA: KIRK DOUGLAS THEATRE / THE PERFORMANCE I
ATTENDED WAS ON JUNE 14, 2011

IN THEIR PLAY *The Method Gun* the Austin-based collaborative Rude Mechs has created a delightful theatrical work that combines satire, whimsy, history, and
naturalist theater in a way that few works today have
attempted.

The subject, or one might say the missing center
of their work, is a drama teacher, Stella Burden, with
whom the five players of *The Method Gun* had long
worked—that is, until she suddenly disappeared into
Ecuador or Paraguay.

Actress Hannah Kenah explains to the audience,
at the play's start, that her Rude Mechs company has
found play texts, lesson books, films, and interviews
about Stella Burden and her method—nicknamed the

"The Approach"—in libraries and other locations near Austin. And, by coincidence, a grant led one of their members to Ecuador, where Stella was evidently last spotted.

As early as August 14, 2006, the company posted a Stella Burden site, explaining that they were "conducting research" for *The Method Gun* to create "a fictional biography and a theatrical production tracing the life and tragic death of Stella Burden (a.k.a. 'the other Stella')," the "other" obviously referencing Stella Adler, whose "Studio of Acting" helped to make famous "The Method" of the Stanislavski system.

The work that the Rude Mechs created centers on the five remaining students (Carl Reyholt, Connie Torrey, Koko Bond, Robert "Hops" Gilbert, and Elizabeth

Johns), now without a leader, but attempting to keep their company together in an interminable rehearsal of several years of a production of *A Streetcar Named Desire*—without the major characters of Blanche, Stanley, Stella, and Mitch. We experience, accordingly, the company's reenactment of some of Stella Burden's principles (most notably on "how to cry" and "how to kiss"), the company members' squabbles, sexual inter-relations, fears, doubts, and, later, questionable fame for being the last students of Burden, as they are inter-viewed, filmed, and trotted out in university theater conferences. One by one they reveal the few objects Stella left behind, including a small plastic tiger and a bird cage wherein sits a gun, suggesting to the actors that everything they do is a matter of life or death.

At the core of these various activities is the almost empty play they are rehearsing—the characters consist-ing of Pablo the Paper Boy, a Tamale Vendor, a Colored Woman, a Mexican Woman, a Negro Woman, Steve, Stella's friend Eunice, the Nurse, and the Doctor—a truly lunatic production, which, nonetheless, is quite revelatory of the play itself.

Every now and then the actors step out of charac-ter, speaking directly to the audience about events or, at one point, asking audience members to take out small pieces of paper and write down the teacher or other person who most influenced them. The action also includes—in contrapuntal reaction to the absurdly strict methods of "The Approach" (hinting at the equally absurd restrictions of Adler's and Lee Strasberg's "The Method")—a ridiculously witty tiger, who from time to time ap-  pears ready to dine on the actors, and in the end, goes off with their most contentious member, Elizabeth Johns. The play also presents a truly gratuitous sex scene, wherein the women begin kissing and the men run in from the wings, stark-naked, except for balloons tied to their penises, thus keeping them seemingly erect.

If this all sounds strangely experimental, it is not. For the Rude Mechs have balanced their play between satire and a sense of modest reverence. They are, after all, actors themselves, and as loony as Burden's techniques may appear, the actor-characters keep a respectful distance from all-out camp.

Of course, the play is a satire at heart, and as much as the audience may wish to believe in such a strict theatrical authoritarian, or that good theater results from such stunted techniques, the play itself pushes against this. Yet the actors (Thomas Graves, Hannah Kenah,

Lana Lesley, E. Jason Liebrecht, and Shawn Sides, who also served as director) have not only a respect for the fiction they have created but have expanded the myth of Stella Burden far beyond the theater stage. In their various web calls for information about this obscure teacher, the group noted her interest in the Los Angeles artist Chris Burden, who not only shared her last name but was himself injured by a gun during an art performance. The artist claims no knowledge of her.

In some reports, Stella is said to have been killed by a gun similar to the one left behind. In still another commentary, a writer notes that when Stella Adler performed in film she added an "r" to her name (Ardler), while Stella Burden dropped the "r" when she performed in that medium (Buden). When asked by a student whether this implied any relationship between the two, Stella wittily and vaguely punned: "Some are and others aren't."

The strangest suggestion is that Burden's close relationship with Marilyn Monroe may have been behind the actress' breakup with Joe DiMaggio!

All of this lovely nonsense reminds me, in part, of Eleanor Antin's creation of her performative dancer, Eleanora Antinova, for whom Antin created photos of works she had choreographed, a series of performed plays, drawings, autobiographical writings, etc., going so far as to lecture on her life with Diaghilev and the

Ballets Russes at the Museum of Modern Art in New York, where several people approached her in awe, one even offering to support her balletic school. It also reminds me a little of my own self-created author, Claude Richochet, whose various works have appeared in books and journals over the years.

In short, *The Method Gun* is not simply a work of the stage but is a grander creation of theatrical history and fiction.

On stage, the actors finally reach what appears to be an impasse, Elizabeth Johns suggesting they sell everything and go away to another country. The others, however, are adamant in their devotion to the single performance of their play-without-a-play the next day. The tension becomes so palpable that one member grabs the gun, shooting it at each of them. It is, after all and fortunately, only a stage gun that shoots blanks.

Yet when they perform Williams' "shell," the actors (both Burden's supposed company and the Rude Mechs) actually do endanger their lives. Swinging several lamps in opposing directions, company members silently enact their roles within range of the missiles with a balletic intensity, balancing the real possibility of being killed or at least knocked out with the concentration on their miniscule roles put into motion. The effect is absolutely stunning, and the audience was truly awed. The company responded to the audience with a projected listing upon the walls of the those figures who had been so important in their lives. Among them was the playwright Mac Wellman. I had written the name of my mentor Marjorie Perloff, which somehow was misread as Penloff—the "r" disappearing just as it had for Stella Burden, she too becoming one of the ones who "aren't."

LOS ANGELES, JUNE 17, 2011
Reprinted from *US Theater, Opera, and Performance* (June 2011).

The Dark Side of the Moon

MAXWELL ANDERSON AND ANGUS MACPHAIL
(SCREENPLAY, BASED ON A STORY BY MAXWELL ANDER-
SON), ALFRED HITCHCOCK (DIRECTOR) **THE WRONG
MAN** / 1956

IT IS STRANGE to think that only two years after making one of his greatest films, *Rear Window*, and in the same year that Alfred Hitchcock directed *The Trouble with Harry*—perhaps his most joyful film of this period—as well as the remake of *The Man Who Knew Too Much*, the 1956 black-and-white movie *The Wrong Man* was a dismal box-office failure.

Several reasons are generally cited for this fact, the most obvious being simply that the film, based on a true story with few of the original facts altered, was simply too bleak. Moreover, in its documentary-like tone and structure, the film does not seem like a Hitchcock product. It has little of the gruesome wit and irony of most of his movies, and lacks, at least superficially, the cinematographic brilliance of the other films mentioned. The director himself seems to back away from the work, appearing in a brief shot before the film begins to tell the audience the movie is based on real events, instead of appearing in a tongue-in-cheek cameo, as he usually does, within the frame of the story. Even the phenomenal composer Bernard Herrmann seems to have become more somber, certainly less flamboyant, in this film—although his stunning jazz piece (Manny works as a string bass player in a jazz group performing at the Stork Club), interrupted by almost sickening moans of the instruments, is highly memorable.

To see the hard-working, good family man Manny Balestrero (intensely played by Henry Fonda) be systematically destroyed by the American justice system is so painful that it is a hard movie to watch. In some ways, *The Wrong Man* combines all of the fears and paranoias of the mid-1950s, a period where the whole country was, in a sense, put on trial, everyday men and women accused of anti-American sentiment and actions. Although I have often suggested that the 1950s was far more interesting than the way in which the decade is usually presented, this particular aspect of the period, along with the angst of nuclear destruction, put everyone on edge. It is little wonder, accordingly, that people did not flock to Hitchcock's dour film. Even a critic writing as late as 2004, Christopher Null, describes it as one of Hitchcock's "most forgettable works of his mature era."

Having recently watched the film again, however, I now think it, along with *Shadow of a Doubt*, is one of his most excellent, if frightening, depictions of American life. Films like *Vertigo*, *North by Northwest*, and even *Psycho* are much closer to European cinema-making than either *Shadow of a Doubt* or *The Wrong Man*, the latter of which is as grounded in the streets of New York as many of the 1940s *film noirs*, and, as we now perceive, highly influenced artists like Scorsese in *Taxi Driver*.

It is not that the police in this film are villains, or that they are even particularly insensitive enforcers. Indeed the dilemma of this film is not that any group of men or women torment Manny, but that—once he has visited the local insurance office to see if he might get a loan to pay for his wife's upcoming dental bills—the whole world order crumbles, truth and memory slipping away into nightmare reality. He is identified by women of the insurance office as a man who twice before held them up. The women can hardly bear to look

at the accused themselves, one of them almost sickening to even glance in his direction.

The police quickly create a line-up made up of persons whom the women might have previously seen in uniform, as justice continues to crack, leaving Manny Balestrero to face the shattering effects upon his life.

In this world turned upside down, coincidences predominate. When asked to write the words that appeared in one of the hold-up notes, Manny makes the same spelling mistake as did the criminal, reinforcing the police's belief in his guilt. His simple statement, "I made a mistake," echoes in a Kafka-like cry of existential guilt, repeated later in his wife's fractured vision of reality that it is she who has made the mistakes by needing dental care or through simply not being a good enough wife. Even Manny's two innocent sons mope about as if they have helped to create the mountain of evidence that appears to insure Manny's imprisonment.

Truth has little significance in this dark world. The fact that during the first robbery the couple had been away on vacation and during the second robbery Manny had a swollen cheek seems to matter little. None of his fellow vacationers can be found, some having died, others disappearing into oblivion. The young lawyer (Anthony Quayle) to whom Manny and his wife are recommended is well-meaning but inexperienced (in this instance, Hitchcock did change the facts, since originally he was a New York Senator at the time of the trial).

As his wife Rose (Vera Miles) slips into insanity, it is as if Manny, a religious believer, were suddenly suffering the trials of Job. The only bit of luck he receives, if one can call it that, is that a juror screams out early in the trial concerning the mundaness of courtroom details, apparently in the belief that Manny's guilt is obvious, thus assuring a retrial, and giving the defense more time to prepare.

One cannot imagine the final events to be anything but fiction, so perfectly do they fit with Hitchcock's sense of moral outrage against institutional systems and individual fate: quite by accident the head detective in this case encounters another recently arrested man in the precinct hall who looks vaguely like Manny, and turns back from his exit to further investigate, discovering that he is responsible for the robberies for which Manny has been accused.

In the movie, however, Manny's new freedom seems hardly to matter. His wife, locked away in an asylum, apathetically ignores his claims that everything will now be all right. She, so the doctor proclaims, is still "on the dark side of the moon."

Only a written after-note tells us that two years later Rose recovered, allowing the family, perhaps, to return to some normalcy. But one doubts, after all they had been through, that everyday life was ever possible again.

LOS ANGELES, SEPTEMBER 3, 2011
Reprinted from *World Cinema Review* (September 2011).

Slightly Sour

JAMES GOLDMAN (BOOK), STEPHEN SONDHEIM
(MUSIC AND LYRICS) **FOLLIES** / LOS ANGELES, AHMAN-
SON THEATRE / THE PRODUCTION I SAW WAS ON MAY
26, 2012

LET ME BEGIN by unequivocally asserting that Stephen
Sondheim is the greatest of living American musical
theater composers and lyricists. In dozens of musical
comedies and dramas, Sondheim has given us a long
string of memorable songs, and he penned notable lyrics in works such as *West Side Story* and *Gypsy* before he
even got a chance to demonstrate his musical talents.

Let me also admit that after seeing the splendid
revival of Sondheim's *Follies* yesterday at Los Angeles'
Ahmanson Theatre, I was sorely tempted to postpone
writing about the experience. I was afraid, however, if I
didn't immediately take on the task that I'd find myself
in the same situation as I am with his *Merrily We Roll
Along*, a production which I saw in 2010 and have as

yet failed to express my thoughts on! I know the reasons for my reluctance; they are similar to those that I expressed about Sondheim's *Company* of 2007 (see *My Year 2007*). But I find it almost mean-spirited that I can't simply let well enough alone, that I can't just soak myself in all those memorably lyrical and witty songs of desire and pluck—which in *Follies* amounts almost to a cornucopia of treasures: "Beautiful Girls," "Waiting for the Girls Upstairs," "Broadway Baby," "In Buddy's Eyes," "Who's That Woman?," "I'm Still Here," "Could I Leave You?," "The God-Why-Don't-You-Love-Me Blues," "The Story of Lucy and Jessie," and "Live, Laugh, Love"—then go home and report, "What a

great show!" And yes, this loving and caring revival was a great show, some of its praises which I'll sing shortly.

But—that terrible three-letter word—let me just repeat: I have problems with Sondheim's vision. After seeing 10 works for which he has written lyrics, music, or both, and after having heard recordings of several others, I have to conclude that Sondheim has one of the darkest visions of humankind of any Broadway composer. In work after work, he focuses on individuals living in unhappy marriages who cheat, lie, and delude themselves; beings who hate the world, murder, and even consume their fellow beings; drunks, vagrants, evil-minded con men, and deviously manipulative women. In a Sondheim musical, hope and happiness are as rare as a full eclipse played out against the northern lights.

Now, I certainly do realize that all these subjects are far more interesting as themes which help to generate larger questions than do the everyday joys and pleasures of life. For a writer who has titled one book of poetry *Dark*, has written a fiction about the kidnapping of children and possible pedophilia, and whose plays, although comic, often include arguing couples and dysfunctional families, my observations may sound somewhat insincere. But even in my very darkest of works there is always some sort of reaffirmation or possibility of real hope. Although my companion and I, who have been in a mostly monogamous relationship now for 42 years, may argue daily, neither of us, we concur, has ever thought of leaving the other for more than a few hours at a time. I have nothing against the darkest of visions, but mightn't that dreary scowl be relaxed just once?

I also know, having now read both of Sondheim's volumes of lyrics, with "attendant comments, principles, heresies, grudges, whines and anecdotes," that, although I often disagree with him, the composer is quite brilliant and thoroughly knowledgeable about his art, able to cite the songs of his predecessors, and point to their successes and failures. Sondheim himself claims Hammerstein as his mentor, and I take him at his word. But as dark as are certain passages in *Carousel*,

Oklahoma! (see *My Year 2003* for a discussion of those darker themes), *South Pacific*, and even *The King and I*—I will pass on making any comments about his saccharine, sugar-coated *Sound of Music*—Hammerstein's lyrics and librettos are joyful celebrations, for the most part, of love and life.

Follies, like so many of Sondheim's works, is a kind of haunted castle of lost loves, dreams, aspirations, and hopes, a testament to a world of deluded people who are desperate to find love and meaning in a world that has failed them. Indeed, as Sondheim tells it, his dramatist and he first intended this musical to be about a reunion in which, the central characters, plastered with equal measures of nostalgia and alcohol, have motives to kill each other; he and Goldman originally set out to write a kind of murder mystery set at a party for aged performers. While they eventually dropped that notion—thank God—the sparsely told plot that remains is still about the four central characters' torturous marriages, their desires for their dreams of the past, and the gradual stripping away of their delusions. It ends, at least in the revival version, with the still-angry but dependent Phyllis and her husband Ben leaving without much hope of true reconciliation, followed by the newly rejected Sally and her disappointed husband Buddy hoping to just get some rest before they begin the next day of their lives.

Such empty relationships, as we know, certainly do exist. Possibly these unhappy folks can all begin again, and they might even revitalize their relationships—although given the dark songs they have just sung about not getting what they want, losing their minds, and the desire to live life "in arrears," it seems highly unlikely. This same ending faces the characters of numerous Sondheim musicals, most notably in *Company* and *Merrily We Roll Along*, while others end in far worse ways: murder, assassination, fiery death, and even cannibalism. One might almost say that in Sondheim's world both characters and audiences are eternally lost in the woods with the knowledge that the wolf is following right behind.

So despite the medley of lovely and witty melodies with which the composer has threaded his works, they are still quite deadly delicacies, laced with heavy doubt and open cynicism.

Having said all this, we must also admit that nearly all of Sondheim's unhappy figures are survivors. They've had their ups (although we rarely see them) as well as their downs, as Sondheim's Carlotta (Elaine Paige) sings:

Good times and bum times,
I've seen them all and, my dear,
I'm still here.

Or as Hattie expresses her pluck:

> I'm just a Broadway baby,
> Walking off my tired feet,
> Pounding Forty Second Street
> To be in a show.

After hearing Elaine Stritch's rhythmic rendition of this song, with the perfect timing of the lines

> At
> My tiny flat
> There's just my cat,
> A bed and a chair.

for a few seconds I was uneasy with Jayne Houdyshell's more lusty and less-nuanced version; but, in the end, her zest for life nearly brought down the house.

Similarly, the whole chorus gets to tap out their troubles in "Who's That Woman?," led by the brass-throated Stella (Terri White).

Sondheim also ameliorates his dark themes somewhat through the clownish behavior of his characters, revealing their own realization of their failures, as in Buddy's (Danny Burstein's) manic "The God-Why-Don't-You-Love-Me Blues" and the haunting "Live,

 Laugh, Love," sung by Ron Raines as Ben Stone, a song of escapism which turns, as in *Cabaret*, into an echo chamber-like house of horrors.

Sondheim's figures, moreover, often express deep feelings that they themselves do not recognize as pleasures. This is particularly true in both of Sally Plummer's (Victoria Clark's) powerful ballads, "In Buddy's Eyes" and "Losing My Mind." In the former, she expresses to her friends why she should be happy with her husband without comprehending, so it seems, that she actually might be happy for those very reasons:

> Life is slow, but it seems exciting
> 'Cause Buddy's there.
> ....
> In Buddy's eyes,
> I'm young, I'm beautiful.
> In Buddy's arms.
> On Buddy's shoulder,
> I won't get older.

And similarly, in "Losing My Mind," Sondheim himself points to her use of the word "to" instead of "and," revealing her deepest problems are of her own making:

> I dim the lights
> And think about you,
> Spend sleepless nights
> To think about you.

Clark sang these with a full-bodied voice that certainly did justice to the song, but after hearing Barbara Cook and Bernadette Peters sing those same lines, it is perhaps impossible to accept anything below their perfection.

Finally, Sondheim's comic wit, even if it is dripping with bitterness, occasionally outweighs the despair of his characters. That is particularly true in Phyllis' (Jan Maxwell's) paean to divorce, "Could I Leave You?," in which she poses alternatives to her unhappy marriage which she's already embraced:

> Could I bury my rage
> With a boy half your age
> In the grass?
> Bet your ass.
> But I've done that already—
> Or didn't you know, love?

Maxwell sang this with such clear diction that all the

song's bitter humor shone luminously, like the crystals which her character daily counts.

For Sondheim, apparently, these stories of survival, self-revelatory slips of the tongue, patter pieces, and comic diatribes are all we have in a world where everything is seen through a glass darkly. Perhaps it's as ridiculous to ask such a dark thinker to show us the sun as asking Ingmar Bergman—whose film Sondheim  adapted in another recent revival, *A Little Night Music*—to show us a way out of deep despair. But then, to my way of thinking, that is precisely what Bergman does, whereas Sondheim entertains us grandly, but just as we begin to have fun, he puts out the light. And there is, finally, nowhere to go but back home again, with the slightly sour aftertaste of too much gin in our mouths.

LOS ANGELES, MAY 27, 2012
Reprinted from *US Theater, Opera, and Performance* (May 2012).

Three Lost Souls

ALAIN RESNAIS AND LAURENT HERBIET (WRIT-
ERS, BASED ON TWO PLAYS BY JEAN ANOUILH), ALAIN
RESNAIS (DIRECTOR) **VOUS N'AVEZ ENCORE RIEN VU
(YOU AIN'T SEEN NOTHIN' YET)** / 2012

IN MANY WAYS, Resnais' late-career film *Vous n'avez
encore rien vu* (with the terrible American title of *You
Ain't Seen Nothin' Yet*) is a quintessential expression of
the themes of his films. Resnais has always focused on
the fleetingness of love and life, and of how the actions
of the past continue to affect and even destroy the joys

of the present and the future.

Here, cleverly, Resnais has chosen two plays by the late French playwright, Jean Anouilh (*Eurydice* and *Cher Antoine ou l'Amour raté*), which themselves deal with those very themes, asking Bruno Podalydès to direct an independent theatrical production of them, and then interwoven the stage actors' performances with those of his fictional characters, gathered together as part of playwright-director Antoine d'Anthac's supposed "will," which calls up the major actors who have,

over the years, performed these same roles.

Some are now quite elderly, others in their middle-age, while the cast in the filmed production, using what appears to be a warehouse as their backdrop, are young figures from La Compagnie de la Colombe.

As the filmed drama gets underway, the renowned actors (who include Anne Consigny, Michel Piccoli, Lambert Wilson, Pierre Arditi, and Sabine Azéma), unable to control themselves, begin to play along with the filmed actors, reciting their old scenes. The variations in their ages and acting styles create a stunning example of just what both Anouilh—who Resnais ad-

mitted highly influenced him as a young man—and the director are trying to express.

For the most elderly actors, we quite literally see the ravages of the past upon their faces, and they recite with a strong sense of sorrowful nostalgia upon their tongues; the middle-aged actors are somewhat more assertive, but they too, we perceive, are now questioning their own choices; while the young stage actors, beautiful to behold, almost declaim their loves and desires.

By alternating these performances, sometimes even using a split screen, and once creating a kind of triangular presentation of texts, Resnais achieves a prism of emotional meaning that brilliantly explores the very ideas expressed in Anouilh's 1941, wartime drama.

I am not so sure I am fond of Anouilh's meeting of the two lovers after the woman's death. Or Resnais' own ending, wherein d'Anthac (acted by Bruno Podalydès) enters the spellbound room, having, apparently,

not really died, but simply having been determined to bring all of his beloved actors together again. It seems too much like a gimmick, even if it's a slightly comical insider joke, since the fictional character is actually the real director of the stage performance. But these are minor complaints about Resnais' otherwise magical tale of artifice and reality, time lost and time regained. If nothing else, Resnais still proves, in this penultimate work, that he is a master of the medium.

And the acting is brilliant. How many times does an audience get to see three versions of a play in one telling? Maybe you truly "ain't seen nothin'" quite like it. Certainly the story of Orpheus and Eurydice will never be seem the same after seeing this and Cocteau's earlier film.

LOS ANGELES, APRIL 25, 2017
Reprinted from *World Cinema Review* (April 2017).

Jack Klugman

SADLY, THIS YEAR, the actor Jack Klugman died of prostate cancer, although he had also suffered from throat cancer in previous years as well. I never quite appreci-ated his roles, which included a juror in *12 Angry Men* and the role of Oscar Madison in the television role of *The Odd Couple* opposite Tony Randall. But over the years, I have come to admire his many television appearances, having watched him again in a television marathon of *The Twilight Zone*, in a lovely role in "A Passage for the Trumpet" from 1960; and I recall him from the TV series *The Defenders*. Of course, he also appeared in a great many Broadway theater performances, in which I never saw him. But I did meet him, when he was an elderly man with throat cancer, in 1993, when

Jerry Lawrence and I were dining, the night before our great celebration of his career, at Sardi's in New York as he came over to our table to greet Jerry. I shook his hand, nothing more, but still was pleased to briefly encounter this trouper of Broadway and television. He could hardly speak, but it was eloquent nonetheless.

For the last several years I have taught one course each year for the M.F.A. program at Otis College of Art. Fortunately, Paul Vangelisti, Director of the Program, and his superiors have been very receptive to my often unusual and sometimes innovative course offerings, which have included author-based courses—one on the works of Gertrude Stein and a second on the fictions of William Faulkner and Eudora Welty—on broad topical subjects such as "International Fiction," and genre-centered courses on "American Satires" and "Autobiographical Writings and Fictions." In 2011 I taught a course focused on what I describe as "Dialogue Fictions," works that center on their characters' spoken words and conversations. Beginning with a couple of Platonic dialogues, we quickly moved into 20th-century British fictions by Elizabeth Bowen, Ivy Compton-Burnett, Ronald Firbank, Anthony Powell, and Henry Green, ending with two US books, James Schuyler's and John Ashbery's Nest of Ninnies *and Jane Bowles'* Two Serious Ladies. *Most of my students and I felt that, although the readings were removed from the style and genre of their own works, the course was successful.*

The essays below were written as short introductions in response to my readings before and during that course.

PRETENDING TO COMMUNICATE

Firbank as Poet

RONALD FIRBANK **VALMOUTH** (LONDON: GERALD
DUCKWORTH, 1919)

IN PREPARATION FOR a fiction course for the MFA
Creative Writing Program at Otis College of Art this
fall, I reread Ronald Firbank's fiction *Valmouth*, and
sought out his biography on Wikipedia, where I read

that the author "produced a series of novels."

Since I consider myself a
sort of authority on the various genres of fiction, I am no
longer surprised to see that any
fiction is described by most
readers these days as a "novel."
And although the genre "novel" seems to me to center on a

central figure, charting his or her relationship (often in symbolic terms) with the larger culture or, at least, the world outside the central figure, I have become somewhat indifferent if people use the term "novel" indeterminately.

The only times it truly upsets me is when readers have difficulty with a work of fiction because it does not meet the standard expectations of a "novel," such as Djuna Barnes' anatomy *Nightwood*, a work that wasted the energies of at least one critic, Joseph Frank, in creating a new form (what he called "spatial fiction") to explain what he saw as anomalies, all perfectly at home in the anatomy genre. Others have approached the epic fictions of Heimito von Doderer and Robert Musil, works whose structures often work more like musical compositions than plot-organized novels, similarly. But when I raise these issues, I usually get blank stares or significant harrumphing.

I might have described Firbank's *Valmouth* as a dialogue fiction, a work that uses conversation as its major structural device, a genre that can be traced back to Plato's *Dialogues*. Indeed I intend to teach this work in a course titled "Dialogue Fictions," which includes works by Elizabeth Bowen, Henry Green, Ivy Compton-Burnett, Anthony Powell, and others.

This time, my reading, however, revealed that perhaps I had been wrong in even presuming to describe

Valmouth and most other Firbank works as "fictions." While it is true that many kinds of fiction contain little or no plot—and Firbank seems unable to close any event, let alone begin it—at least most fictions have a narrative. If there is one in *Valmouth*, it can be summarized by saying that the book is primarily about a group of elderly women, women who have survived longer than those in other English communities either because of the Valmouth air or its water. The major "event" of *Valmouth* consists of a grand dinner party for these women and most of the town's citizens in Hare Hall. Little of importance happens at this occurrence—indeed it is often difficult to know throughout the work what indeed might be "happening"—but it is significantly placed near the center of the work (p. 78 of 127 pages).

There also appears to be no "central" character, indeed no "real" characters, Firbank preferring names (Teresa Twisleton, Rebecca Bramblebrook, Flo Flook, Simon Toole, Tircis Tree, Mrs. Hurspierpoint, etc., listed sometimes for entire paragraphs) over characterization; but three quickly drawn figures do predominate, namely the black masseuse Mrs. Yajñavalkya, her mysterious niece Niri-Esther, and Mrs. Thoroughfare's son Dick—a sailor who is away from home for most of the fiction. If one must point to a single central figure, it would have to be Yajñavalkya, since it is clear that she is the most intelligent and exuberant figure in the book.

Firbank clearly loved blacks, and writes about them in several of his "fictions." His admiration for blacks, however, does not mean that he escapes the prejudices of his time (*Valmouth* was first published in 1919): the word "nigger" appears once or twice in this book, and in the title of his *Prancing Nigger*. The elderly women seem to be of two minds concerning Yajñavalkya as they praise her ointments and the touch of her fingers, alternating with disdain for her race.

In fact, we don't ever truly know Yajñavalkya's ethnic background. At times she is simply from "the East," at other times she appears to have traveled from Africa or India, while at the end of the work, it appears, she is Tahitian, her niece born of Tahitian royalty. It hardly matters, since it is apparent that what Firbank most enjoys is the possibility of using his "black" figure to create another kind of voice, in this case a strange mélange of dialect and argot. At least she is given a few full sentences.

> We Eastern women love the sun...! When de thermometer rise to some two hundred or so, ah dat is de time to lie among de bees and canes.

The rest of the figures utter half sentences, phrases, overheard remarks. Most of this work is so utterly fragmented that—although we glean that the conversation is usually about societal behavior and love—the meaning and significance of the dialogue are impossible to detect.

Mixed with Latinate sentences, French phrases (some of them poorly put together), and an occasional German word or two, the fragments coming from these figures' mouths is less a dialogue than a series of signs, linguistic clues to what might or might not have happened:

There uprose a jargon of voices:
"Heroin."
"Adorable simplicity."
"What could anyone find to admire in such a shelving profile?"
"We reckon a duck here of two or three and twenty not so old.
And a spring chicken *anything to fourteen*."
"My husband had no amorous energy whatsoever; which just suited me, of course."
"I suppose when there's no more room for another crow's-foot, one attains a sort of peace?"
"I once said to Doctor Fothergill, a clergyman of Oxford and a great friend of mine, 'Doctor,' I said, 'oh, if only you could see my—'"
"*Elle était jolie! Mais jolie!... C'était une si belle brune...!*"

"Cruelly lonely."

"Leery...."

"Vulpine."

"Calumny."

"People look like pearls, dear, beneath your wonderful trees."

This goes on for several pages, and such passages dominate the entire text.

At several other moments we overhear the whispered conversations of servants:

"Dash their wigs!" the elder man exclaimed.

"What's the thorn, Mr. ffines?" his colleague, a lad with a face gemmed lightly over in spots, pertly queried.

"The thorn, George?"

"Tell us."

"I'd sooner go round my beads."

"Mrs. Hurst cut compline, for a change, to-night."

"...She's making a studied toilet, so I hear."

"Gloria! Gloria! Gloria!"

"Dissenter."

"What's wrong with Nit?"

The younger footman flushed.

"Father Mahoney sent me to his room again," he answered.

"What, *again*?"

"Catch me twice—"
"*Veni cum me in erra coelabus!*"
"S-s-s-s-s-s-sh."
"*Et lingua...semper.*"

At least we can sense what's behind their gossip, namely the sexual attacks of the priest on the young footman; but just as often these conversations offer up no real information.

Similarly, there are passages of fragmented readings, the one below listened to by Mrs. Hurstpierpoint between the *Aves* of her beads:

Music, she heard. Those sisters † a ripe and rich marquesa † strong proclivites † a white starry plant † water † lanterns † little streets † Il Redentore † Pasqualino † behind the Church of † Giudecca † gondola † Lido † Love † lagoon † Santa Orsola † the Adriatic——

Again, we get the idea, the satiric mix of the sacred and the mundane, a romantic love story set against the movement of the prayer beads, but there is no other significance, and even that has been revealed to us through signs and symbols.

Niri-Esther speaks throughout in a language of her own, using phrases such as "*Chakrawakt—wa?*" and

"Suwhee?" A passing drunk sings an entire song in a near-nonsense language:

> Lilli burlero, bullen a-la.
> Dar we shall have a new deputie,
> Lilli burlero, bullen a-la.
> Lero lero, lilli burlero, lero lero, bullen a-la,
> Lero lero, lilli burlero, lero lero, bullen a-la.
>
> Ara! but why does he stay behind?
> Lilli burlero, bullen a-la.
> Ho! by my shoul 'tis a protestant wind.
> Lilli burlero, bullen a-la.
> Lero lero, lilli burlero, lero lero, bullen a-la,
> Lero lero, lilli burlero, lero lero, bullen a-la.
>
> Now, now de heretics all go down,
> Lilli burlero, bullen a-la
> By Chrish! and Shaint Patrick, de nation's our
>   own—

Similar songs appear in his other works, like this little gem from *Prancing Nigger*:

> *I am King Elephant-bag,*
> *Oh de rose-pink Mountains!*
> *Tatou, tatouay, tatou...*

My point in mentioning these numerous fragmented passages (and I might have selected nearly any page in *Valmouth* for examples) is that it is clear Firbank is not at all interested in telling or even circuitously *conveying* a story. His pleasure is in language, not in fiction. Even when he has set up a scene, as he does at the end of the book, gathering all the work's figures together for the marriage of Niri-Esther, the black Tahitian princess, to the fair-haired inheritor of Hare Hall, Dick, nothing comes of it. Dick suddenly disappears from the scene and book, while the community impatiently waits within the church, Niri-Esther wandering outdoors to follow a butterfly. The work ends with no attempt at conclusion or even a suggestion of one. Absolutely *nothing* happens. It is as if Firbank were toying with any reader who might seek an interrelated narrative.

Yet Firbank's works, for some (for me), are highly enjoyable, delightful forays into linguistic silliness, as somehow both the old and the young of this work come together again and again to talk, to share idle gossip, gripes, complaints, and tales of illicit or imaginary love. Although we never know the full content of any of these, we can—the author requires it of the reader—fill in the blanks, turning Firbank's characters' words into our own desires and disappointments. In short, anyone coming to Firbank expecting a story, a kind of "novel"—no matter *how* one defines that—will be disappointed. For Firbank is closer to being a poet than a storyteller, a man interested more in the play of language than in what it means.

LOS ANGELES, JULY 28, 2011
Reprinted from *Or*, No. 7 and *PIP Poetry Blog*.

Caught in the Whirl

ELIZABETH BOWEN **EVA TROUT** (LONDON: JONA-
THAN CAPE, 1969)

THE TITLE CHARACTER of Elizabeth Bowen's deli-
ciously written fiction of 1969 is an outsized woman,
described variously by the author as "monolithic," "a
giantess," and "an Amazon," along with other unflat-
tering appellations. From the very first action, as Eva
Trout drives the Dancey children past the castle she
owns and where she
was schooled for a
short while, Bowen
fixes her figure in our
minds as a purposeful
being constantly on
the move: at the mo-
ment at the wheel of
her Jaguar. The book
is subtitled "Chang-

ing Scenes," a suggestion of the numerous shifts in location and emotional states of its hero. Even Eva's position in the car, as the author puts it, is "not, somehow, the attitude of a thinking person."

As we first glimpse this towering and overpowering figure, she is about to bolt from the household in which she had originally asked her guardian to place her: Larkins, the run-down farmhouse wherein reside the Arbles. Iseult Arble, a former teacher of the girl, is perhaps the first and only person who attempts to actually educate her; while Iseult's husband, the less-than-brilliant Eric, has grown comfortable with Eva's presence, he feels a growing tension with his wife, a shift that Eva interprets as Eric's attraction to Eva.

In preparation for the move, announced to the Dancey family, while kept secret from the Arbles, Eva's London-based guardian, who has gotten wind of Eva's plans, calls Iseult to the city in order to plot a way to keep his charge from running off before inheriting, a few months later, the fortune left to her by her father, Willy. And the interchange between the two is one of the great moments of the book, as these most intelligent figures of the work attempt to comprehend and outwit one other. Constantine is a darker and more sinister version of Iseult, a man who clearly is used to hatching plots—although in this case he fails. For Eva rushes to the small town of Broadstairs, purchasing a house by the sea. But it is clear that this woman, incapable of even boiling water, will not be able long to care for herself.

Eva has left behind numerous clues to her destination, and both Eric and, soon after, Constantine follow her, the latter believing he has found the two in an uncompromising situation (in fact, Eric has simply taken a nap). Eric and Iseult divorce, just the first of numerous negative effects that this giantess will have on all the figures around her.

After gaining her inheritance, Eva travels again, this time to the US to purchase what is presumably an illegal baby, there coincidentally meeting up with her first love, a former fellow classmate, Elsinore, who is now married to a traveling salesman. Her encounter with Eva results in an expression of great unhappiness with her current circumstances.

Eva soon returns to England with her young son in hand, this time staying in a series of hotels. The child is a deaf mute, perfect for a mother who has little of intelligence to say, and who throughout the fiction is searching for someone upon whom to shower love. In short, Eva continues to wreak havoc upon all those with whom she becomes involved.

For Eva, we gradually discover, is not so much a realist character for the author as she is a metaphor of pure action, a big, clumsy, thoughtless whirlwind of a figure. Those least able to act, the emotionally complex and introspective Iseult and the eldest Dancey child, Henry, a bright and witty boy who ultimately enrolls in Cambridge, are naturally attracted (if slightly disgusted) by this energized force. Eva represents precisely what these two are missing in their lives. Yet by nature they both fear her: Iseult is not at all amused by Eva's blank stares, and Henry chastises Eva several times for her failure to think things out. Yet both enter into strange commitments with this force. Iseult determines to read to the young Eva in hopes of opening her mind and, later of course, opens her house to her. Against his better judgment, Henry agrees to play her husband in order to fulfill the fantasy of love and marriage for which Eva has so longed.

The disaster with which Bowen's fiction ends, the child murdering his mother with Eric's loaded and *real* gun, is somehow inevitable. For in a sense, the great vortex that Eva symbolizes must be destroyed so that other, more normal figures, can survive. Ultimately Eva's son, Jeremy, would have suffocated in Eva's fantasy of love, and he would never have been able to return enough to fill the vacuum at its center.

Bowen reiterates the tension between the two kinds of people she has created with references to Victorian literature that both Iseult and Henry mention. Broadstairs, the town to which Eva first retreats, is the home of Charles Dickens, a place which Iseult later visits. Henry mentions Browning's narrative poem-play, *Pippa Passes*. These two authors could not be more different.

Dickens' works, filled with orphans desperately seeking for love, are played out on huge stages of vast action that catch up the characters into circumstances that are nearly always extremely bad or good.

Pippa, of Browning's carefully rhymed poem, walks through the city, singing songs that almost no one hears, but changing everyone for the better as she invisibly passes. While the figures of Browning's work may be contemplating divorce, rape, murder, revenge, and other horrible acts, Pippa's very existence, for the most part, alters their awful plans.

Iseult must certainly see herself more as a Pippa than a Dickensian figure, while Eva, it is clear, is a 20th-century equivalent of more than one of the great novelist's desperately needy beings. Iseult's feeling that she is somehow magically connected to Eva's son Jeremy is perhaps a kind of Pippa fantasy. But Iseult, in the end, does find some sense of balance, returning to Eric.

Henry, like Constantine, is too cynical to see himself as aligned with either, but the family in which he has grown up behave much like a series of Dickens' comic characters. But he, like Constantine—who changes in the process of the story from a wicked controller of others to a man in love, in his case with a priest—is so thoroughly affected by Eva that, by work's end, he is ready to really marry her instead of simply mimicking the act. Eva, drama itself, may be wonderful to contemplate, but is impossible to have and to hold.

LOS ANGELES, JULY 18, 2011
Reprinted from *EXPLORING* fictions (August 2011).

The Man Who Would Not Die

IVY COMPTON-BURNETT **MANSERVANT AND MAIDSERVANT** (PUBLISHED IN THE US AS **BULLIVANT AND THE LAMBS**) NEW YORK: ALFRED A. KNOPF, 1948; REPRINTED BY NEW YORK: NEW YORK REVIEW BOOKS, 2001)

IT MAY SOUND by my title as if I am calling up shades of the Russian monk Rasputin to describe events in Ivy Compton-Burnett's masterful dialogue fiction. Horace Lamb, the dictatorial and peevish husband and father at the center of her fiction, certainly outlives all manner of possible murders. Although none of the family or servants actually plot or enact Horace's brushes with death, they certainly all harbor some reticent desire for his demise.

The fiction begins with the rather tyrannical father arguing with his cousin Mortimer about whether or not the fire is smoking. Mortimer's suggestion that the fire "appears" to be smoking outrages Horace, who cannot tolerate nor think of abstractions. For him, everything is concrete, "black or white," "yes or no"; and that problem is at the heart of his difficulties with others, who dream and plot, wish, scheme, or just desire!

That first morning already hints of his own wife's exasperation with him. Called away to her ill mother, she is only too happy, it appears, to escape Horace's temper. What we don't yet know, but soon discover, is that she plans to leave Horace and marry Mortimer, hoping that the children may join her.

That is the first of the dark events that permeates Compton-Burnett's fiction, and builds up a web of near melodramatic incidents that often seems at odds with the intelligent and witty commentary through which the story is told. Of the British dialogue fiction writers (Elizabeth Bowen, Ronald Firbank, Anthony Powell, Henry Green, and Evelyn Waugh among them), Compton-Burnett is the purest in the sense that almost all of her tale is told through conversation rather than description. And since almost all of her figures—except perhaps for the lowly servants George and Miriam—speak so literally, it is not hard to imagine them playing in what at times appears to be a Victorian gothic romance.

Certainly there are no ghosts in the Lamb house, just the personal secrets and frailties of the entire family. While Horace is obviously the most flawed and the least likeable figure, he perceives himself to be the most rational being in the house. Once he has gotten wind of his wife's intentions, he begins also to see himself as a kind of tortured man, betrayed, a bit like Lear, by his family members.

Rather than railing against events, however, Horace determines to change his relationship with his children, which he achieves, bringing them from open fear and opposition into a more-loving family circle wherein he reads to them, embraces them, and opens himself to their expressions in a way he had not previously done. Despite her intentions, his wife, Charlotte, *does* return, and discovering the changes in family life, realizes she cannot now leave without losing her children.

Mortimer perceives that his relationship with her cannot persist, particularly since she is more in love with her children than with him. While accepting Charlotte, Horace sends Mortimer away, hoping he will marry a local girl and live in the mill house. But Mortimer breaks with the girl when he discovers that it was she who had read his letter from Charlotte and revealed the truth to Horace. With a small allowance from Horace (who controls his wife's money), Mortimer leaves the Lamb house, staying in a rented room in another town.

While neither Mortimer nor Charlotte have sought Horace's death, they were certainly ready to spiritually and emotionally destroy him through their acts. And from these events Horace gives rise to new suspicions he might have previously been unable to imagine. At times his fears grow into a kind of paranoia.

Nonetheless, Horace is secretly pleased when Mortimer unexpectedly returns to the house, having missed their conversations.

Hardly has family life returned to normal, however, before Horace, trying to sort out events, takes a walk in the direction of a bridge which most of the family members know is ready to collapse, but have failed to notify Horace. His two sons, Marcus and Jasper, watch him as he passes, and soon recognize that he is on the way to the bridge. At first they think about warning him, but realizing it is probably too late, they instead ponder what his death might mean to them and the family. Within a few moments, however, they are penitent for their thoughts and come running into the house with tears and cries of fear.

People are called forth to check on Horace, as the

family waits in horror. But Horace returns unscathed, a recently placed sign having warned him away from crossing. When he hears the series of events, however, he is shocked by what he quickly perceives was his sons' momentary desire for his death. His reaction, as of old, is extreme. He threatens no possibility of communication or even, in their minds, expulsion from the family.

While Mortimer and Charlotte argue for their innocence and his patience, Horace grows angrier and angrier:

> So I am placed like this. My children desire my death. That is their feeling for their father. I have escaped from it to find it is what is wished for me. And I can honestly say that I have never wished it for anyone else. I have never grudged anyone the right to live.

This from a man who has seldom allowed others to be what they might.

As Marcus later retorts:

> We are afraid of you. You know we are.... Your being different for a little while has not altered all that went before. Nothing can alter it. You did not let us have anything; you would not let us be ourselves. If it had not been for Mother, we would rather have been dead. It was feeling like that so

often, that made us think dying an ordinary thing. We had often wished to die ourselves.

A third "attempt" on Horace's life occurs when the young servant George, ill-treated by the head butler, Bullivant, and virtually ignored by the family, is discovered stealing treats from the cupboard which he plans to award to his friends. Called into a conversation with Horace, the boy refuses to attend, claiming his day off. What he plans to do is kill himself by leaping from the bridge, leaving Horace to suffer the consequences of guilt.

George cannot bring it off, but instead removes the "Danger" sign. Again Horace approaches the bridge, wondering if it might now be repaired, before discovering the sign a ways off along with a knife that he has given his son.

Accusations again resound throughout the Lamb home, only to be cleared when neighbors report having seen George with the knife a few hours earlier in the town general store. George, who has returned to the house, is upbraided—although in kinder terms than Horace might have accomplished—by Bullivant.

Pneumonia, a far more dangerous opponent, takes over Horace's body, and, as the family quietly suffers in silence, his end seems to be near. The wonder of Compton-Burnett's tale is that, as Horace finally encounters a real threat to his life rather than the imaginary ones he has battled throughout the story, family members and servants grow more and more contrite, expressing their need for and love of their tyrannical father, who has been just if not wise in his behavior. And experiencing the weakness of his own body somehow changes Horace as well, as if he begins to perceive the human frailty in himself, not simply in others.

Horace's miraculous resurrection is also a family reconstruction, each of them returning to their proper roles. Marcus and Jasper, along with Avery, Sarah, and Tamisin, can return to being children. Aunt Emilia, Charlotte, and Mortimer again become the core of love in this cold house. Bullivant, Cook, George, and Miriam remain in loyal service to the whole. Horace, for all of his weaknesses and blunders, has once again survived.

LOS ANGELES, AUGUST 21, 2011
Reprinted from *EXPLORING*fictions (August 2011).

International Relationships

ANTHONY POWELL **VENUSBERG** (LONDON: DUCK-
WORTH, 1932); REPRINTED BY (LOS ANGELES: GREEN
INTEGER, 2003)

THE FIGURE AT the center of Anthony Powell's satiric
"dialogue fiction" is Lushington, far too serious and
lugubrious for the events he encounters. Like Henry
Green's *Party Going*, this book begins in a pea-soup
fog in London, involving, just as in Green's work, an

affair with a woman, the
beautiful Lucy, who allows
Lushington to observe her
during her bath; yet, just as
in Green's fiction, little occurs since she is apparently
in love with Lushington's
close friend, Da Costa, who
represents England in an
unnamed Baltic country.

At least Lushington has consummated his relationship with Lucy; it is unclear whether Lucy's beloved Da Costa has ever had sex, since he seems utterly uninterested in women, attending to them—just as he attends to foreign service—distractedly and ineffectually. If Lushington seems confused and without direction, Da Costa is an absolute fool whose major attentions appear to be focused on his overly eager-to-serve and ridiculously loquacious valet, Pope, known to his former army comrades as "the Duke."

Nearly everyone in Powell's delicious put-down of "international relationships" is an out-sized type, nearly all of them desperately seeking love, with few of them knowing how to achieve it. On the boat over to the mysterious Baltic country, Lushington, sent there by his newspaper, meets several of these figures, including the sad and disintegrating Russian Count Scherbatcheff and the far more outrageous and pretentious Count Bobel, both of whom will be ostracized from the society of this Baltic country, which is suffering the later stages of an attempt at Russian takeover. Throughout the work, there is an underlying fear of murders and bombing, which at first merely intrigues Lushington, but later thoroughly involves him and ends in his necessary escape from the scene of which he is supposed to be reporting.

Also on the voyage over, the reporter meets two

women, Baroness Puckler and Frau Mavrin, the latter a handsome and elegantly poised woman with whom he becomes sexually involved. It is his relationship with Frau Mavrin and his pretended friendship with Mavrin's clueless, academic husband, Panteleimon, that lend Lushington any dimension, and stir up, from time to time, Powell's otherwise rather static plot.

Indeed, it is as if all of these figures and others were attempting to play out their lives simply to be brought into the pages of Lushington's newspaper. For behind the scenes nearly all their lives are empty and quite meaningless. When Lushington visits his friend Scherbatcheff we encounter a kind of hellish apartment wherein various members of his family go about their paltry lives trying to walk round and ignore each other's presence. Despite the Count's good-natured acceptance of his condition, the visit is one of the most painful scenes of Powell's book, and through it we suddenly comprehend the character's depressive and, ultimately, consumptive state of mind and body. His death is cruelly announced in Powell's work: "And then one day Count Scherbatcheff died."

Frau Mavrin's homelife is hardly better. She, Lushington, and others, visiting one late night, must awaken her husband, who, forced to dress, appears only as his guests are about to leave, and is left with little to do but help them take the unresponsive elevator down to the street. Later, Panteleimon pours out his fears of his wife's affairs to Lushington, all his suspicions pointing to Da Costa, with whom he seems determined to fight a duel, while Lushington, the guilty one, feeds him platitudes.

Bobel is clearly a fool who cannot even attain a central table at the local cabaret, Maxims. Cortney, an American, is as clumsy and empty-minded as they come, while the militaristic stooge, Waldemar, is more concerned with his uniform than any ideas he might express.

While one might worry about the fate of this small Baltic country, there is so little at the center of this outlandish place that, like Lushington, we are hard-pressed to care about its affairs. While in reality, I cared very much about and loved my visits in Lithuania, Latvia, and Estonia, Powell's non-existent Baltic spot seems to survive on a series of nightly parties in which very little happens and even less is intelligently discussed. But then, to be fair to Powell, neither have we heard any intelligent conversation in the London presented in this book!

It is only a tragedy that lends any significance to Lushington's stay in "Venusberg," a world where love seems to matter more than anything else. After attending the annual grand ball, Lushington, tired and disturbed by Frau Mavrin's foul moods (she is furious about his imminent departure), decides to walk home in the cold, while his friend Da Costa escorts her home.

Assassins, supposedly attempting to kill Police Commissar Kuno, attack a droshky, and end the lives of both Da Costa and, as Lushington later discovers, Frau Mavrin instead. But we also must question whether Panteleimon might have had a role in this. Called up in the middle of the night by Pope, Lushington serves as a witness to his friends' respectability.

As meaningless as has been his trip to this country, the reporter travels back to face what will clearly be an always slightly disinterested Lucy, where he will surely settle into a homelife as meaningless as all those lives he has just witnessed.

As in all Powell's works, the slightly bitter satire is infused with a brilliance of language that redeems the characters' lack of significance.

LOS ANGELES, SEPTEMBER 6, 2011
Reprinted from *EXPLORING*fictions (September 2011).

So and So

HENRY GREEN **PARTY GOING** (LONDON: THE HO-
GARTH PRESS, 1939)

THE ELDERLY MISS FELLOWES begins this wonderful
comic novel as she walks through a thick London fog
toward the train station where she intends to see her
niece, Claire, off on a trip the younger woman is making to the continent with several other friends. Suddenly, a dead pigeon falls from the murky sky to her
feet below. For some inexplicable reason, Miss Fellowes
picks up the dead bird, washing it in the lavatory sink,
and wrapping it up in brown parcel paper. Soon after,

> Miss Fellowes did not feel well, so, when she got to
> the top of those steps she rested there leaning on a
> handrail.

Slightly recovering, the woman decides to order
tea at the busy station food shop, but when no one will

come to wait on her, she decides to go over to the counter and order a whisky instead.

Meanwhile, the partygoing group gradually arrives, each member finding it difficult to make their way to the others, but eventually gathering, with their luggage, at a central point. Their host, Max, is the latest to arrive, after having considered not even going. The others, Claire, Evelyna, Angela, Julia, Alex, and Robert, gradually do link up, but by the time they encounter each other, the trains have been long delayed because of the fog, and Miss Fellowes has fallen into a faint at the restaurant. Max arranges for their party to inhabit rooms at the nearby station hotel, into which they also sneak Claire's ill aunt, before the management pulls down the gates over the entrances to protect the premises from the potentially marauding crowds beginning to gather at the station.

So begins Green's satirical work. The rest of it is spent in close rooms, where the women each gossip and try to out-wit one other, manipulating the men in their group, while trying each to vie for the eligible, wealthy, and handsome Max. Alex, who is gay, spends most of his time whining and complaining, Robert retreats to the hotel barroom, and Angela's equally incompetent boyfriend mopes nearby, sorry that he had not wished her a better farewell.

Green's work, accordingly, is centered primarily on

the women and their subtle and, more often, obvious put-downs of one another, just as they pretend long friendships and admiration for each another. Into this group, the beautiful and legendary Amabel miraculously finds entry, claiming her right to join them, even though she has been rather specifically uninvited by Max. Her visit, moreover, ratchets up the heightened tensions between these competitive harridans, and ultimately threatens to break up the party. Nothing much else happens in this fiction, but the war of words and these women's mindless and often meaningless actions and disparagements of one another, along with Alex's aspersions, and Angela's discomfort (she is a first-timer in their party), create enough comic energy to match any boulevard farce.

All the ninnies gathered at the hotel, wealthy and/or spoiled, are, at heart, mean and bored, having no ideas with which to entertain their empty heads. And Green's satire soon turns somewhat vicious as we observe their selfish manipulations. Only the gravely ill Miss Fellowes, cared for by two of the women's nannies who have also come to see the group off, perceives anything of significance. In her fight against alcohol and possible death, she undergoes a kind of spiritual journey that transforms the empty connections made by the others into something meaningful and possibly salving.

Claire, as well as the others, is described as being incapable of caring for her aunt, and, we gradually discover, she is only too ready to leave her behind in the strange hotel room and escape, Green revealing that Miss Fellowes herself cannot stand her niece, nor Claire's mother, the older woman's sister—feelings we share.

The vast void of these individual's lives is less revealed in their catty statements and petty behavior than in Green's own impeccable style—through the very language Green uses to convey their feelings. Among the author's several rhetorical devices, the most obvious is his use of the word "so" to convey the weak link of their logic. The conjunction and, at times, adjective, seems to convey an underlying relationship of events where there are actually no real connections. Three examples from many dozens of instances throughout the work will have to suffice:

> She called him darling, which was of no significance except that she had never done *so* before, and he did not at once tumble to it that her smiles and friendliness for him, which like any other girl she could turn on at will *so* that it poured pleasantly out in the way water will do out of taps... (p. 117) [italics mine]

So she came over to where he was sitting, and, his hands taken up with pouring out his drink, she kissed his cheek and then sat down opposite. (p. 113) [italics mine]

They made noises which could be taken to mean yes and Julia explained to Miss Henderson how Max had already ordered tea *so* that it would be easy to carry two cups along to them without Angela knowing. (p. 71) [italics mine]

One need only compare that false connection of "so," with the adjectival and adverbial connections, that actually suggest a subsequent relationship, used to describe Miss Fellow's nightmare adventures:

And Miss Fellowes wearily faced another tide of illness. Aching all over she watched helpless while that cloud rushed across to where she was wedged and again the sea below rose with it, most menacing and capped with foam and as it came nearer she heard again the shrieking wind in throbbing through her ears. In terror she watched the seas rise to get at her, *so* menacing her blood throbbed unbearably, and again it was all forced into her head but this had happened *so* often she felt she had experienced the worst of it. But now with a roll of drums and then a most frightful crash lightning came out of that cloud and played upon the sea,

and this repeated, and then again, each time nearer
till she knew she was worse than she had ever been.
One last crash which she knew to be unbearable
and she burst and exploded into complete insensi-
bility. She vomited. [italics mine]

Here there is a specific relationship between events.
The mental vision Miss Fellowes encounters, a kind of
apocalyptic tempest, results in an actual physical action. The mental vision she encounters directly relates
to her own actions and behavior.

For the others, there is "no significance," as they
speak of pointless actions such as smiling, kissing a
cheek, or carrying two cups of coffee. For the partygoers, action is pointless, and ideation, accordingly, has no
real connection with the petty things they accomplish.

Whereas Max's gathering of nitwits can only wait,
twittering away their time before an equally meaningless adventure in the south of France, Miss Fellowes has
responded to nature in her attempt to give the dead
bird—itself a kind of symbol for the others' spiritual
deaths—a properly ritualized burial. It is she, accordingly, who must suffer the storms and waves of angst
that the others will not and cannot face.

When the news finally reaches the group that the
trains are running again, Julia—who throughout the
early part of the fiction has worried over what she calls

her charms, meaningless tokens from her childhood that she carries with her wherever she goes—rushes into Miss Fellowes' room, bursting out with the news, oblivious of Miss Fellowes' presence:

> "children we are to go, they've telephoned to say it's all over, isn't it just wonderful and we're to get reading, darlings, just think."

But, obviously, she and her friends cannot "think," for they have no "fellow" feelings, no empathy for anything or anyone in the world around them. Julia's tokens are all inanimate objects, *things*, as opposed to Miss Fellowes' formerly living bird. In the world of the party-goers there are no true connections between anything they might do as opposed to something else, and, therefore, no difference between present or past. As Embassy Richard says, after he is asked to join their party:

> "But weren't you going anywhere?" Amabel said to Richard, only she looked at Max.
>
> "I can go where I was going afterwards," he said to all of them and smiled.

The relationship between Julia and her friends is summarized, again with the recurrent word "so," a few sentences earlier:

So like when you were small and they brought children over to play with you and you wanted to play on your own then someone, as they hardly ever did, came along and took them off *so* you could do what you wanted.

LOS ANGELES, SEPTEMBER 12, 2011
Reprinted from *EXPLORING*fictions (September 2011).

Life in Duluth

JOHN ASHBERY AND JAMES SCHUYLER **NEST OF NINNIES** (CALAIS, VERMONT: Z PRESS, 1975)

ASHBERY AND SCHUYLER begin their fiction in what seems, at first, an almost conventional mode. Two people, Alice and Marshall, sit at the dinner table, gently arguing, a conversation that appears to be between husband and wife. He, quite obviously, goes to the city every day to work, while she, a 1950s housewife, it seems,

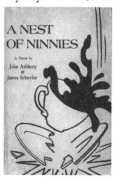

is dissatisfied with life in a New York suburban community, "fifty miles from a great city."

Alice seems bored, languid at the very least, uninterested in the leftovers that Marshall has pulled from the refrigerator for their supper. Poutingly, she refuses to eat, wanting to go to the city. Marshall himself is described as sulking, seeking a missing bread basket in which to serve hot bread. Indeed, pouting, sulking, and wounding seem to be the major activities of these two, until they are interrupted by a woman, Fabia, from next door, at which point Marshall seems to come alive while Alice retreats to the basement to shake their furnace into action. Before long a fuse has blown and a snowstorm has begun, the three heading off to a hardware store and to a nearby Howard Johnson's for a drink.

Throughout *Nest of Ninnies*, in fact, storms—both meteorologically and emotionally—are abrew. None of the characters might be described as emotionally stable, and the weather, no matter where these figures go, is generally filled with rain, snow, ice, and wailing winds. And many of the characters perpetually drink.

In this first chapter, moreover, we quickly discover that whatever one might think are the facts have nothing to do with reality—if there is a reality in their world. Language, in particular, makes no true connections. In the first few pages I've described above, the characters speak more by association than with any attempt to truly communicate:

"We of course made no attempt to alter this old place when we took it over, beyond a few slight repairs," Marshall seemed aware of the young woman for the first time. "I wanted to have the fireplace bricked up because it cools the house, but so many people commented on it we decided to leave it."

"You don't seem to see so many people."

"Look, snow is coming down it now."

An especially loud clang from the basement caused them both to start. "You sit down and I'll get you a cup of coffee. I'll put on the lights and call Alice," Marshall announced.

Alice's dim form appeared in the door. "I think I've just blown a fuse. Hello, Fabia."

"That's very funny. The fuses at our house blew out too. It must be general."

As we move forward into this strangely charted territory, we gradually begin to meet other characters—Fabia's brother Victor, who has just dropped out of college, and her parents, The Bridgewaters—while we discover that the quarreling couple of the first scene are not husband and wife, but sister and brother, Marshall being somewhat attracted to Fabia, while Alice is interested in the wayward Victor.

As these characters (types more than flesh-and-blood figures) are established, we begin to suspect that the fiction will be a kind of domestic story of their interchanging relationships and lives. But after a few chapters, in which the characters half-heartedly attempt to settle down (Marshall is the only one, it appears, who has a job), Ashbery and Schuyler take the work in an entirely different direction.

Just as we grow used to the small cast of figures the authors have presented us, they quickly move forward in space, first to Florida, then to Paris, Italy, back to New York, and away again, floating in an out of their original home while adding more and more figures as they go.

One might argue that, after the first few scenes, Ashbery and Schuyler pick up where Henry Green's marvelous *Party Going* ended, with a large party of figures finally ready to move on. That group of ninnies is perhaps more British than this American grouping, but there are enough French acquaintances, Italian pick-ups, Pen Pals, schoolgirls, and numerous others to create a hilarious international "nest" into which and out of which the figures come and go, just as in Green's fiction.

If the language these characters use is absurdly associative and self-centric, so too are their actions. Time and again characters meet and accidently re-encounter each other as if the whole of Europe and the US were just as small as the suburban New York community in which the work begins and ends.

Just as absurdly, in the latter part of the book, the figures pair off in odd combinations we might never have expected, Alice marrying an Italian pick-up, Giorgio, and together opening a restaurant; Irving Kelso, a mama's boy and Marshall's co-worker, marrying a French woman the group has met in Florida, Claire; and Claire's sister pairing up with Victor.

Victor's Pen Pal, Paul, meanwhile, arrives at novel's end with Marshall, the two having evidently traveled to Duluth and South Bend! As all the other figures move off in the various directions their lunatic behavior leads them, Marshall announces that he may move to Duluth; Duluth, he reveals, is big in plastics, and his company (evidently producing or using plastics) wants to open up a new branch in that northern Minnesota city.

I have eyes only for Duluth. That's a place where they really know how to relax and get the most out of life. I could even live there myself. You never saw such steaks.

Paul announces, in turn, that he likes the US and may not return to his home in France. Both speak of the delights of South Bend.

Meanwhile Fabia was saying to Paul, "What *was* there in South Bend, anyway?"

"You won't believe this," Paul said, "but it's true: a Pam-Pam's!"

"Oh," Fabia allowed.

The cryptic reference to the international bar and restaurant chain suggests far more than it appears to, perhaps even hinting at how to read through the characters' scatter-brained references.

Bar Pam-Pam's was a kind of early bar and coffee house scene, as popular in its time as Starbucks today, except that several of the Bar Pam-Pam's operations played cool jazz and catered to special audiences.* Cartoonist Joe Ollmann writes in *The Paris Review* about a local Pam-Pam's in New York which he describes as an "old man bar," suggesting to me that its clientele, while not exclusively, included elderly gays. What Ashbery and Schuyler seem to suggest, accordingly, is that suddenly Marshall and Paul are a couple who perhaps may be the first to escape the loony nest into which the dozens of characters have fast settled.

After having just feasted on Giorgio's special courses, Victor suggests in the final lines of the book, perhaps hinting at the new relationship between the two men:

I'm so hungry I could eat a wolf. Why don't we go over the Gay Chico and have some refried beans?

And so these "cliff dwellers" bid their goodnights, moving off toward the parking lots and shopping plazas of their empty lives. Life in Duluth might be just the tonic.

———

*Steve Fletcher describes a Bar Pam-Pam in England on the internet:

The refectory in the college had about as much atmosphere as a cemetery with lights, so a girl student with whom I was highly smitten, Diane, suggested we go to the Pam Pam. A coffee bar.

It was just across Oxford Circus at the junction with Hanover Street and Hanover Square and the exterior had a South East Asian look about it which was continued on the inside with low lighting, bamboo and palm trees in jungle browns and greens.

The Pam Pam was quite small; it had about half a dozen very low tables and behind the counter was the first coffee machine I had ever seen. (There was a small upstairs section too over the counter with no more than three tables.)

Scandinavian open sandwiches were the house speciality (and the only ones on offer) consisting of a piece of rye bread topped with a piece of lettuce, a tomato and a hard boiled egg or a sardine—very exotic.

A bit pricey too, I seem to remember. But the owner, a Spaniard, was never in a hurry to get rid of poor students. He also played music: jazz. Not on a juke box but on a Dansette 78 r.p.m. record player behind the counter.

He had great taste and I was always asking him what the records were, his favourites being the boogie inspired piano pieces by Oscar Peterson. Cool sounds in a cool place.

The Pam Pam was different and quite unlike the other coffee houses I was now also frequenting—the infamous French coffee/newspaper shop near the corner of Old Compton and Charing Cross Road, and the Gyre & Gimble at Charing Cross.

There one could rub shoulders with hookers, villains and dealers—plus the likes of Victor Passmore, Francis Bacon, Lucien Freud and demimonde characters like Quentin Crisp and Ironfoot Jack.

Because it was just outside Soho and on the edges of Mayfair, which was relatively quiet at night, the Pam Pam seemed a bit exclusive to the art students of RSP. I hung out there for about a year and became an ardent modern jazz fan.

LOS ANGELES, NOVEMBER 8, 2011
Reprinted from *EXPLORING* fictions (November 2011).

Prophets of the Ordinary

JANE BOWLES **TWO SERIOUS LADIES** IN **MY SIS-TER'S HAND IN MINE: AN EXPANDED EDITION OF THE COLLECTED WORKS OF JANE BOWLES** (NEW YORK: THE ECCO PRESS, 1978)

THE TWO SERIOUS LADIES of Jane Bowles' title are, in many ways, as different as they could be; and, although they know one another slightly, they are not good friends.

Bowles presents us with a brief history of Christina Goering, daughter of a wealthy American industrialist. Even as a child Christina was not appealing, most children refusing to play with her because of the puritanical religious games she demanded along with a bizarre series of punishments, in one case involving being packed in mud before swimming in a small stream. Yet, as with almost all Bowles' women, she is strong-minded, opinionated, and feels no regret for speaking forthrightly. She is, in some senses, an absolute monster. Yet,

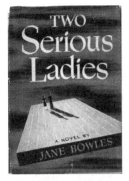

throughout her life, she attracts people to her, or at least they are attracted to her because of her money. Lucy Gamelon, despite not having any real connection to Miss Goering, visits her one day, only to move in with her the next day. At a party, Miss Goering meets a sweating, overweight man, Arnold, who soon also moves in with her and Miss Gamelon.

But hardly has this tale begun, with its completely unexpected results, before Bowles interrupts it to tell another story, about Mrs. Copperfield. Miss Goering and Mrs. Copperfield meet momentarily at the party, but other than that, there seems to be little connection, and one can only wonder at the structural logic of Bowles' fiction.

We do, however, sense a link between the two, other than the authorial declaration of them both being "serious" ladies. Mrs. Copperfield is far more hesitant in doing new things than is Miss Goering, yet it is she who actually travels, with her husband, to Panama. And once she is ensconced in the run-down hotel in the middle of town to which he has taken her—determined to forgo the expense of the more popular tourist hotel—she appears far more adventuresome than anyone else in the fiction.

Certainly her first foray into Colón street life is characterized as a Kafka-esque nightmare:

> They were walking through the streets arm in arm. Mrs. Copperfield's forehead was burning hot and her hands were cold. She felt something trembling in the pit of her stomach. When she looked ahead of her the very end of the street seemed to bend and then straighten out again.... Above their heads the children were jumping up and down on the wooden porches and making the houses shake. Someone bumped against Mrs. Copperfield's shoulder and she was almost knocked over. At the same time she was aware of the strong and fragrant odor of rose perfume. The person who had collided with her was a Negress in a pink silk evening dress.
>
> ..."Listen," said the Negress, "go down the next street and you'll like it better. I've got to meet my beau over at that bar." She pointed it out to them. "That's a beautiful barroom. Everyone goes in there," she said. She moved up closer and addressed herself solely to Mrs. Copperfield. "You come along with me, darling, and you'll have the happiest time you've ever had before. I'll be your type. Come on."
>
> ...The Negress caressed Mrs. Copperfield's face with the palm of her hand. "Is that what you want to do darling, or do you want to come along with me."

"...Wasn't that the strangest thing you've ever seen?" said Mrs. Copperfield breathlessly.

It is precisely scenes like this, or even more normal-seeming meetings wherein the characters say totally unpredictable things, that entice us into Bowles' story and help us to comprehend Mrs. Copperfield's actions. For no sooner has she encountered this strange world than she is truly sucked up into it, joining, ultimately, the prostitute Pacifica, who encourages her to move into the Hotel de las Palmas where she lives.

Giving up her husband's hotel, and, finally, even her husband himself, the timid and frightened Mrs. Copperfield discovers the friendship and love of the local prostitutes and shares time with them drinking in bars. By the end of her story, we recognize that she, like Miss Goering, is a woman on a mission to challenge herself, to alter her life, and survive in conditions she might never have imagined. Similar to Miss Goering, this serious woman is rushing into the unknown as a kind of punishment and test for her own fears. As Mr. Copperfield writes, in his goodbye letter to his wife:

Like most people, you are not able to face more than one fear during your lifetime. You also spend your life fleeing from your first fear towards your first hope. Be careful that you do not, through your own wiliness, end up in the same position in which you began.

In short, as we are about to discover, Mrs. Copperfield—although a much more charming and, at times, disarmingly sensual woman—is of the same breed as Miss Goering, both of them being strong strictly-raised women of great eccentricity who test themselves over and over again to challenge the patterns of their lives.

When we return to the story of Miss Goering, accordingly, we read her increasingly bizarre shifts in perception with the knowledge that, as in the case of Mrs. Copperfield, it can result in significant sensual changes.

Yet, as we have been told, Miss Goering's seriousness is more of the religious type than Mrs. Copperfield's inconsistencies. She is determined to challenge almost all her fears. She sells her lovely house, despite the outcry of the parasitic Miss Gamelon and challenges of the dependent Arnold, moving to an industrial island near Staten Island, into a house with little charm and hardly any heat.

When a third man, Arnold's father, determines to join their strange little community, Christina begins traveling to the larger island, visiting a local derelict bar and accepting the offers of its male customers to join them in bed.

After her first adventure, she reports that she intends to return, admitting that she may not immediately come back. One by one, the remaining trio who have lived with her, and off of her fortune, abandon the house, Arnold having discovered a new love, Miss Gamelon having moved into another house, and Arnold's father returning to his wife. In the end Miss Goering, who has gone off with an ugly man who believes she is a prostitute, must face a future even more undetermined than Mrs. Copperfield, who has returned to New York with Pacifica in tow—although it does appear that Pacifica may soon bolt.

Even Miss Goering, although believing that the challenges she has set before her, have made her "nearer to becoming a saint," wonders if she hasn't been piling "sin upon sin as fast as Mrs. Copperfield." For these strong women have both become dependent upon the flesh.

The marvel of Bowles' strange tale is its complete originality. Although the events she describes are often strange, even a bit surreal, they are played out in such a seemingly logical way that they seem even more incredible for having occurred. Most importantly, the central figures speak in their own linguistic pattern, mixing a kind of 19th-century rhetoric with a language which might be at home on the street. In a very odd way, Bowles' language is as outlandish as Damon Runyon's—like Runyon's, these characters are not particularly educated, however their talking is a process of thought instead of simple communication. And in that sense, they are always participating in a dialogue—socially or internally—with everyone around them, with the entire world.

At times, in fact, it seems that the whole world might potentially be pulled into Bowles' tale as the two serious ladies travel about, gathering up friends and lovers as they go. Both are heavy drinkers who prefer to sit at the bar, who and seem able to attract anyone they speak to. Critics have mentioned the pattern of twos and threes that accumulate around Mrs. Copperfield and Miss Goering, but I would argue that, while the two do tend to alternate between duos and trios, like magnets they might equally attract dozens of willing partners, men and women. And, in that sense, these highly wrought women are a bit like latter-day prophets, missionaries who, in preaching to the natives, willingly take on the attributes and behavior of those they seek to save, transforming themselves, in the end, into absolutely ordinary human beings. Yet both, strangely, have become something larger simply through their abilities to change their lives.

LOS ANGELES, NOVEMBER 29, 2011
Reprinted from *EXPLORING* fictions (December 2011).

Living in the Details

SAMUEL BECKETT **WAITING FOR GODOT** / LOS AN-
GELES, MARK TAPER FORUM / THE PRODUCTION I SAW
WAS ON APRIL 7, 2012

WITNESSING the brilliant production, directed by Michael Arabian, of the Mark Taper Forum's *Waiting for
Godot*, I was struck by something that I had not noticed
from previous viewings or reading the play. Watching Alan Mandell (as Estragon), Barry McGovern
(as Vladimir), James Cromwell (as Pozzo), and Hugo
Armstrong (as Lucky), one gets the sense that, except
for an occasional overlong pause which slowed down
this production a bit, the performances were close to
perfect. The long-time Beckett thespians, Mandell and
McGovern, spout the often fast-paced dialogue in a
rhythm that is pitch perfect, along with bodily motions
that reveal their every thought.

For the first time in this moving production, I
became aware of just how spare Beckett's great work

truly is. My companion Howard, enjoying the first act, commented on the obvious: "Beckett seems to have presented all his themes in the first few minutes. I can't imagine what he might have to say in the second act."

"Well," I mused, "that's true. But his themes are really not what matter most. The fact that we live in a universe promising the return of a missing God, that some men, like Pozzo, are entirely wrapped up in themselves, mean men of power who do nothing but rule over others' lives—is not central to the play at all. Suffering, despair, pain, boredom...yes, these are the givens of Beckett's universe, but they are not what makes his work so remarkable. It is the various ways, the numerous things we do each day to get through the suffering, despair, pain, boredom, loneliness, etc., that are at the center his plays and fictions. And that is everything, isn't it?"

By the end of the second act, Howard, who had never before seen a production of the play, understood what I was talking about. Beckett, more than nearly any other playwright, takes chances in *Waiting for Godot* by so pruning down the play's large themes that the work almost mocks itself. Estragon, who is always about to leave—even though his time apart from his long-time companion, Vladimir, results in endless beatings in a ditch—is reminded again and again by his friend that their existence on this bleak plateau with only a tree and a rock is to wait, to wait for Godot. That is their only purpose, despite the seeming meaninglessness of that. Whoever this Godot is—whether a personal God of vengeance (if they don't wait, Vladimir suggests at one point, they will be punished) or a New Testament God of love—it is clear that Godot may never come, may never return their patient and often impatient waiting on earth. He may not even be a loving God; after all, so we are told by the messenger boy, he beats the boy's brother. What kind of deity is that?

It hardly matters, so reverent are these two clowns who represent us. What is important is the waiting itself. But how to survive that? How to live through each day? That is at the heart of Beckett's play, is at the center of Beckett's melodious language. How might these two men—not necessarily "gay" men, but men who have, nonetheless, lived together for 50 years—get on? While fighting, contradicting one another, attacking each other, cajoling, complaining, laughing, watching, hugging, comforting, hating, threatening to part, and even contemplating suicide, they entertain one another, they talk and haggle, and cry and laugh the way each of us does daily. Godot may be what they think they are waiting *for*, but what these men *do* with their lives is try to communicate in the hundreds of ways man communicates with others and himself. The play is such a moving work of art not because of its over-arching thematics, not through its structure, but because of its presentation of everyday life, its barebones revelation of how mankind converts the emptiness of daily living into something of worth, of meaning, sometimes even into rapturous joy, but mostly into ridiculous acts.

Living, suggests Beckett, is not played out in the tectonics of great ideas, but in the details of everyday life. It can be the accidental encounter of two ridiculous strangers, Pozzo and Lucky, the second tortured by the first, while the power-hungry man is equally dependent upon his servant, a kind of lesson in Marxist-like theory. Or it can focus on the simple rediscovery of one's own boots. For Didi and Gogo—their personal nicknames for each other—getting through each day is sometimes even centered upon just talking about how they *might* get on, the contemplation of separating, or the observation of a tree suddenly spouting leaves. For Vladimir, surviving depends upon memory, while for Estragon, survival requires sleep. Beckett moves his play forward, in short, through his characters' attempts to move forward, to get on through just one more day, and another after that.

Such a structure, wherein the author reveals the creative act itself, is a dangerous

one, particularly for an audience which may desire to be told everything, to be led forward. In *Waiting for Godot*, however, the audience is put on edge, wondering what these two fools will come up with next. How will the plot move forward, how will they get through yet another day? But in that wonderment, the audience members are forced to re-imagine their own lives. Even the theater piece they are attending is a way to pass the time, to move forward through the day. They too must go home, eat a carrot, chew on a piece of radish, crawl into the ditch of their beds to be pummeled in lonely dreams throughout the night. Some may even contemplate bringing it all to an end. But most will arise to meet again, to work, to talk and haggle, to cry and laugh, just like the two clowns of Beckett's play do throughout the two days we witness of their lives.

LOS ANGELES, MARCH 9, 2012
Reprinted from *US Theater, Opera, and Performance* (March 2012).

Moving Forward by Standing Still

SAMUEL BECKETT **MERCIER AND CAMIER**, TRANS-
LATED FROM THE FRENCH BY THE AUTHOR (NEW YORK:
GROVE PRESS, 1974)

WRITTEN ORIGINALLY in 1946, Beckett's first novel after World War II did not have an easy time getting to press. Although it was accepted by the French publisher Bordas in 1947, Beckett withdrew it before it was printed, insisting that, according to biographer Deirdre Bair, it was "a working draft or preliminary attempt to evolve a new technique of fiction." After years of forbidding its publication—during which various critics quoted from it and wrote about it in their studies—Beckett was finally convinced to allow its 1970 publication in French. He still resisted translating it, the English-language edition not appearing until 1974.

Perhaps that delayed publication helped the work receive its proper due. Had it appeared earlier, it would

have seemed a very strange fiction indeed. It is now one of my favorites of Beckett's works.

The two characters, whom Beckett describes elsewhere as a pseudo-couple, in many respects are early versions of Vladimir and Estragon from *Waiting for Godot*. Like the couple of his famous play, they are vagabonds, opposites in appearance—one, "small and fat...red face, scant hair, four chins, protruding paunch, bandy legs, beady pig eyes," according to Conaire; the other, "a big bony look with a beard, hardly able to stand, wicked expression"—who come together, talk, speculate, argue, wonder, doubt, and attempt time and again to separate, only to return to one another's side. Like the famed dramatic duo, they seem to be awaiting something or, at least, seeking something they never find. Some passages, in fact, seem to be directly repeated in the later drama.

Like Vladimir and Estragon, their pairing belongs to a long tradition of inseparable comic figures dating back at least to Flaubert's Bouvard and Pécuchet, and embracing 20th-century figures such as Laurel and Hardy.

But these two, in other respects, are quite different from Gogo and Didi, for they do not simply remain on an empty plain with one tree in sight, but move forward and backward through a town that is similar to Dublin, venturing out and returning to rediscover their pasts and the dejecta they have shed in moving forward: a sack, a bicycle, a raincoat, an umbrella. Even more than Gogo and Didi, these two are a couple, not only through deep friendship, but sexually as well. They sleep together, side by side, hand in hand throughout the story (the dramatic couple of *Godot* separate each night), and, at least at one point, at Helen's place—the brothel to which they return again and again—Beckett describes their activities as such:

> They passed a peaceful night, for them, without debauch of any kind. All next day they spent within doors. Time tending to drag, they mansturprated mildly, without fatigue. Before the blazing fire, in the twofold light of lamp and leaden day, they squirmed gently on the carpet, their naked bodies mingled, fingering and fondling, with the languorous tact of hands arranging flowers, while the rain beat on panes. How delicious that must have been!

While this passage, and others in the fiction, seems to indicate homosexual bonding between the two, we must not make too much of this, since Camier describes a former marriage, and Mercier, momentarily left alone, is confronted early in the book by two children who, upon seeing him, call him "Papa." More importantly, in many respects Mercier and Camier, despite their physical differences, are one: both aspects of Beckett's own persona, an inner and outer portrait of a lost being in search of some place to which he might escape.

Yet, the intensity of their relationship, the deep emotions they feel for each other—despite their attempts, at times, to escape each other's presence—is important to the work. For without each other and the kind of yin and yang they represent, the other is nothing; and when they do part near the end of the book, Beckett introduces a character from a previous fiction, Watt, to temporarily bring them back together, reintroducing them to one another all over again. Just as Beckett's tale cannot begin until the two, on slightly different timetables, have comically matched their arrivals and departures to meet up with each other, so when they finally part—"Well, he said, I must go. Farewell, Mercier. Sleep sound, said Mercier."—the story goes dark:

Alone he watched the sky go out, dark deepen to full. He kept his eyes on the engulfed horizon, for he knew from experience what last throes it was capable of. And in the dark he could hear better too, he could hear the sounds the long day had kept from him, human murmurs for example, and the rain on the water.

In short, the fiction ends with a kind of death, not that very different, however, from the experiences of the couple throughout their "adventures."

What their so-called "adventures" consist of, obviously, makes up Beckett's tragicomic story. In one sense nothing happens except little oddities such as, early on, two dogs having intercourse in the same small archway where they wait out the rain, later the appearance of a businessman who claims they had made an appointment, and the violent intrusion and attempt to arrest them by a busybody constable. They are not precisely elements of plot, but random events that serve as counterpoints to the two figures' questions and speculations, as interruptions to their elementary summations. Indeed, as Beckett makes clear, there is in *Mercier and Camier* no story to be told, a reality he brilliantly satirizes with a ridiculously abbreviated summary after every two chapters. Yet for all that, it is as if these two lived out an entire life in their few days of travel. While Beckett's later figures often hardly move, living out the fictions they tell in their minds, these two move without getting anywhere, moving forward sometimes by standing still, yet becoming strangely exhausted by their seemingly Herculean ambulations. And, by fiction's end, not only have they rid themselves of all possessions, they have drained their bodies of the desire to move forward—or even backward for that matter. Like the characters in later Beckett

works, they have transformed their busy activities into abstract motions of thought. In this sense, Beckett truly does create in this marvelous work a kind of blueprint for his new fictional techniques, demonstrating just how much can happen in a world in which nothing of importance seems to transpire. The little voyages taken by Mercier and Camier are journeys more vast than those of the rest of humankind.

LOS ANGELES, APRIL 27, 2012
Reprinted from *EXPLORING*fictions (April 2012).

Be Again

SAMUEL BECKETT **KRAPP'S LAST TAPE** / LOS ANGE-
LES, PRODUCTION OF THE GATE THEATRE DUBLIN AT
THE KIRK DOUGLAS THEATRE / THE PERFORMANCE I
SAW WAS ON NOVEMBER 4, 2012

ACTOR John Hurt's portrayal of Krapp in Beckett's
1958 play is absolutely brilliant, except for, perhaps, the
near interminable pause before the actor begins speaking. The stark setting of the play, with a single spot of
bright white light, gives a grand theatricality to Krapp's
world, a world in which, under the light, he feels safe,
surrounded by darkness wherein, as Beckett himself de-
scribed it, "Old Nick"
or death awaits. Hurt
reiterates this once or
twice by daring, with
some humor, to enter,
momentarily, the sur-
rounding darkness.

On his 69th birthday, Krapp, yet again, forces himself to interact with a younger incarnation. It is clear that Krapp has a fixation with his former selves. For years he has recorded tapes describing his life's events, most of them quite meaningless, but some revealing great poetry and sensibility. The tape Krapp chooses on this particular rainy night is "Box 3, Spool 5," the day Krapp turned 39.

Director Michael Colgan reveals that what leads up to his playing the tape is as important in some senses as what is actually on the tape. The ritualistic acts, Krapp's continual checking of the time, his strange way of eating a banana—he puts the entire banana into his mouth, holding it there for a while before biting it off, clearly a bow to the fruit's sexual suggestions—and his nearly falling on the banana peel he has tossed into the dark reveal him to be a kind of eccentric fool—in short, the typical Beckett figure. As his name suggests, he is "full of shit."

Hurt presents Krapp with a kind of valor despite obviously distancing him from the human race. Clearly Krapp's mother has been a monster, living for years in a world of "vidiuity"—the condition of being or remaining a widow. The small things he describes are both comical and life-affirming: playing ball with a dog as his mother dies, awarding the ball to the dog as he hears of his mother's death, attending a vesper service as a child, falling off the pew.

Krapp is an everyday man with romantic aspirations, or at least he was, it is apparent, at age 39, the time when we all have arrived in the prime of life. Krapp at 39 is a smug bore—

> Spiritually a year of profound gloom and indulgence until that memorable night in March at the end of the jetty, in the howling wind, never to be forgotten, when suddenly I saw the whole thing. The vision, at last. This fancy is what I have chiefly to record this evening, against the day when my work will be done and perhaps no place left in my memory, warm or cold, for the miracle that...(hesitates)...for the fire that set it alight. What I suddenly saw then was this, that the belief I had been going on all my life, namely—(Krapp switches off impatiently, winds tape forward, switches on again)—

—a man who will not regret any decision of his life. But he is also a man amazingly come alive through the love of a woman, whom he describes lovingly in a scene where the two lie in a small punt as it floats into shore through the reeds.

The older Krapp, who realizes that his younger self could not imagine the loneliness and emptiness of the life ahead, has no patience at times with his past. His new tape, which he begins after impatiently winding the older tape ahead to escape his previous self's blindness, is filled with bitterness and anger for a failed life:

> Nothing to say, not a squeak. What's a year now? The sour cud and the iron stool. (Pause.) Reveled in the word spool. (With relish.) Spooool! Happiest moment of the past half million. (Pause.) Seventeen copies sold, of which eleven at trade price to free circulating libraries beyond the seas. Getting known. (Pause.)

He has failed, obviously, even in his writing career. Unlike his younger self, so unregretful of his past, the old Krapp is filled with the detritus of his life, all those materials left over from his disintegration. If the younger Krapp declares himself to be only moving forward, the older desires to "Be again!"

> Be again in the dingle on a Christmas Eve, gathering holly, the red-berried. (Pause.) Be again on Croghan on a Sunday morning, in the haze, with the bitch, stop and listen to the bells. (Pause.) And so on. (Pause.) Be again, be again. (Pause.) All that old misery. (Pause.) Once wasn't enough for you. (Pause.) Lie down across her.

He gives up this, his last tape (or perhaps simply his

latest), to listen again to his former self describing his sexual moment with the woman in the punt.

Hurt so painfully suffers and loves his former self—at one moment even embracing the machine during his young speeches—that one can almost hear his heart crack.

LOS ANGELES, NOVEMBER 6, 2012
A slightly different version of this piece about the filmed version with John Hurt was published in *Reading Films* (Los Angeles: Green Integer, 2012).

The Dapper Irishman

ON APRIL 12, 2012 our friend Ronan O'Casey (known to his close friends simply as Case) was playing poker at one of the small gambling parlors south of Los Angeles. He was, evidently, an extraordinary poker player, and that day he won $300, which he called to report to his wife, Carol Tavris; "I'm on my way home," he announced. Our friend Roz Leader, through whom we had long ago met Case and Carol, reported that she could just see him proudly driving away in a bright blue blazer, perhaps a purple or dark blue handkerchief sprouting from his coat pocket; Case was, with regard to dress, somewhat of a dandy.

A few minutes later, he called Carol again to report that he had suddenly begun to feel strange, quite awful in fact. She advised him, since he was already on the freeway, to pull over to the side. The phone went dead. She attempted to call the police, but since she didn't know his precise whereabouts, a search was nearly impossible. A short time later, however, the police called

back. A car had been spotted on one of the freeways, half on and half off the shoulder, with a body slumped over in the front seat. Having freed Case from the car and brought him to a local hospital, rescuers flew him by helicopter to UCLA hospital; he was pronounced dead upon arrival. So, at the age of 88, ended the life of Ronan O'Casey.

One cannot say that his death at that age was exactly a surprise. Case had been suffering the indignities of small strokes and other ailments for some time. But, as author Murray Pomerance—to whom I'd introduced Case and Carol a few years back—observed: "He seemed in some way, for all his fragility, immortal, as perhaps all Irishmen are."

By the time Howard and I had been introduced to Case at one of Roz's numerous dinner and holiday celebrations a number of years ago, he was, in some respects, a "man of the past," lovingly retelling his numerous stories of working with Michelangelo Antonioni in *Blow Up* (he played the dead body, a role which I describe in detail in *My Year 2007: To the Dogs*). But Case could also spin dozens of other stories, new and old, regarding his rich past as an actor (on the London stage in *Kiss Me, Kate, The Odd Couple*, and *Detective Story*; on TV as the well-known character of Jeff Rogers in *The Larkins* from 1958-1963; and in films such as Nicholas Ray's *Bitter Victory*, with Richard Burton and Christopher Lee). Besides  his acting career, Case had had an incredible life, was a marvelous cook, and could boast of having one of the most intelligent and perceptive wives anyone had ever met, author and social psychologist Carol; she remains one of my very favorite acquaintances.

Beyond this, Case had "style," which many described at his memorial service on April 22, 2012 as "grace." Case was a dynamic individual—no one can deny him that—loyal to friends, vociferously outspoken against whatever he saw as pretention—which sometimes, one must admit, could be directed at things simply outside his imagination. He was gloriously melodious of voice, charming and handsome, stubborn and, on rare occasions, plain irritating. Anything said against the Irish—despite the fact that Case, himself, was born in Montreal—was met with a flurry of abuse. I have already reported his outburst over my dislike of

 the Irish Nobel Prize-winning poet Seamus Heaney. Yet, when I later approached him for an interview about his experiences with Antonioni, Case came to lunch fluttering like a peacock, sweet and appreciative of my attentions, filled with knowledge and engaging tales.

Moreover, Case never stopped making new friends. Pomerance, who met him when he was writing a book on Antonioni, reported, "I felt close to him." That was the way with Case: if one liked the man, one felt embraced.

As Jay Perry described at the memorial ceremony for Case at a private home on Rising Glen Road, he was for many not just a friend, but a *great* friend, one for whom people went out of their way. Martha Bluming recited a long and charmingly written testimonial letter to Case's superb cherry pie. A lover of jazz, Case was celebrated at his memorial with a beautiful rendition of "Love is Here to Stay" by the duo Terry Trotter and Chuck Berghofer. Actor Theodore Bikel reminisced about his and Case's close friendship (more like brothers than just friends) in their early days in London and read, almost channeling Case's euphonious voice, Yeats' "Song of the Wandering Aengus." Carol read one of Case's favorite poems, e e cummings' "the great advantage of being alive." Case's son Matt read letters from relatives and friends unable to attend the ceremony.

Everyone was moved to tears. And, ultimately, when we looked around the room, seeking out the ghost of the man we knew would always hover over our lives, many of us muttered to ourselves, in a language characteristic to the man, "Fuck!" The dapper Irishman had died.

LOS ANGELES, APRIL 23, 2012
Reprinted from *Green Integer Review* (April 2012).

DINOSAURS

Whatever Happened to Willy Loman?

ARTHUR MILLER **DEATH OF A SALESMAN** / NEW YORK, ETHEL BARRYMORE THEATRE / THE PRODUCTION I SAW WAS THE EVENING PERFORMANCE OF MAY 4, 2012

AS BEN BRANTLEY noted in his *New York Times* review of this revival of the noted American play *Death of a Salesman*, one gets shivers from the first rise of the curtain just to be able to see the magnificent set from the original production by Jo Mielziner and hear the original score by Alex North. In some respects, this entire production, directed by the renowned Mike Nichols, seems a bit like a museum piece as the obviously able cast of Philip Seymour Hoffman, Linda Emond, and Andrew Garfield tiptoe through their lines with a kind of muted reverie. One certainly can respect Nich-

ols' quiet reverence for this play, given the many boisterous and mannered productions that have come before it, such as Dustin Hoffman's quirky 1984 interpretation (I saw only the filmed version); and, every so often, Nichols' rendition soars in its dramatic intensity. Andrew Garfield's tearful embracement of Willy as he admits his life's failures brings tears to the eyes of anyone who still has the capacity to feel. But for much of the production, I felt almost like Willy's wife, Linda, who admits in one of the last lines in the play: "Forgive me, dear. I can't cry. I don't know what it is, but I can't cry."

Holding back and holding in occasionally give new meaning to some scenes as well. Hoffman (usually an over-actor who here is utterly demure) plays Willy, in the scene where his son Biff (Garfield) visits him on the road only to discover a woman in his room, with devastating understatement, so skillfully in fact that it is hard to believe Biff when he later denies he is holding a grudge against his father. Similarly, the more naturalistic relationship between Willy and his ghost of a brother, Ben (John Glover), gives new resonance to what is usually a booming statement of the new potentials to be found in Alaska. Under Nichols' direction, the missed possibilities of Willy's life  seem never to have been real options, his family and his desire to die like the green-slippered salesman he encountered early in his life dominating Loman's middle-class vision of the world. Here too we perceive the other son Hap (Finn Witrock) as a kind of latter-day carbon copy of his uncle Ben, a fluttery profligate, perfectly willing to stand up his dinner appointment with his father and run off with the first woman he encounters, only to promise again and again that he will soon marry someone. If mendacity rules the Loman house, Ben is Willy's true heir.

But finally, one recognizes, that such a quiet production also allows one to hear all of the play's many creaks and ghostly moans. It is strange just how "stagey" is Miller's *Death of a Salesman*, given that this "realist play" was carefully grounded in everyday life, perhaps even more so than the utterly theatrical and highly exaggerated expressionist world of Tennessee Williams' *A Streetcar Named Desire* (a multicultural production of which is playing just three blocks away, a version drubbed by the critics). Stanley Kowalski—a worker from the lower class—literally soars as a character into the stratosphere of believable  American anti-heroes, while Willy Loman remains, 53 years after his first Broadway appearance, ploddingly grounded to the theater boards out of which he sprang, a concoction of Miller's deeply impassioned but, nonetheless, theme-driven social consciousness. Despite his wife's plea that "attention must be paid," time has turned our heads. The middle class which Willy so poignantly represented in 1949 has now nearly disappeared from American society, along with its mythical "American Dream."* And, in that respect, this play is not only dated, but outdated.

We might almost conclude that in this one instance Miller was prophetic in his ability to foresee as early as the late 1940s that the remnants of the vast American sales force—so crucial to the advance of capitalism in the early 20th century (and lovingly remembered in musicals such as *The Music Man*)—would ultimately disappear from the American landscape.

Today I have traveled to New York to spend a few minutes as a publisher with my sales representatives,

 among the very last of that dinosaur species. Within just a few years, as we know in our bones, all personal sales people will have disappeared, to be replaced with the computer and other as-yet-unimagined devices. Willy Loman must seem to most younger viewers—very few of whom made up the audience of the Friday evening performance of Miller's play—as unrecognizable as a typewriter, an obsolete thing of a forgotten past. By contrast, the Stanley Kowalskis of the world, outrageously larger-than-life second generation immigrant Koreans, Armenians, Haitians, Mexicans, Russians, Indians, Pakistanis, and others—sexually dynamic men and women temporarily locked into poverty—still exist in our culture by the millions. One might simply summarize the differences between these two mid-20th-century US playwrights by saying that while Miller focused on the aspirations of a man seeking a petit-bourgeois existence, Williams—as always, embracing the wretchedly comic outsiders—put all his chips on a man of sweat who preferred to bathe in the sappy fizz of a beer while facing brutal reality.

I suppose, had I been asked to sit down to dinner with either, I'd have chosen Willy—which I almost felt I was doing in attending this production—who, after all, is a coarser version of my own father. But had I been asked to go to bed with either, I'd have jumped into the sack with Stanley, just like Stella, in the blink of an eye—even if Marlon Brando weren't playing the role that night. And as far as I'm concerned, that is the important difference between Miller's and Williams' visions.

———

*Some of these sentiments, particularly regarding the disappearance of the middle class in relationship to Miller's play, where addressed in a *New York Times* op-ed essay by Lee Siegel on May 3, 2012, two days before I wrote this essay. However, I did not have the opportunity to read Siegel's piece until after I had completed my essay, when, after sharing my sentiments with Susan Bee, she pointed the similarities out to me.

NEW YORK CITY, MAY 5, 2012
Reprinted from *USTheater, Opera, and Performance* (May 2012).

The Compromise

GORE VIDAL **THE BEST MAN** / NEW YORK, GERALD
SCHOENFELD THEATRE / THE PERFORMANCE I SAW WAS
A MATINEE ON MAY 5, 2012

THE BEST MAN is a play of political demands, subterfuge, lies, blackmail, and, most importantly, compromise—although the hero of Vidal's witty political parable, William Russell (John Larroquette), refuses compromise with his arch-enemy, Joe Cantwell (Eric McCormack), or with his own conscience. In that respect both Cantwell and the out-going President Arthur Hockstader (James Earl Jones) are correct in insisting that Russell is not a political beast!

The compromise that Russell makes is a rare one for any political contender, sacrificing his own career and his political battle for power, moral victory and, possibly, a reaffirmation of his relationship with his wife.

In this star-studded revival of Gore Vidal's 1960

comic-drama, Candice Bergan, Kerry Butler, Angela Lansbury, and Jefferson Mays (together with Larroquette, McCormack, and Jones) act up a storm, somewhat cloaking the fact that, for all its noise and hoopla (the sound of booming applause of convention-goers and cackling reporters being broadcast through the theater's sound system even during intermission), the play is really a series of drawing-room comedic skits of wit and bluff.

Like Arthur Miller's *Death of a Salesman*, the revival of which I witnessed a night earlier, *The Best Man* encapsulates, moreover, a vision of a world that no longer exists: the whirl of backroom politics, where decisions for party nominations were played out in convention hotel suites, and votes were bought and sold through a series of brokerings based on individual reputations smeared with lies, rumor, scandal, and partial truths.

If, given today's preordained presidential campaigns where all has been long decided before the convention's bland rhetorical flourishes and flag-waving remonstrations, we feel superior to the nasty bloodbaths of earlier party gatherings, we might take note that, at least in Vidal's fantasy, politics still mattered, and the individual candidates, freed from appealing to the whole of the American populace, could at least imagine (even while recognizing the reality was something far different) that their personal values matter.

While Vidal remains, ultimately, cynical of that process—awarding the nomination to a "best man" whom neither of the leading candidates seem to know anything about—both Russell and Cantwell, as different as they are, attempt to forge their campaigns based on very personal visions.

Today elections are won more on "general" appeal—which one might describe as campaigns based on generalities and artful waffling as opposed to personal integrity and individual history. One need only note how current Republican candidate Mitt Romney attempts to cover over his own tracks regarding his Massachusetts support of health coverage; or how he keeps silent about his family roots in Mexico—where his

 ancestors engaged in polygamy; or perceive Obama's attempts to downplay his Indonesian childhood and diminish his real accomplishments on such issues as health care, currently unpopular with right-leaning independents, and aspects of which may soon be overturned by the Supreme Court.

It is true that in Vidal's play both major candidates have something to hide: Russell, his nervous breakdown and its attending medical history, as well as the subsequent failure of his marriage; Cantwell, his possible involvement in his young military days with a homosexual roommate. But, in reality, it hardly matters whether the latter was involved in sexual acts or in merely squealing on his roommate, for in the context of the play either action demonstrates his moral hypocrisy and his commitment to "the ends justifying the means." Russell's bout with mental exhaustion, it is clear, has little to do with his career, including his more recent performance as Secretary of State, and, in reality, may simply indicate his inability to accept simple solutions to complex issues. And both men, despite their real and implicated blackmail, still stake their claims on the personal values reflected in their public service. While Cantwell's politics are ruthless, opportunistic, and play directly to the ignorance of public perception, he is nevertheless a man of action, a true political beast who will clearly accomplish whatever he sets out to do. Despite Russell's superior sense of ethics and his erudite comprehension of American and world history, he is, as his campaign advisor and the current President point out, a man who wavers when faced with critical choices. Or, to express it another way, he is a man who stops to think before acting—a fatal flaw, evidently, for any leader.

While one might be tempted to compare Vidal's characters with today's presidential candidates, accordingly, Obama is no Russell, despite his intelligent projection of moral issues, just as Romney is no Cantwell, despite his obviously expedient shifts to the far right in order to appeal to those constituents. We live today in a time where everything is far more prepackaged and, consequently, morally blurred.

The politics of Vidal's parable, represented by the enormous compromise of candidate Russell, are no longer possible in our society of political and social extremes. As in the Miller play, I suspect, very few members of the audience under 60—and there were none whom I spotted at the Schoenfeld matinee I attended—would be able to comprehend a drama so centered

on one man's moral scruples. "When did morality and politics ever share the same bed?" today's voters might scoff. While in 1960 Vidal might have pointed to John Kennedy (even if mistakenly), today we have "hot mic" statements from our President admitting to Russian President Medvedev that during the election he needs the "flexibility" of not saying what he eventually might want to. And anyone reading the daily papers perceives that even expedient political compromises rarely occur in the chambers of congress. Morality today, apparently, often has little to do with a truly thought-out position. A man like Vidal's Russell, sad to say, is either a political dinosaur or a literary fabrication at best. And a man of compromise, as Republican Senator Dick Lugar's defeat yesterday confirmed, is someone to be shunned.

MINETTA TAVERN, NEW YORK, MAY 6, 2012
LOS ANGELES, MAY 8, 2012
Reprinted from *US Theater, Opera, and Performance* (May 2012).

The World Comes in Quite Fast

ANDRE GREGORY AND WALLACE SHAWN (SCREEN-
PLAY), LOUIS MALLE (DIRECTOR) **MY DINNER WITH
ANDRE** / 1981

MY DINNER WITH ANDRE was a kind of perfect match
between two friends working in the theater, since Andre Gregory was seeking a way to share his experiences
and Wallace Shawn was looking for a project that was
structured around a dialogue—almost inconceivable
outside the most experimental of film endeavors. How
that was transformed into a film with a well-established
international director such as Louis Malle is almost
a miracle. And that the film succeeds, that we can sit
back and enjoy this exhilarating conversation between
the two men, is even more astounding!

Although the experiences that both are sharing
come from actual events in their lives, the pair argued
that they were not, necessarily, playing themselves, and
that they would have loved to switch roles to prove that

fact. Yet we sense a bit of exaggeration here, particularly in the case of Andre Gregory, simply because the experiences he relates are so utterly original that it would be hard to link them with another person; and they are so brilliantly recounted that it is difficult to imagine another playing his role.

For nearly half the film, Gregory is dominant as, answering occasional questions Shawn poses, he explains why he left a successful career in the theater and his own family, moving temporarily to Poland to work with the famed Polish experimental theater director Jerzy Grotowski. When Gregory asks to join Grotowski's acting seminar, Grotowski turns the tables and asks Gregory to run the seminar. The American agrees on the condition that the actresses consist only of 40 Jewish women who speak neither English nor French; Grotowski agrees, and organizes a retreat in a Polish forest (although men are included in the group). The theatrical experiences and the descriptions of Grotowski's "beehive" reveal the elemental and spiritual changes that these actors undergo in creating a new kind of theater, one that alters the soul.

Yet Gregory goes even further in seeking new enlightenment, joining an unusual agricultural community of men and women in northern Scotland, traveling to the Sahara desert with the Japanese monk Kozan in an attempt to create a play based on seemingly miraculous coincidences with regard to the fiction *The Little Prince* by Antoine de Saint-Exupéry, and being buried alive on Halloween by a theatrical group in Long Island. In short, Gregory's life is a search for enlightenment, as many individuals attempted throughout the later 1960s and early 1970s. His vision is akin to aspects of the hippie movement, in which society was declared dead or destructive, wherein personal possessions, cultural habituations, and political dogmas were perceived to have destroyed the individual, turning people into robots instead of thinking and feeling beings. Speaking of the culture of his time, Gregory notes:

> They've built their own prison, so they exist in a state of schizophrenia. They're both guards and prisoners and as a result they no longer have, being lobotomized, the capacity to leave the prison they've made, or to even see it as a prison.

In such an unfeeling world, the speaker summarizes, "It may very well be that 10 years from now people will pay $10,000 in cash to be castrated just in order to be affected by 'something.'" As Gregory notes, for a few moments during love one loses oneself. In a moment of ecstasy, one is merged with the other, but then a few seconds later the everyday routine of being returns, "the world comes in quite fast."

During the second half of the film, the more nerdy Shawn takes over, arguing that, although he comprehends what Gregory has been saying, the kinds of experiences that his friend has sought out are not available to most people, and that most people do not take Gregory's seemingly startling insights and coincidences in the same way. There is, he argues, a difference between a world of magic or science. Although he might think twice about taking a trip after receiving a fortune cookie saying, "Beware of a voyage," he would still take the trip: "That trip is going to be successful or unsuccessful based on the state of the airplane and the state of the pilot, and the cookie is in no position to know about it."

After Gregory argues that we have lost touch with the moon and the sky and the stars through our demand for being surrounded by things of pleasure, such as the electric blanket his friend has mentioned, Shawn speaks out:

> Yeah, but I mean, I would never give up my electric blanket, Andre. I mean, because New York is cold in the winter. I mean, our apartment is cold!

It's a difficult environment. I mean, our life is tough enough as it is. I'm not looking for ways to get rid of a few things that provide relief and comfort. I mean, on the contrary, I'm looking for more comfort because the world is very abrasive.

Ultimately, what Shawn argues for is simple, a cup of coffee, the presence of his girlfriend, Debbie.

In his wanderlust, the brilliant raconteur Gregory has surely convinced those of us from a generation who grew up after World War II of his moral position. Many of us might agree with his summaries of life in the latter half of the 20th century. When I shared this film, however, with a class of students, most of whom were born after this 1981 film was made, there was almost no sympathy at all with Gregory's activities. My students nearly all sided with Shawn.

And why should they not? These are young people in a depressed economy who have paid hard-found money to get a higher degree to help them in their careers and, maybe, allow them to find a market for their creative endeavors. They *are*, despite the differences of their cultural experiences and perceptions, the character Wally Shawn portrays.

In fact, Gregory himself later questions his mad search for a new reality, for a way of living outside of what he sees as the frozen world of dead thought. "Who

did I think I was?" he asks of himself, outrageously comparing his activities to those of Nazi architect Albert Speer, a cultured man who thought the everyday rules of life did not apply to him. Gregory, despite his declared perceptions, seems to have returned to the groove of everyday life, living with his wife Chiquita and dining in fine restaurants such as the one the men are sitting in, eating quail, drinking good wine.

There is throughout the film, despite its serious philosophical questions, a slight sense of satire about the whole thing. Gregory, after all, could only undertake his immense searches throughout the world by having enough money to do so, although others sought out such international enlightenment with little more than a knapsack and thumb. He is, quite obviously, a man with connections and some wealth. In one of the earliest speeches of the film, Wallace Shawn describes his own changed life: "I've lived in this city all of my life. I grew up on the Upper East Side. And when I was ten years old, I was an aristocrat. Riding around in taxis, surrounded by comfort, and all I thought about was art and music. Now, I'm 36, and all I think about is money." One does not necessarily need to know that Shawn is the son of *The New Yorker* editor William Shawn and journalist Cecille Shawn to comprehend that he has undergone his own big changes in life. If theater has made Gregory successful, for Shawn it has made life difficult, forcing him to live at an almost impoverished level.

> The life of a playwright is tough, it's not as easy as some people think. You work hard writing plays and nobody puts them on. You take up other lines of work to make a living—I became an actor—and people don't hire you. So you just spend your days doing the errands of your trade.

His girlfriend, Debbie, works hard at two different jobs. The wonderful dinner Gregory offers him of two quails results only in Shawn's observation that he didn't realize that they would be so small.

While Gregory hates what people call reality because it reconfirms the ordinary and deadening of life, Shawn argues that serious plays are about human alienation and help to make people aware of reality.

Does our acceptance of the ordinary destroy our lives, turning what might have been the extraordinary into an inability to think, even to feel?

These philosophical opposites have been at the

heart of great, literature for centuries, from Plato's cave to Lear's madness. It is less important to find a definitive answer to the questions these two viewpoints pose, I suggest, than it is to ask ourselves these questions again and again. In the end, Gregory goes home, it appears, to what has now become a rather comfortable existence. Shawn, having the last word, observes:

> I treated myself to a taxi. I rode home through the city streets. There wasn't a street, there wasn't a building, that wasn't connected to some memory in my mind. There, I was buying a suit with my father. There, I was having an ice cream soda after school. And when I finally came in, Debbie was home from work, and I told her everything about my dinner with Andre.

And so the banal is linked to the sublime.

LOS ANGELES, DECEMBER 8, 2011
Reprinted from *World Cinema Review* (December 2011).

Something Bad is Happening

WILLIAM FINN (MUSIC AND LYRICS), WILLIAM FINN
AND JAMES LAPINE (BOOK) **FALSETTOS** / LOS ANGELES,
THIRD STREET THEATER / THE PERFORMANCE I SAW
WITH HOWARD FOX WAS A MATINEE ON SUNDAY, OCTO-
BER 16, 2011

THERE HAVE BEEN numerous revivals of William
Finn's operetta-like musical since its long 1992 run on
Broadway (487 performances). Unlike most American
musicals, Finn's work, broken into two parts—*March
of the Falsettos* and *Falsettoland*—has basically no spoken words, the story being told through the music and
lyrics.

Finn's story of the late 1970s and early 1980s in
New York is almost a textbook of social issues expressing correct attitudes towards its two major focuses,
American Jews and gays, and was highly appreciated by
its audiences. With its further introduction of AIDS,
along with the difficulties the characters face with mari-

tal relationships—a young son being very much at the center of this work—it elicited more than its share of empathy, resulting in tears (falling even from own eyes).

The work begins with the main character Marvin (Jesse Einstein), his son Jason (the talented young

Major Curda), his psychiatrist Mendel (Chip Phillips), and his lover Whizzer (Richard Hellstern) singing "Four Jews in a Room Bitching," a piece laying out the difficulties each are facing. Marvin has left his wife, Trina (Lani Shipman), for Whizzer, but continues to insist upon a "tight-knit family," demanding that both he and Whizzer continue to play an important role in Jason's life.

For her part, Trina is obviously hurt by the series of events, but still attempts to create a conciliatory relationship with her former husband and his boyfriend. A trip to the psychiatrist Mendel, however, creates a new series of events, as Mendel, singing "Love is Blind," attempts to help her while at the same time falling in love. In "Marvin at the Psychiatrist, a Three-Part Mini-Opera," Marvin details his relationship with Whizzer, concluding that he is in love with him, Mendel moving the conversation to Trina's bedroom habits, as Marvin and Jason reply in counterpoint.

Jason, in turns out, is having his own difficulties, wondering whether his father's homosexuality can be inherited ("My Father's a Homo"). Whizzer suggests that Jason also visit Mendel, who now is in what might be described as personal relationships with the entire family.

Meanwhile, tension is building between Marvin and Whizzer, as the former attempts to put Whizzer in the position of homemaker. At the same time, Trina is increasingly feeling alienated by the situation, growing fearful that she is becoming less and less prominent in her family's life ("I'm Breaking Down"). A visit from the psychiatrist for dinner and therapy results in further involvement between Mendel and Trina, and before long he has made a marriage proposal to Trina.

Trina has mixed feelings, which she expresses in "Trina's Song," but she realizes that Mendel's love is sincere, and, in need of support, she realizes she could do worse. The men, all realizing their failures, together sing "The March of the Falsettos," admitting that their roles as "masculine" examples represent a great deal of bluff.

Trina and Mendel announce their marriage plans, and Marvin reacts with anger, violently slapping his ex-wife, both painfully singing "I Never Wanted to Love You," a sentiment Whizzer repeats to Marvin, and Marvin relays even to his innocent son.

By the end of the first part, Marvin has broken with Whizzer and created a gap between himself and Trina. Attempting to salvage his connections with his son, he sings "Father to Son," reassuring Jason that he will always love him, however he turns out.

If the first part has been almost brittle with dilemmas, Finn presents us with the second part which is even more distressing. It is now 1981, two years later. The cast has grown by two others, lesbian neighbors of Marvin: Dr. Charlotte, an internist, and Cordelia, a kosher caterer. These two women offer support and love to the lonely Marvin, but create new problems of their own.

Although Marvin has grown wiser ("About Time" being a song about growing up and getting over his selfish behavior), and managed to retain a close relationship with Jason, the issue of his son's Bar Mitzvah creates new tensions with Trina, she attempting to plan a large event, while Mendel and Jason encourage a more simple party. Caught in the middle, Jason is furious with both parents, which Mendel assures him is absolutely natural ("Everyone Hates His Parents").

Both parents, Cordelia, and Dr. Charlotte attend a baseball game in which Jason is playing, and in "The Ball Game" all make fun of themselves for watching Jewish boys "who can't play baseball" and getting caught up in the event. To everyone's surprise, Whizzer shows up—invited by Jason—which creates new tensions and reveals to Marvin just how much he has missed him.

In the midst of these adult dilemmas, Jason somehow manages to hit the ball, but is so nonplussed that he forgets to run!

Another "falsetto" piece relates their new traumas. And soon after, Marvin and Whizzer return to their relationship. The war between Trina and Marvin, however, continues, until suddenly, in a racquetball game, Whizzer collapses and is taken  to the hospital. Dr. Charlotte has already warned us through song that "Something Bad is Happening," young men increasingly becoming ill and dying. And we soon discover that Whizzer has AIDS.

In the trauma of the new situation, both parents offer Jason the option of "Canceling the Bar Mitzvah," while all four of the gay figures, Marvin, Whizzer, Charlotte, and Cordelia, musically muse on how their love can last in "Unlikely Lovers."

As Whizzer's condition worsens, Marvin turns to God, singing—a bit like Tevye in *Fiddler on the Roof*—"Miracle of Judaism." Suddenly, all break into Whizzer's hospital room, Jason having decided that the Bar Mitzvah should be celebrated there, with Cordelia catering the event. For a few happy moments, "The Bar Mitzvah" lifts everyone's spirits, but suddenly Whizzer can no longer continue in their company, and is wheeled from the celebrations.

Left alone, Marvin sings his major love song of the work, "What Would I Do if You Had Not been My Friend?," a piece which might melt away all the icebergs in Greenland, as we hear the news that Whizzer has died.

Marvin and his friends surround Whizzer to bid the audience farewell without another round of "Falsettoland."

Finn's work is, as I mention above, often touching and certainly affecting. The audience with whom I saw the production clearly loved the work. But the constant stereotypes of both Jewish and gay issues the musical presents often transform it from a serious dialogue into a kind of saccharine and even sanctimonious affair. At their best, the lyrics remind one of Stephen Sondheim, with their cleverly satiric purposefulness, but just as often they can't hold up the significance they attempt to portray, and the music—never reaching the heights of Sondheim in works such as *Follies, Merrily We Roll Along* (which is closest in spirit to Finn's work), or *Sweeney Todd*—seems all to be of one piece without creating the variance of sound and structure that would lend the musical a richer sheen.

The cast I saw were all quite capable, at moments even wondrous, with the small musical combo on stage creating a feeling of a much larger cast. Their acting also created a sense of absolute delight. So what if it's not a perfect work? It certainly is worth a visit to the theater any night.

LOS ANGELES, NOVEMBER 4, 2011
Reprinted from *US Theater, Opera, and Performance* (November 2011).

Hoarding Nature

METIN ERKSAN, KEMAL İNCI, AND İSMET SOYDAN
(SCREENPLAY, BASED ON A STORY BY NECATI CUMALI),
METIN ERKSAN (DIRECTOR) **SUSUZ YAZ (DRY SUMMER)**
/ 1964

THE TURKISH FILM *Dry Summer* features an outright
old-fashioned villain, Osman (Erol Taş), who suddenly
one day maliciously decides to dam up a spring on his
property, the source of water for his tobacco-farming
neighbors as well.

His more handsome and caring younger brother,
Hasan (Ulvi Dogan), attempts to dissuade him in his
decision, explaining that such an act will surely not
bode well with the neighbors and the community at
large. But Osman refuses to listen, and goes ahead with
his plan. As the younger brother, Hasan—and his local
fiancée Bahar (Hülya Koçyiğit)—has little choice but
to go along with him.

Besides, the young couple, desperately in love,

have wedding plans on their minds. In one of the earliest scenes, director Metin Erksan depicts their lovemaking in a patch of tall reeds, wherein Hasan must discover her before they can make love, that scene emphasizing the force of nature that has overtaken them and their rapport with it. Soon after, they are married, despite the wishes of Bahar's mother.

Rather than accept the natural world in which he lives, Osman has determined to steal what the villagers describe as "earth's blood," holding onto the natural resource for use only on his own land. Obviously, in attempting to go against the dictates of nature—the water naturally flows from the spring to the farms below—Hasan's prediction comes true: things do go terribly wrong. At first, the locals take Osman to court, where they win, the dam being removed by authorities.

But when Osman countersues, and the verdict is reversed by a higher judge, the same authorities are forced to restore the small, homemade dam. As their crops shrivel up in the title's dry summer, the neighbors take things into their own hands, moving towards Osman's spring *en masse*; amazingly, he battles them off. But when, later, a couple of the men return to remove the dam, he demands that his brother join him in a shooting expedition that ends with the death of one of the men.

Erksan carefully shows Hasan refusing to fire, so that we know Osman has killed the villager. Yet Osman insists that Hasan take on the guilt, assuring his brother that because he is younger and married, he will get a lighter prison-term.

In this fable-like story, the innocent is sent to prison, while the greedy brother remains at home to tend the farm and lust after Bahar. When she and Osman attempt to visit Hasan in prison, we discover that Hasan has been sent to another prison further away. And soon after, we discover that Osman has been ripping up his

 brother's letters instead of passing them on to his wife.

Like a hungry panther, Osman circles Bahar, watching her undress through a slat of wood, intensely staring at her—at one point, while milking a cow in her presence, sucking on the beast's tits—and finally touching up against her, ready for the rape. When she finally hears that Hasan has died in prison, she gives in to Osman's demands.

Hasan, we discover soon after, has not died, and upon being given his freedom, is warned by a lawyer to lie low.

Clearly, however, in his bitter isolation, Hasan has been changed, and we can tell as this former gentleman storms across the fields that he plans for revenge. Bahar, attempting to undo the dam yet again, is shot by Osman. Hasan nonetheless proceeds to his brother, finally drowning him in the water he has attempted to claim for his own, Osman's body slowly being dragged downstream as the water is released for all to use.

As I have suggested, there is a fable-like quality to this work—and it ends in that magical world: Bahar has not been killed, but only wounded, and is carried to safety by her husband.

Clearly, Erksan's work was highly influenced by Italian Neo-Realism; yet, with its surrealist-like images and fabulist  trappings, it is a great statement of Turkish cinema, winning the Golden Bear Prize at the Berlin International Film Festival.

Never before had a Turkish film been so highly awarded, and one might have thought that this film would lead to a new level in Turkish filmmaking. But its very success caused a huge uproar among international film directors for the Turkish government to permit the showing of European and American works, resulting in a near abandonment of serious local filmmaking. Only in the last years of his life did the director—who was censored and finally left the film industry, producing primarily TV—see his 1964 film restored and his countrymen giving new respect to his and other Turkish film pioneers' works.

Erksan died this year at 83 of complications from kidney disease.

LOS ANGELES, NOVEMBER 21, 2012
Reprinted from *World Cinema Review* (November 2012).

Locked Up

JACK RICHARDSON **GALLOWS HUMOR**, REPRINTED
IN DOUGLAS MESSERLI AND MAC WELLMAN, EDS. *FROM
THE OTHER SIDE OF THE CENTURY II: A NEW AMERICAN
DRAMA 1960-1995* (LOS ANGELES: SUN & MOON PRESS,
1998)

WITH THE ANNOUNCEMENT of the death of American playwright Jack Richardson on July 1, 2012, I recalled how delighted Mac Wellman and I had been to rediscover his play *Gallows Humor* and reprint it in our 1998 drama anthology. I immediately reread the play, and enjoyed it even more this time round.

Richardson's play in two parts is really a study in early 1960s marital relationships rather than about a murderer soon to be hung. There is a murderer indeed, Walter, locked away for beating his wife to death with a golf club—"forty-one strokes from the temple to the chin." But Walter was clearly locked away even before his tempestuous reaction. He cannot abide the pros-

titute sent to him by the Warden to take the prisoner's mind off the gallows and lead him to his death with a smile on his face. Walter, who has also just been served up a large chicken dinner, cannot even think of eating it, and is horrified by Lucy's carnal appetites, which include not only bedding down with him, but consuming the chicken and tossing its bones into the center of Walter's cell.

Walter is clearly a man of order, determined to clean and organize his cell up to the very moment of his State-determined death. It is not that he is unattracted to women, simply that he has no intention of detracting from the system that has put him into the cell and now has determined the end of his life. Walter is a number, 43556, and like Zero of Elmer Rice's *The Adding Machine* he is thoroughly a man of the system, a man who after the murder of his wife has clearly abandoned the dizzying world outside the prison walls, and who now is disturbed by the "perfume and overpowered flesh" of the female with which he has been provided. We can only suspect that self-imprisonment, being locked away in an unhappy life, is what led to his frenzied act.

Lucy, on the other hand, has a job to accomplish,

and with philosophical relish attempts to convince Walter to change his ways: to, after 20 years of living a meager existence, seek out his reward in her "mouth, fingertips, and breasts." The first part ends, obviously, with Walter being seduced by the joys of life which he was clearly seeking in his wife's murder.

On the other hand, the Warden and Hangman are even more locked away in their lives than has been Walter. At least he has gone temporarily mad, has left the confines of normalcy. Phillip, the unhappy Hangman, is so frustrated with his life that he has, as his wife describes it, begun to do hundreds of little things— tossing ashes into his slippers, skipping club meetings, purchasing a pair of red socks—that reveal his determination to change his life or, as he puts it, his desire to "open the window and slither down the drainpipe to disappear forever."

The morning of Walter's hanging, Phillip is determined to wear a black mask over his head, like a Medieval figure—an idea met with hardy resistance from the Warden and Martha, Phillip's wife. As Phillip goes off to slip on the mask, the Warden and Martha discuss Phillip's behavior. Sympathizing with what she has had to endure, the Warden reveals his long-time love for Martha, and, eventually, she admits her love for him. The Warden also lives in an unhappy relationship, his own wife having had various sexual encounters with plumbers and other working men. The two determine to have an encounter, but hilariously cannot even find a date when they might meet, so involved are they with the society in which they live. As Phillip returns with his mask, he discovers the two kissing, and, outraged, insists that he will now leave as he has long desired.

Martha offhandedly invites him to first help her with the dishes, and before he can even comprehend what he has agreed to, he perceives he is trapped, locked away in his own staid identity, unable to even open the kitchen door. When it comes time for him to attend the hanging, Martha must pop the door open, promising him "something very special for dinner."

At least Walter has had the courage of his convictions, while these "free" figures are more locked away in their determined patterns than Walter is in his cell. As the Prologue, performed by Death, suggests, they too will ultimately die. Walter has lived a freer life in the short time he has to remain on this earth than the Warden, Hangman, or his wife.

If Richardson's little masterwork seems cynical, it also represents the intense dissatisfaction with everyday existence that animated other American playwrights of the time such as Edward Albee, Arthur Kopit, and Jack Gelber—precursors of the later 1960s generation that would ultimately, if only temporarily, alter definitions of freedom and love.

Unfortunately, *Gallows Humor*, was to be the last of Richardson's successful plays. Two further works, *Lorenzo* and *Xmas in Las Vegas*, closed on Broadway after only four performances each. Although he long served as drama critic for *Commentary*, the author wrote no new plays. However, he did help his friend Elaine Kaufman establish her East Side restaurant, Elaine's, suggesting larger tables and promising to provide writers, which he did.

LOS ANGELES, JULY 11, 2012
Reprinted from *US Theater, Opera, and Performance* (July 2012).

How to Tell a Film

JAFAR PANAHI AND MOJTABA MIRTAHMASB
(DIRECTORS) این فیلم نیست (THIS IS NOT A FILM) / 2011,
USA 2012

FOR THE LAST several years, because of his house arrest and his inability to make films, the film director Jafar Panahi has been creating works that "are not what they seem," directing films that subvert the genre and save him from the censors. *This is Not a Film* is precisely that, not a film but a film about film, about how one might direct a film and how one might tell a film narrative without actually realizing it.

Locked up in his comfortable Tehran apartment on a day his family members have traveled to celebrate the Iranian festival Chaharshanbe Suri, preceding New Year's Eve, Panahi turns on his camera to record,

 in documentary style, a day in his life, including his awakening and breakfast. Determined to find a way around his ban, Panahi calls up his friend Mojtaba Mirtahmasb and asks him to take up the camera, while he begins, through the use of masking tape and imagination, to realize a movie that he was planning, but can no longer make, about a young girl, much like him, who has been locked up in her home because she has determined to attend the university.

The parallels between the locked-away girl and his personal condition are crucial, in that they convey the impossible frustration and desolation of a society barring individuals from their destinies and creative endeavors. But almost as soon as he has begun to play out the scenario of the young girl locked away in her small room with a view only of a young boy who appears outside her window, the director gives up, realizing that, of course, you cannot "tell" a movie. As evidence he gives an example from one of his earlier films, showing a scene where an amateur actor suddenly behaves in a strange way that the director might never have imagined possible. A shot from yet another movie shows how a simple set design reveals much more about the character than he might ever have imagined.

In short, the director shows us how film is not just about its narrative, the script, but about how the actors, cinematographer, art director, and others work together to transform what might have been imagined. Telling a movie is impossible. Or is it?

Although billed as a sort of documentary, Panahi's and Mirtahmasb's film, pretending to be shot in a single day—the film was actually shot over a period of four days for a cost of around $4,000—incorporates a great many personal and political events which come together to make a far larger statement. Panahi's daughter's pet lizard, Iggy, plays a large role as he roams the rather posh apartment, crawling up bookcases filled with books and clawing his way behind them, casting a rather eerie presence which, clearly, is not unlike the Iranian officials. He refuses to eat his usual diet of lettuce and seems to be only happy when he is fed a few pieces of cheese, evidently a lizard delicacy. As Panahi complains at one moment, "Your claws, Iggy, are hurting me, get off me, you're hurting me." And the very presence of the lizard fills anyone who is not a lizard lover with the sense of reptilian danger.

As usual on this Iranian holiday, people set off enormous fireworks—even though they have been recently banned. And the city, which we glimpse through the apartment's many windows, seems to be entirely on fire. His phone mates and his visitor complain of not only the impossible traffic but seem to suggest the entire city of Tehran has gone slightly mad.

And the final appearance of a garbage-collecting young man, a student in Art Research, substituting for his sister, brilliantly introduces us to another perspective in the Iranian underworld. This handsome young

 man, embarrassed for his appearance (he keeps asking if he can change his shirt) and the smell of the garbage he is collecting, recognizes the famous director immediately, and is stunned by Panahi's interest in him. The filmmaker accompanies him in his garbage-gathering rounds floor by floor, until he reaches the lobby.

If nothing else, we see hope for the future in the grace and comprehension of this young man, who, once they reach the lobby, advises Panahi to remain behind so that he will be safe. It's clear the limits of reality are perceived by all.

In the end, Panahi has found a way to "tell" his film visually with amateur actors who do precisely what he has advertised: behave in way that you might not expect. *This is Not a Film* is a totally understated work that profoundly  makes its message clear through all the elements of cinema, while pretending, nonetheless, not to use them. It is, quite clearly, a radical expression of what it means to make movies in a society that cannot accept them, yet has an audience desperate for their messages. Panahi put his movie on a flash drive, which was snuck out of Iran in a birthday cake. The movie was shown, as a surprise entry, in the 2011 Cannes Film Festival, and later appeared at the New York Film Festival, demonstrating that the collapsed society cannot truly censor an imaginative mind.

LOS ANGELES, JULY 13, 2012
Reprinted from *World Cinema Review* (July 2012).

Pomp and Circumstance

JOSEPH ROTH **RADETZKYMARSCH** (BERLIN: GUSTAVE KIEPENHEUER VERLAG, 1932), TRANSLATED FROM THE GERMAN BY JOACHIM NEUGROSCHEL AS **THE RADETZKY MARCH** (NEW YORK: THE OVERLOOK PRESS, 1995)

ONE IS IMMEDIATELY STRUCK when reading Joseph Roth's masterwork, *The Radetzky March*, at just how amazing is the author's ability to transform rather unlikeable figures into characters who emotionally involve his readers. Perhaps it even begins with the title. When I answered my companion, who asked me what I was reading, with "*The Radetzky March*," he turned up his nose in disgust: "I hate that piece. I think it is my least favorite of all march music." "Mine too," I replied, "but I love this novel."

One might be tempted to say similar things about the novel's characters: the three generations of the Trottas, beginning with the infantry lieutenant, Joseph, who saved Franz Joseph's (the Supreme Commander in Chief's) life by pushing him down at the very moment, at the Battle of Solferino, when the Emperor had put binoculars to his eyes. Joseph suffered a shattered clavicle and a bullet lodged in his left shoulder blade. In appreciation for his  brave deed, Trotta is decorated with the Order of Maria Theresa and knighthood, and is now called Captain Joseph Trotta von Sipolje, in honor of his native town. Neither a great military man nor, for that matter, particularly gifted in any specific profession, Joseph Trotta, however, is a thoroughly honest man, becoming outraged when he reads of his alleged salvation of Franz Joseph in a children's history:

> An enemy lance bored through the young hero's chest, but most of the foes were already slain. Gripping his naked sword in his hand, our undaunted monarch could easily fend off the ever-weakening attacks. The entire enemy cavalry was taken prisoner. And the young lieutenant—Sir Joseph von Trotta was his name—was awarded the highest distinction that our Fatherland has to bestow on its

heroic sons, the Order of Maria Theresa.

Against the advice of all his friends and the authorities, Captain Joseph Trotta petitions the government for changes in the text, but is unsuccessful. Youth needs heroes, the authorities and the Emperor proclaim. In response, Joseph retires to a country house, puttering around the place for the rest of his life, his only bequeaths to his son amounting to the family title and a painting by his son's friend, Moser, during one of his visits home.

The son, a central character of Roth's novel, grows up to be the District Captain, Franz, Baron von Trotta und Sipolje, a man of no great imagination, but of superior character and obedience to the demands of the society. Joseph sends his son to military school, where the son dutifully relays the laws of the Habsburg Empire to his local populace. But Franz's greatest achievements are the absolute regularity of the Sunday concerts by the famed conductor Nechwal—concerts beginning always with the renowned "Radetzky March"—his morning constitutionals, and his afternoon visits to a local bar where he plays chess with the garrison medic, Dr. Showronnek. Franz's life, in short, is the regularized life of a dying generation, a world of moderated pomp and circumstance, played out upon the backdrop of the small town of W in Moravia.

Franz's son, Carl Joseph, in turn, is raised as a military man, serving first as a member of the cavalry, later as an infantryman. He too is unimaginative, a nonreader, who basically obeys authority. But Carl Joseph, the hero of Roth's epic tale, has none of the backbone of his father and grandfather, but rather is a weak man who, as the tale moves forward, finds love with two motherly older women, Frau Slama and, later, the wealthy married Frau von Taussig. He becomes an alcoholic, and assumes others' gambling debts—all of which result in scandals and in the deaths of some of his only friends. In the end, like nearly all the figures of this fiction, he dies in battle in the prelude to World War I, a death that is so banal that it reminds one of the children's nursery rhyme, "Jack and Jill" ("Jack and Jill went up the hill to fetch a pail of water"), an act Carl Joseph undertakes from the embankment in which he and his men are holed up in order to slake the thirst of his soldiers.

In short, the Trottas are representative of just those figures in the great Austro-Hungarian Empire who outlived their era, contributing to the fall of the empire, a world of Romantic ideals without any substance. As my friend Marjorie Perloff mused, "How does Roth, then, make us care so much about these people, people whom you might detest in real life? Yet we do care intensely about the Trottas, and we are moved by the events in their lives."

One might simply attribute this ability to feel for Roth's insignificant characters by pointing to the author's narrative capabilities. Yet, on the surface at least, Roth's fiction is simply a realist work, with no great flourishes of narrative technique to explain why, as late as 1932—long after the great narrative experiments of Proust, Woolf, Kafka, Stein, and numerous others, and in the very same period as Faulkner's greatest works, *The Sound and the Fury* (1929), *As I Lay Dying* (1930), and *Absalom, Absalom!* (1936)—Roth's more traditional-seeming fiction still holds its own, seeming even to be part of that modernist sensibility.

In part, it is Roth's ability to present his numerous figures within a cinematic-like structure, interconnecting them with all the art of a great cinematographer moving through time and space. The entire fiction is brilliantly played out between two crucial events in Habsburg history: the salvation of Franz Joseph in Solferino—which permits him to reign longer almost than any European monarch—and the assassination of the heir apparent, Archduke Franz Ferdinand, an event which would soon end the Austro-Hungarian Empire. These two points in time—1859 and 1914, 11 years after Franz Joseph's coronation and two years before his death—link the Trottas to the Emperor through 55 years of his reign, more than a half-century.

Within this matrix, Roth moves freely back and

forth in space, from Solferino to the small town of W, from Vienna to the small borderlands town where Carl Joseph is stationed. There are many examples of Roth's abilities to cut and intercut with great exactitude, but none so startling as the series of events that begins with Carl Joseph's involvement with the killing of local factory workers on strike. Presenting Trotta in bed with encephalitis and other injuries, Roth cuts to the Kaiser in his castle at Schönbrunn vaguely recalling the Trotta name and associating it with the name Solferino, before writing on Carl Joseph's dossier the words *settle favorably*. A brilliant chapter about the aging Franz Joseph follows, presenting his isolated life in which the wise monarch is forced to play the simpleton and fool. Despite having a cold, Franz Joseph is determined to attend war-games and maneuvers in the distant borderlands, at which point the author moves him forward in space so that by the end of that chapter he meets up with Carl Joseph himself, associating the young lieutenant with his grandfather, and mistaking him for his father, the District Captain. It is as if history itself has intervened in the Trotta family's life, all accomplished with a few splices of narrative ingenuity.

A similar event occurs when the ever-troublesome Carl Joseph is forced to pay up on loans and gambling debts (debts he has taken on for others), writing to his father for help. The father, we are surprised to discover, has no money—like his son, he is incapable of balancing accounts. Here also, Roth suddenly moves his small-town figure—often described as a near look-alike of the Emperor—into the royal court as the dashing elderly man, dressed in his white military attire, seeks out and is finally permitted an audience with the Emperor in order to plead his son's case. When the two finally do meet they not only look like brothers but appear to be looking into a mirror, forcing the reader to recognize that they are not only similar in appearance but that the District Captain, son to the man who has saved Franz Joseph, and the Emperor are mirror images of one another in their beliefs, their demeanors, and their lives—reiterating the fact that the son of the "hero of Solferino" has remade his life in the image of Franz Joseph. By bringing the two face to face, Roth has cinematically demonstrated that time and space have become one: over time, the elder man has seemingly spawned his double in the surrounding societal space, which is, of course, the desire of any despot, beloved or not.

Another device Roth uses to develop his characters is to imbue them with special eccentricities or endow them with sudden perceptions which link them to us. Once he has established the Trottas as types—as blustery remnants of a romantic past—the author suddenly recasts them against type as they are faced with special perceptions and exceptional circumstances. Most of these scenes are also laden with irony, not only because of our realization that they are not usually like this, but because, through the exceptionalness of their emotions and the situation, they are not so very different from ordinary folk, confused and very human beings. One of the most notable of numerous such occasions is when Carl Joseph returns home to be told that the woman, Frau Slama, with whom he has had a long affair, beginning in his youth, has died in childbirth. Carl Joseph is stunned by the news, and even more troubled by his father's insistence that he visit and present his condolences to Sergeant Slama himself. Carl Joseph puts off the event as long as possible, but ultimately encounters Sergeant Slama in his now-empty house. The two uncomfortably share bits of conversation, the young Lieutenant having to pretend a near ignorance to the objects in the room in which he has spent long hours. Offered a raspberry drink, Carl Joseph must almost unendurably sit through Slama's attempts to find where the liqueur is kept, looking in all the wrong places, Carl Joseph knowing of its exact location in the kitchen. The pain and frustration of this scene is almost unbearable, as we feel the deep tension between the two men. But Slama turns the tables, so to speak, as Carl Joseph attempts to make a hasty retreat, calling him back to hand his wife's love letters over to the young Lieutenant. Although Carl Joseph has saved Frau Slama's letters, he clearly has never imagined that she might save his, and that not only has Sergeant Slama known of their affair but so too has his own father. Such situations, in short, intrigue the reader and involve him, as we first feel for the figures involved and then delight in the ironic humor of the situation.

At numerous times throughout his work, Roth creates similar situations: each time father and son come together in what begins as a formal and rather distant relationship, the two increasingly reveal and even display their love for one another. Carl Joseph, on his final visit, for the first time not only takes his aging father's arm, but holds it, walking home arm in arm. At other times, Roth attributes these two figures with sudden flashes of perception: Carl Joseph, for example, coming to realize his great love and compassion for his friend Max Demant; the District Captain, upon his trip to visit his son in the borderlands, discovering through the pessimistic observations of Chojnicki that the empire is indeed about to collapse. Similarly, the emotional complexity of both men's deep relationships with the most worldly and least-traditional thinking figures in the book—Moser, Demant, Chojnicki, and Skowronnek—gives dimension to the obedient and unquestioning Trottas.

In the end we begin to see that, despite their simplicity, their obvious weaknesses, even their stupidity,

 the generations of the Trottas are not so very different from anyone else. Indeed, had they been left to their origins as simple peasants, they might, like Carl Joseph's orderly, Onufrij, have survived very nicely. Certainly Carl Joseph seems to be at his happiest in the few days when he lives in natural solitude in Chojnicki's woods, keeping out of sight of his former infantry friends and greeting the local peasants.

Finally, in a book with all the hoopla of military parades, rattling sabers, and heel-clicking (one of the most painfully revealing scenes in the book is when the District Captain's loyal servant Jacques, ill in bed, attempts to click his heels under the covers when visited by his employer), and, yes, the blaring trumpets of "The Radetzky March," the dominant images and sounds are strangely those of the natural world. From the canary's beautiful songs that accompany both Jacques' and the District Captain's deaths, to the croaking frogs of the borderland swamps, the strange honking early migrations of the geese, the constant murmur of crickets, and the eerie silence of the ravens signifying to the locals the end of their world, it is nature that has the final say in the noisy dissonance of Roth's Austrian society. And, in the end, it is not the marches, the clashing swords, the explosion of rifles, or plod of feet that define this dying world, but silence, the mouthing of words that cannot be heard as the Kaiser lies dying, the empty silence that settles over a son's death.

Roth's great fiction may seem almost artless, a simple—if epic—tale of the death of the Austro-Hungarian Empire, but it is, finally, a domestic drama most carefully crafted in its vast cinematic movements, its delicate shadings of characters, and its skillful juxtaposition of human and natural voices. And by fiction's end, the blare and bluff of "The Radetzky March" is drowned out by the rich and various cadences of living and dying men.

LOS ANGELES, MAY 1, 2012
Reprinted from *EXPLORING* fictions (May 2012).

Angel of Death

SKIP HOLLANDSWORTH AND RICHARD LINKLATER (SCREENPLAY), RICHARD LINKLATER (DIRECTOR) **BERNIE** / 2011, GENERAL US DISTRIBUTION 2012

RICHARD LINKLATER's *Bernie* was based, in part, on a *Texas Monthly* magazine article by Skip Hollandsworth about the small, East Texas town of Carthage, whose residents expressed enormous support for a self-confessed, gay murderer, Bernie Tiede, who shot his then-companion, 81-year-old Marjorie Nugent, in the back four times. So popular was Tiede, and so unloved was the mean, money-hoarding Nugent, that the deed went unreported, her absence mostly unnoticed for nine months before the body was discovered—by greedy relatives and Nugent's financial advisor—hidden beneath frozen meats and vegetables in her garage freezer. After a trial—whose venue was changed to a small community 47 miles away from Carthage because the prosecutor felt he could not get a fair trial, most of the city's citizens proclaiming that they were determined to acquit—Tiede was found guilty and sentenced to life imprisonment.

If this sounds like improbable material for a cross-genre comedy-musical-love-story-courtroom drama, you'd find a champion in the real-life District Attorney, Danny Buck (played in the film by Matthew McConaughey), who argued, "This movie is not historically accurate. The movie does not tell her side of the story." And some Carthage residents would agree, including Toni Clements, who spoke out: "If it was fiction it might be funny, but this was a real person in a real town and no, I don't think it's funny at all."

But you, along with the two figures I just quoted, would also be mistaken. For Linklater's movie is not only hilarious, but a sad and moving piece of cinema, revealing, more successfully perhaps than most sociological or psychological studies, what is at the heart of small-town community life that defines its pleasures and failures.

Bernie (Jack Black), a mortician by trade, may be a kind of harbinger of death, even, as Danny Buck describes him, "an angel of death," but he is also, from the moment he sets foot on East Texas soil, a sympathetic citizen who goes out of his way for his fellow Carthage citizens, a man who not only knows everyone by name and asks about their friends, family, and illnesses, but is there in their times of joy and sorrow alike. Akin to *The Music Man*'s Professor Harold Hill, Bernie may have been a kind con man, but once he insinuated himself into small-town life, he created things for people to do, ways in which community folk could show their caring for one another. Directing the local Methodist Church choir, Bernie lifted his own voice in song. As a director of and actor in local community theater productions (including Meredith Willson's *The Music Man*), he not only helped others dance and sing out for joy, but performed with equal exultation in various roles. He advised little league baseball players and proffered financial tips to factory workers and farmers. Not only could he transform cold corpses into presentable funeral apparitions, he could eulogize the dead and sing lovely songs over their frozen forms. Most particularly, he was there to hold the arms and offer bereavements to the small town's numerous widows. At one point, the film hints at the real Bernie Tiede's ability to offer sexual satisfaction to some of the town's heterosexual males (when the police later searched the real Tiede's home, they found videotapes of him engaged in homosexual acts with married men). But so beloved was Bernie in this East Texas outpost that many of its citizens could have cared less about the fact that he was, as one resident put it, "a little loose in the loafers." "He only shot her four times," one resident equivocates. He was one of them.

Through a brilliant mix of actors' and actual town citizens' testimonies to Bernie, Linklater uses the first part of his film to help us comprehend why almost everyone so loved this man, and, more importantly, how dependent small-town citizens are on people who respect and support their communal values. How easy it might have been (just ask the Coen brothers) to turn this series of short interviews—particularly given the accented vernacular of the East Texas twang—into a satiric put-down of rural Americana. Instead, Linklater, obviously in love with the very eccentricities his unsophisticated characters so readily display, helps us to comprehend that they are as desperately in need of love and social communion as the most isolated urban dweller. Bernie offers nearly everything, except a beautiful face and shapely body, that anyone might desire. He is, as several of the town residents repeat, a total "people person," a man of, for, and created by the people. "If the people of Carthage were to make a list of people most likely to get to heaven, Bernie'd be at the top," summarizes one local.

If we realize in his readiness to please that he is

himself a lonely person, so too does Bernie comprehend this in nearly everyone he meets, even in the mean-spirited Marjorie Nugent (wonderfully performed by veteran Shirley MacLaine), whose wealthy husband has just died. True to form, Marjorie at first rejects Bernie's attempts to console her. When he comes to her door bearing flowers, she scoops them up and slams the door in his face. But nothing seems to deter this gentle man, who appears again with a gift basket of toiletries. Even the devil himself would have to invite Bernie in. Before you can shake a stick, Bernie has put a smile (slight as that may be) on Marjorie's sourpuss, and before long he is ushering her to church and concerts. Within a few weeks the couple are traveling—first class, of course—on jaunts to Russia, France, New York, and elsewhere, taking in the delights of saunas, operas, and theater

fare. With her help, Bernie buys nine cars, an airplane, and jet skis. If the residents are busy gossiping, it is more out of incredulity than suspicion. That Bernie has transformed their very meanest citizen into a semi-human specimen is only evidence once more of his powers as a genuinely nice human being.

But the devil, unfortunately, as a Carthage resident might have expressed it, cannot change her spots. Before long, the ready-to-please Bernie has been converted by the stiff-necked, constantly chewing harridan into a lackey to cut her nails, iron her clothes, even clean and fold up her flowery new panties. The desperate-to-please Bernie goes along with everything until she begins to cut off his connection with all the others to whom he has already demonstrated so much love! She will clearly have him only for herself. So this nonviolent lover of all mankind one day discovers himself, in a kind Jekyll and Hyde transformation, possessed with the necessity of taking up a small gun she has purchased to kill an armadillo, aiming it and shooting into her permanently armored hide.

With the evil villain of this piece dead, Bernie uses

her wealth as perhaps it should have always been spent: supporting the community at large, a Western clothing shop on Main Street, build-ing a new church wing, buying homes for poor folks, awarding twin girls a birthday gift of a backyard playhouse. Bernie himself continues to live in a small, mortgaged house, paying his monthly installments for his original run-down car late.

In the final vicious courtroom scenes, played out before jurors who one Carthage resident quips "have more tattoos than teeth," the salacious cowboy-booted and Stetson-hatted County District Attorney twists Bernie's good-willed intoxication with everyday life into that of a suave city-slicker's pre-mediated acts based on the fact that Bernie can pronounce the name of the musical he has seen in New York, *Les Misérables*, and that he vaguely knows that white wine goes with fish. It is enough to make one cry!

The glue to Linklater's quite amazing moral screed is Jack Black's near flawless and notably subtle recreation of Bernie Tiede. Instead of his usual naughty-boy antics, his anarchic defiance of society, this time round Black immerses himself thoroughly into a character who, while appearing like a model citizen, reveals the dark hollows of the American heart. As the credits began to scroll across the screen (which, incidentally, should not be missed), the three women behind me verbally concurred that Jack Black should be nominated for an Oscar for his performance. And, although I doubt the Academy would ever be so clairvoyant in their sensibilities, I must admit that the thought had just a few moments earlier crossed my mind.

LOS ANGELES, MAY 25, 2012
Reprinted from *N^th Position* [England] (July 2012).

A World of the Dead

JEAN RENOIR AND CHARLES SPAAK (SCREENPLAY),
JEAN RENOIR (DIRECTOR) **LA GRANDE ILLUSION**
(**GRAND ILLUSION**) / 1937, USA 1938

SEEING *GRAND ILLUSION* the other day upon the large screen of Los Angeles' Laemmle's Royal Theatre, I perceived this film in a new way than I had when I watched it as a young student years before. In the interim, I had attempted to view an old VHS tape, but the quality was so washed out that the subtitles were impossible to read and it was painful even to the eyes. This 1999 restoration was, in every way, a revelation.

If I had originally perceived this film as an almost comical anti-war statement from the great film director, this time around, provoked by comments from my companion, Howard, I realized that, despite the film's international admiration, it is a work that is not entirely self-contained; that particularly for the young, without a strong sense of history, its meaning might be blurred.

Despite what we generally know about the savagery of the first modern war of the 20th century, Renoir's work depicts the wartime situations from the strange vantage point of officers in various German prisons where, although we are shown some deprivations and the utter boredom of prison life, for the most part the officers from various countries—Renoir focuses primarily on the French—are treated relatively humanely, particularly when they are transferred to Wintersborn Prison under the command of Rittmeister von Rauffenstein (the imperious Erich Von Stroheim). Indeed, in some respects, given the hefty food packets received from home by Lieutenant Rosenthal (Marcel Dalio), their gastronomical condition is far better than the Germans, who survive primarily on cabbage. Yes, they are all prisoners, forced at times to endure painful punishments, but they are given liberties not even conceived of in Billy Wilder's World War II encampment of *Stalag 17*, which, along with numerous other films, owes much to Renoir's 1937 work. Although there are certainly outbreaks of anger and even violence between the various prisoners and their captors, Renoir's work has none of the frontline futility of a film like *All Quiet on the Western Front* of seven years before.

Even the film's final escape into German territory, where the two survivors, Lieutenants Maréchal (Jean Gabin) and Rosenthal are forced to cohabit a small cottage with a widowed German farm woman (Dita Parlo) and her daughter, is presented as almost idyllic, and the two men's final escape into Switzerland is greeted with respect and appreciation by the German soldiers attempting to track them down.

In short, one might ask, what is this film, so obviously cinematographically well-conceived, really about? War, at least from Renoir's perspective, is certainly not hell and, at times, is even lauded, particularly by the aristocratic career officers, Captain de Boeldieu (Pierre Fresnay) and von Rauffenstein. Even if we accept Renoir's own statement that his film is "a story about human relationships" that demonstrates that the commonality of mankind is far more important than political divisions, *Grand Illusion* seems, at first sight, a timid statement of pacifism.

The film's seeming relativism, moreover, seems even more strange given the movie's date, 1937. Although World War II, if one ignores the Japanese-Chinese War already raging in 1937, is generally dated as beginning in 1939, there was no question at the time of the work's filming that Europe was moving in the direction of another violent encounter between countries. Hitler had become Chancellor of Germany four years earlier, the Italian Fascist party under Benito Mussolini had seized power nearly a decade before, France had allowed Italy to conquer Ethiopia, and in 1935 the Territory of the Saar Basin was reunited with Germany, repudiating the Treaty of Versailles. In return for Germany's support of their Ethiopian invasion, Italy dropped their objection to Germany's desire to absorb Austria. By 1937, almost anyone, except perhaps for British Prime Minister Neville Chamberlain, would have recognized that the whole continent was again about to explode into war.

Renoir's gentlemanly depiction of the previous war's prison camps, accordingly, seems almost cowardly in retrospect. Yet, Nazi Propaganda Minister Joseph Goebells named *Grand Illusion* "Cinematic Public Enemy No. 1," ordering all prints be confiscated. The French authorities banned the film in 1940 for "as long as the war should last." When the German army marched into France that same year, the Nazis seized every print and negative of the film for its ideological criticisms of Germany. What are we today missing in that picture?

In part, it is simply Renoir's great sense of irony that has been lost. For years now I have maintained that irony has disappeared in the young, to be replaced instead with satire or camp exaggeration. A long tale told through vignettes that subtly play out a conflicted statement is perhaps hard to comprehend in a time of pastiche.

Let me attempt to explain Renoir's masterwork by suggesting that the world it portrays was recognized by most intelligent viewers of the time as a world that had long before been destroyed, that the characters of *Grand Illusion* existed, at the time of the film's making, in the world of the dead. Accordingly all their values, whether fascistic or humane, were "grand illusions," visions of a world that would be destroyed by the war in which they were engaged. By moving us away from the front lines, removing us from the playing fields, so to speak—and Renoir's work is very much one about the relationship between soldiers and children at play (consider Captain de Boeldieu's statement: "Out there, children play soldier.... In here, soldiers play like children.")—we can more vividly see the delusions of all concerned.

The most obvious of those delusions involves the absurdity of class: the belief, epitomized by both Captain de Boeldieu and von Rauffenstein, that in their aristocratic commitment to their military world, they stand somehow apart and superior to the political divisions which they are ordered to impose. Having just finished reading Joseph Roth's wonderful fiction *The Radetzky March* a few weeks before seeing *Grand Il-*

lusion, I am struck by the parallel conclusions of Roth's and Renoir's visions. If nothing else, World War I completely shattered the smug presumptions of moral superiority embedded in militaristic nations such as Germany, Austria, and even France. As grand as these gentleman officers might have perceived their world to be, it was they who brought war into existence, and it was they, as a class, who were most obliterated by their involvement. The only difference between de Boeldieu and von Rauffenstein is that the former comprehends that he represents a world of the past that is being replaced by the working class officers like Maréchal and outsiders such as the Jewish Rosenthal, while the survivor, von Rauffenstein, lives on as a kind of mad Frankenstein, his body made up of metal and wood, many of his bones having been destroyed in battle after battle. But even von Rauffenstein knows what lies ahead: "Believe me, I don't know who is going to win this war, but whoever it is, it will be the end of the Rauffensteins and the Boeldieus."

Sacrificing his life to what he perceives is a new future, de Boeldieu finds a more graceful "way out," playing the clown as he runs up and down the castle staircases, flute in hand, cigarette in his mouth, to serve as a decoy for his escaping soldiers. Although de Boeldieu is described as a "regular guy" by Rosenthal (whose family is *nouveau riche*), Maréchal comprehends throughout that the Captain is a man apart, a remnant of a world that has been an illusion all along, a world of the *belle epoque* shared by von Rauffenstein, and represented in the film by the Paris restaurant Maxim's, *Frou-Frou*, and a woman they both loved.

Yet, Renoir does not stop here in revealing his characters' personal illusions or delusions. War has already made them comprehend numerous realities that they had previously not conceived. Most of their wives back in France have taken up with other men, and their own sexualities, once so completely defined, have come into some question. One of the most touching moments in the film is the arrival of theater costumes, women's dresses, by which the men, who will soon don them for the joy of entertainment, are amazed, given their short length and their silky textures, changes in styles since they have left home. As one young man puts on a dress and wig, the others stare, jaws locked in wonderment: for them he is clearly the reincarnation of womanhood, the stunning object of their desires. Renoir goes no further in this revelation of gender transformation, but we, as perceptive theatergoers, comprehend its significance.

If class differences seem to have truly been obliterated, racial, religious, and social differences are still very much alive, as, fed up with each other, the escapees Maréchal and Rosenthal suddenly turn on one another, hurling epithets that no longer have meaning. They reunite, but the pain of those abuses never quite heals.

Renoir's gentle German farm woman, Lotte, is only too pleased to invite the two invaders into her home; after all, her own husband and brothers have been already killed in the war—in the horrible battlegrounds Verdun, Liège, Charleroi, and Tannenberg, from which Renoir has kept his audience—and she is lonely.

Although Maréchal may be the better lover, bedding Lotte soon after their arrival, Rosenthal is the bet-

ter father, a man who talks with and even educates her young daughter, going so far as to create a Christmas crèche for the child, an act that goes against his faith. Both delude themselves, in their short stay in paradise, that they may return for Elsa and the child, bringing her and Lotte of the "blaue augen"—the dominant symbol of Hitler's pure German—back to France after the war. As Maréchal expresses his hope that this war will be the end of all wars, Rosenthal argues that such thinking is another "illusion."

Although they both escape into Switzerland, the last few images are of them attempting to move forward as their feet become entrenched in the deep snow. And we recognize, as Renoir certainly did in 1937, that in the world to which they return, if they make it, they once more will be conceived of as a "rough" mechanic and a "rotten" Jew; certainly Rosenthal might not have survived what came after. In an early version of the script, Rosenthal and Maréchal, near film's end, agree to meet in a restaurant at the end of the war, with the final scene, celebrating the armistice, showing two empty chairs at a table.

In short, what might have appeared as a gentlemanly world based on codes of honor, valor, and trust is just as destructive, so Renoir suggests, as the bombs and gas in the trenches at battle's front, offering no more hope for the future than a bullet to the heart.

LOS ANGELES, MAY 24, 2012
Reprinted from *World Cinema Review* (May 2012).

Falling Trees

THOMAS BERNHARD **HOLZFÄLLEN** (FRANKFURT AM
MAIN: SUHRKAMP VERLAG, 1984), TRANSLATED FROM
THE GERMAN BY DAVID MCLINTOCK AS **WOODCUTTERS**
(NEW YORK: ALFRED A. KNOPF, 1987)

AMERICAN WRITERS, particularly poets, often complain that their communities are viciously divided, and
decry the fact that at the center of their art is a great
deal of vicious commentary, particularly between different literary sensibilities. My reaction to the various
attacks from one front or another has always been a
simple acceptance of the fact—although I have seldom
willfully contributed to these assaults. Why shouldn't a

poet or fiction writer,
if she or he is truly
committed to art and
a perception of what
art consists of, feel
a sense of affront by

those who do not have that same commitment? If art matters, so does the territory; all art is necessarily not equal, unless one doesn't truly care about that art.

In Thomas Bernhard's 1984 fiction, *Holzfällen*, moreover, we perceive that the feeling of disgust by some writers for others is not just an American phenomenon, but, if we are to take the voice of Bernhard's narrator as an example, perhaps even more virulently experienced in Austria. And, unless we are somehow involved in that scene, the petty hatreds and disgust (amounting almost to nausea) felt by the central character make for great fun, as he cattily attacks his fellow dinner partners gathered together in Vienna's Gentzgasse for what the hosts, the detested Auersbergers, have described as "an artistic dinner." For Bernhard's Viennese counterparts, some of whom recognized themselves in his satiric attacks, the presentation of their failures, however, was not at all "fun," one going so far as to sue the author and prevent his book from sale.

There is certainly no question that Bernhard, bearing a close relationship to the narrator, presents a devastating portrait of his fellow artists—writers, musicians, tapestry weavers, dancers, actors, and just plain hangers-on. The drubbing they receive and the recounting of the narrator's intimate relationships with many of these figures are almost maniacal as he recounts over and over how he came to know each figure, what role they played in his life, and how they ultimately came to be the truly "hated" figures he regurgitates up before us. Bernhard's book, in short, is precisely what its title suggests, at least in the German: a wood-cutting exercise, *Holzfällen* suggesting in the original not just the noun "woodcutters," but the verb for a critical denunciation.

Bernhard's narrator, having himself suffered an emotional breakdown and, consequently, having spent a period in a mental hospital, has a great deal in common with the author; and the major event of the day of the "artistic dinner," a graveside ceremony for the narrator's friend Joana upon her having committed suicide at her childhood home in Kilb, is similar in some ways to Bernhard's own reported suicide in Upper Austria only five years after publishing this fiction. The reader, accordingly, recognizes the narrator's attacks as highly personal and, at times, nearly hysterical, as the character admits that for years he has gone out of his way to steer clear of his old friends from the 1950s and early 1960s upon his return to Vienna from years abroad. But even if the narrator did not admit to these personal vendettas—which, in fact, lie at the heart of this fiction—the reader would be forced to recognize the subjectivity of the narrator simply by the grammatical structures and intense repetition of his sentences. Each attack on his hosts and their guests, particularly the Austrian Virginia Woolf, Jeannie Billroth, and the Austrian Marianne

Moore and Gertrude Stein (in my mind, two diametrically opposed figures), Anna Schreker, is repeated over and over again in detail, each time the narrator adding a bit of new information, so that we soon recognize the separated figure sitting, as he tells us dozens and dozens of times in the narrative, in a wing-tip chair, clearly obsessed with these beings.

As well he might be, given the fact that as a young man he was pulled into artistic and sexual relationships with nearly all the central players. These include his hostess—a woman from a wealthy bourgeois family who uses her money to help buy her and her husband's way into the cultural scene—he, a composer "in the Webern tradition"—along with the Austrian Virginia Woolf, the Austrian Marianne Moore and Gertrude Stein, and the talentless Joana who spent her life transforming her tapestry-maker husband into a world-renowned artist only to have him bolt to Mexico just as he reached the pinnacle of his profession.

While the narrator may seem utterly ruthless in his attacks, quite viciously recounting the demise of each of these figures, unable to even tolerate them because of their abandonment of whatever talent they might have had, he somewhat redeems himself by being as brutally honest about himself, admitting how they each helped mold him into the artist he is today, while also attempting, in a Tennessee Williams-like metaphor, to emotionally and spiritually "devour" him, equating it to the way all of Austrian culture grinds down its most talented young artists. The Auersbergers have used him sexually to "help save their marriage," Jeannie has taken him in as a kind of devotee of her artistic endeavors, Joana has created a relationship with him to help her develop her failed career as a dancer/actress. In order to survive, he proclaims, he has had to abandon them, while they have vilified him to all their acquaintances for that very abandonment, Joana perhaps even through her death expressing her sorrow over her loss of her once dear friend. So while the narrator may seem to be selfishly satisfied with his tale of his friends' immense failings, he is equally brutal about his own hypocrisies, and praises the talents they once possessed—including Herr Auersberger's musical abilities, his wife's singing talents, and even Jeannie's early devotion to literature before she sold out to the State officials who award stipends and literary prizes, one of which the Austrian Marianne Moore and Gertrude Stein has just been recipient of.

At the center of the "artistic dinner" is a third-rate actor playing Eckdal in the Burgtheater's production of Ibsen's *The Wild Duck*, who, when he finally arrives well after midnight, shifts the narrative to a comic realization of the same boorish "artistic" conversations against which the narrator has been railing. Most of his commentaries are ridiculous statements of the difficulty of the actor's life, criticizing nearly everyone—directors, writers, fellow actors, and the theater itself—while exalting his own innumerable talents. When Jeannie Billbroth attempts to turn the conversation upon herself, "tastelessly" posing provocative questions, the actor turns from performing as a simple ham, endlessly recounting tales he has told dozens of times, to a kind of outraged philosopher, lambasting "the Austrian Virginia Woolf" for her rude impertinence, lashing out against her obvious attempts to put down anything of value. In short, he voices just the criticisms that the narrator has privately held yet, hypocritically, failed to publicly express. The aging actor desires a kind of return to nature—what anyone who has read Austrian fiction realizes is at the very center of that country's romantic ties to a kind of peasant simplicity—a world of *"the forest, the virgin forest, the life of a woodcutter,"* perhaps Bernhard's ironic condemnation of the culture's (as well as the narrator's) own self-destructive desires.

Indeed, Bernhard's narrator, ultimately, does not come off much better than the dead folk of his memories, as he waits until everyone has left, kissing the forehead of his hostess, and murmuring wishes that he might have heard her sing, while promising another visit—all of his actions and words representing more hypocritical mendacity. Or perhaps his actions do represent a kind of truth, as he goes racing down the stairs as if he were still in his 20s, running away from his current home toward the city, determined to write down everything he has just suffered "*at once...now—at once, at once,* before it's too late." At the same time, he admits that as much as he hates these people and Vienna, he, just like the Burgtheater actor, loves them and the city:

> This is my city and always will be my city, these are
> my people and
> Always will be my people...

an admission that almost instructively contradicts his deep hatred of all he has just recounted to us.

In this sense, finally, Bernhard's *Woodcutters* is not just a critical attack; while it is that, it is also an intense dialogue with the narrator's self over his and his society's failures, a public airing of his and his compatriot's laundry, so to speak. And so the fiction is transformed into a kind of loving portrait of a failed world, the world which, after all, all artists are forced to encounter, endure, and write about: never an easy task.

NEW YORK CITY, MAY 4, 2012
Reprinted from *EXPLORING* fictions (May 2012).

A Body Transfixed by the Noonday Sun

PETER SELLARS (LIBRETTO, BASED ON OLD AND NEW TESTAMENT SOURCES AND TEXTS BY DOROTHY DAY, LOUIS ERDRICH, PRIMO LEVI, ROSARIO CASTELLANOS, JUNE JORDAN, HILDEGARD VON BINGEN, AND RUBÉN DARIO), JOHN ADAMS (COMPOSER) **THE GOSPEL ACCORDING TO THE OTHER MARY**, CONDUCTED BY GUSTAVO DUDAMEL / THE PERFORMANCE I SAW WAS ON SATURDAY, JUNE 2, 2012

THE NEW OPERA-ORATORIO by John Adams and his often-time collaborator Peter Sellars, if nothing else—and there is a great deal more to be said for this work—is a serious and mature contribution to orchestral and vocal music of the 21ˢᵗ century. This work is focuses on Mary Magdalene, the "other" Mary, in legend from the town of Magdala, but in this version described as being, along with her sister Martha and brother Lazarus, from Bethany.

The Gospels mention her very few times, primarily in the Gospels of *Luke* and *Mark*; but her importance is clear, particularly through the apocryphal texts which refer to her several times. She is one of the strongest and most important women who was close to Jesus, remaining with him beneath the cross until his death and accompanying his body to the sepulchre wherein he was buried. Most important, however, are the Biblical texts that describe Mary Magdalene as the one who discovered that Christ had risen, reporting the news to his doubting disciples. In connection with this role, particularly from the 10th century on, she is referred to as the "apostle to the apostles."

Adams' and Sellars' piece recounts some of this Biblical history, particularly Mary Magdalene's suffering at the feet of Jesus during the Crucifixion and her later discovery of the missing body. Jesus, who she mistakenly took to be a gardener, calls her by name, the event which ends the work. But through the libretto's collage of texts, this piece takes Mary Magdalene out of Biblical context and drops her into numerous 20th-century contexts, presenting the two sisters first as women who have been arrested and jailed, later as women who run a "House of Hospitality" for homeless girls, and in the second act as women picketing along with civil rights activist and union leader Cesar Chavez—a far different Cesar from Caesar Augustus, whose call for a census brought Mary and Joseph to Bethlehem for their child's birth. This shuffling back and forth in time is an attempt, obviously, by the librettist and composer to link the immediate lessons of Jesus with those who carry his message forth into our own time. And in several ways their condensation of time successfully presents these two important women embodying Christ's teachings, while at the same time emphasizing—particularly in Martha's complaint about being forced to serve alone while her sister lies at the master's feet—the special role Mary Magdalene played in Jesus' life.

Adams' music, particularly in the first act as he follows these women's lives and the resurrection of their brother Lazarus, is lush and beautiful, his constantly shifting rhythms reflecting the pushes and pulls of the demands these special followers put upon Jesus. The composer's brilliant concept of carrying much of the narrative through the voices of three countertenors (Daniel Bubeck, Brian Cummings, and Nathan Medley) allows the story to move forward, while the central figures, Mary Magdalene (Kelly O'Connor), Martha (Tamara Mumford), and the strong-voiced Russell Thomas as Lazarus, sing of their own psychological experiences and their personal relationships with Jesus.

From the beginning we come to understand Mary Magdalene as a woman of special intensity, having evidently attempted suicide and isolated herself from others after her brother's death—the injuries to her arm healed by the Messiah—while later showering her love upon Jesus by washing his feet with the herbs and ointments in her hair. Far different from the hard-working and more sensible Martha, Mary is clearly a woman of passion: as the women's chorus put it (in Spanish), "a body transfixed by the noonday sun," which becomes a metaphor of her love for and personal relationship with Jesus. This Mary—without specifically being portrayed as a former prostitute—is very much an embodiment of Jesus' teachings about love.

There are numerous powerful moments in the first act, including the prophet Isaiah-inspired "Howl ye," sung by Lazarus and the chorus, the passage in Spanish I just referred to ("En un dia de amor yo bajé hasta la tierra"), the intense resurrection of Lazarus ("Drop down, ye heavens, from above"), again sung by the chorus, Lazarus' own impassioned outburst ("For the grave cannot praise thee"), Mary's "I wash your ankles," and the chorus' response ("Spiritus sanctus vivificans vita"), and the absolutely splendiferous Last Supper, sung by Lazarus ("Tell me: how is this night / Different from all other nights?"), a piece, ending the first act, which I almost hoped might never cease.

Unfortunately, not all of the passages that Sellars chose for his collage are as excitingly poetical as those I mention, and, particularly in the second act, when the Biblical narrative begins to dominate, so too does the music turn a bit turgid, occasionally reminding one of the numerous Hollywood film epics of Jesus' life and

crucifixion. Here the countertenors and their narration dominate, while the personal viewpoints of the work's three major figures is diminished by the swelling of larger events, including Jesus' own arrest and Mary's and Martha's agitated protests.

Accordingly, the action is described in a kind of secondhand manner that affects not only the libretto

 but the music as well. Only with the Crucifixion does the work again reach the heights of the first act, particularly in Scene 4, with Mary's recounting of the falling rain on Jesus' body, and Lazarus' interpretations of the dying Christ's words: "I want no shelter, deny / the whole configuration." And both librettist and composer redeem this act with the stunning introduction of a resurrection of nature itself: "It is spring. The tiny frogs pull / their strange bodies out / of the suckholes," sung by both the chorus and Mary. The final graveside encounter between Mary and the gardener who calls her name is so marvelously understated that the audience with whom I saw *The Gospel According to the Other Mary* was not sure whether to applaud as Dudamel brought the orchestra to a quiet cessation.

What I have said above, however, cannot to do justice to the instrumental variations of this piece, which uses numerous percussion instruments not usually found in modern-day orchestras, along with the employment throughout of the cimbalom, creating the sound of an instrument contemporaneous with the Biblical events. Some of the narrative difficulties, moreover, may be solved when the production is transformed from a piece for the orchestra hall into a blend of opera and oratorio performance, which is being planned for the future. I cannot wait to rediscover this work in its new form, and feel blessed to have experienced it in this early manifestation.

LOS ANGELES, JUNE 3, 2012
Reprinted from *US Theater, Opera, and Performance* (June 2012).

By coincidence I chose seats for this performance in the last row facing the orchestra head-on, one of the few choices remaining—apart from the less preferable side and back views—after the subscription-goers' choices of months earlier. We soon realized, however, that these seats were probably also saved as complimentary seating for the work's artists and their friends. A few moments later I spotted Peter Sellars greeting several of our neighbors. When he saw Howard and me, he came joyfully over, hugging and greeting us too, claiming that he had been thinking of us for the past several weeks. I, in turn, had been thinking of him. He, along with Master Chorale director Grant Gershon, sat directly in front of us. The accident seemingly reconfirmed the affection that both Howard and I have felt for Peter over all these years.

Contradictions and Communication

NICK PIOMBINO AND TONI SIMON **POETRY READ-INGS** / OTIS COLLEGE OF ART + DESIGN, M.F.A. PROGRAM, SEPTEMBER 5, 2012

ON THE EVENING of September 5, 2012 I attended poetry readings for poet Doug Kearney and friends Nick Piombino and artist Toni Simon.

I had never before read or heard Doug Kearney's work, which is heavily performance-based, centered in his own theatricality and the collage of voices he brings to his work. On the page, some of his works seem vaguely concretist, with numerous ways of approaching the text when reading. There is an excitement in the numerous possibilities to read down, across, up, or to read certain passages, inserting them into others. And the theatricality of the work gives it an energy that's missing from the often tone-deaf poetry readings without any emotive voice (numerous poets seem determined

to not read any meanings or intentions into their work). The fact that his work also embraces collaborative possibilities, operatic performance, etc. adds weight to each particular poem. Unfortunately, the subjects of his poems are rather obvious and work against his clear delight in finding various voices in which to express them. His themes are primarily about race and racism, confining his work, at times, to categories or genres that have been brilliantly mined already by writers as diverse as Amiri Baraka, Suzan Lori-Parks, and lesser figures such as Lucille Clifton and Toni Morrison.

Piombino and Simon read from their collaborative work, *Contradita: Aphorisms*, which consists of pairings of aphoristic sentences that set up subtle, and occasionally more obvious, oppositions. Several of these are accompanied by quirky collages (reconstructed for the purposes of the tour into well-drafted drawings) that sometimes skew the "contradicta" in yet new ways. Below are a couple of examples:

All that titters is not bold.

Listen to the whispers—all the bold voices have had their say.

*

The mean teach the kind how to hide their pain so as to corrupt and enlist them in their ranks.

Small disappointments revive the child in us, which would be an equal recompense if we could but see it so.

Simon, as I mentioned to the students, had also just released her own book of drawings and poetical works, *Earth After Earth*, published by Lunar Chandelier Press in Brooklyn.

Although I prefer Piombino's masterwork, *Theo-*

retical Objects, I very much love this work. But then, I am a close friend of Nick's and Toni's and, I must reveal, am the publisher of both the books I mention, as well as Piombino's early *Poems*.

What was perhaps most interesting about the event was that, during question time, both poets answered audience questions, but also created an interchange between themselves, at moments almost developing an interview-like atmosphere, during which they ruminated as fellow authors and shared concerns. The kindness in their observations of each other's work—so rare when such poets of radically different sentiments read together—perhaps also reveals the fact that when he is not writing poetry or poetics, Piombino works as a psychologist, a man very used to listening to others.

Later, Piombino, Simon, Kearney, and I joined poets Dennis Phillips, Paul Vangelisti, and an old friend of Toni's at Deck 33, a pleasant outdoor bar and restaurant overlooking the pool of the Custom Hotel, where the poets were staying.

A couple of days later, I met them for lunch at Ray's at the Los Angeles County Museum of Art where Toni had freshly made gazpacho (it is high tomato season in Los Angeles), Nick had their always excellent hamburger, and I truly enjoyed their fresh pasta with crumbled fennel sausage and kale.

Afterwards, we joined Howard for a brief tour of

Los Angeles from the heights of Mulholland Drive, where they could look into both the San Fernando Valley and the LA Basin. Making our way downtown, we pointed out the Los Angeles Cathedral, the Mark Taper Forum, the Dorothy Chandler Pavilion, MOCA, and the always impressive Frank Gehry-created Disney Hall. We also took them on a tour of the marvelously well-kept Union Station, and Howard dropped us off at the marvelous Bradbury Building, for what seemed to be the highlight of the trip—since both Toni and Nick are avid science fiction fans and love Ridley Scott's *Blade Runner,* which shot scenes there. After a renewal of wine and cheese at our house, they crossed the street again to spend hours at the Los Angeles County Museum of Art.

LOS ANGELES, SEPTEMBER 10, 2012

Translating Heaven

ALTHOUGH I KNEW that my friend Michael Heim was dying of cancer, I was still shocked to hear of his death, at the age of 69, on September 29, 2012.

I don't remember where I first met Michael, most likely at a party by my former mentor and dear friend, Marjorie Perloff. What I do remember is that, as a scholar and major literary translator, Michael immediately attracted me, since my publishing houses—both Sun & Moon Press and Green Integer—featured international literature in translation; and we soon became good friends, Michael inviting me to be the lead speaker at one of his UCLA translation seminars. These seminars, held in the summer, invited major translators from around the country to gather for a few weeks, where they shared works they had translated or were currently working on, receiving from their fellow colleagues and a man who spoke and translated from many languages, critical advice and affirmation.

I bravely proffered an introduction from volume

4 of my ongoing *Anthology of World Poetry of the 20ᵗʰ Century*, advocating and defending the publication of international works*, which re-  ceived a great deal of response from the young translators in search of possible publication. After all, both my presses had perhaps published more translations than any American press in those days, with the exception of Dalkey Archive. Many of our publications, moreover, had received awards for translation, and I had received an award as publisher from the American Translators Association. My good friend, Suzanne Jill Levine, translator of Spanish-language literature, was also a guest speaker, and followed my introductory speech.

That event led, through meeting Efrain Kristal, to a two-semester teaching position at UCLA in the Comparative Literature Department—an experience I thoroughly enjoyed—and further resulted in my teaching two courses in the UCLA Scandinavian Department in later semesters.

Michael, born in New York City in 1943, the son of a Hungarian immigrant father (who studied music under Béla Bartok), was the kind of person who naturally nurtures. But he was also an imposing figure, somewhat conservative in the world of open-minded translators, and had graduated from Columbia with a degree in Oriental Studies before gaining a Harvard degree in Slavic languages and literature. Along with French, Spanish, German, and Russian, Heim later expanded his linguistic abilities to include Czech, Slovak, Croatian, Serbian, Danish, Norwegian, Swedish, Dutch, Hungarian, Italian, Latin, and Romanian! And his translations, from several of these languages, were brilliant. When Nobel Prize-winning writer Günter Grass lost his long-time translator, he invited 15 international translators to come together; Heim was selected to translate his book *My Century*. Heim also translated major works by Milan Kundera, Hugo Claus, and numerous others. For me, he translated only one poem (without any remuneration), an original work sent to me by the Czech poet Miroslav Holub.

His stern vision of the original text differed a bit from my own commitment to present a text that, while true to the original had to be recreated, in part, into the translated language:

> The postmodern stance is that the translator creates a new work. That's where I disagree. I believe that the translator is a creator, but I'm not sure that I'd want to create a new work. I would like as much as possible, the *same* work.

Over the last years, I met Michael at several of Marjorie and Joe Perloff's parties, and at events at his own home with his always gracious and intelligent wife, Priscilla. Michael, a tall, lanky, lean-looking man who, one was always tempted to compare, in appearance, with Abraham Lincoln, despite his literary and academic successes, clearly had little interest in money. His very aspect (Lincoln excluded) spoke of the kind of patch-coated academic who hadn't ever given a thought to his costume. Michael, it was apparent, was averse to the smell of dollars.

What we didn't know until the appearance of his obituary in the *Los Angeles Times* was that he and his wife had anonymously given away a small fortune of $734,000, left to him by his father and mother, to establish a fund for the PEN American Center to be awarded to translators over the past decade. I had seen several of the translations that had resulted from his generosity without ever knowing that he had been behind them.

Over the last years, with wracking back pain and then, suddenly, the inoperable cancer, Michael was, occasionally, an oppositional discussant, impatient perhaps with some of the more contemporary figures I published. He was, after all, a kind of classicist, a perfectionist, a mentor for generations of young talents devoted to the often unrewarding job of translating fiction, poetry, and drama that might otherwise receive little reader attention. But I felt only love and admiration for him, a man who had done so much for writers and their translators.

Today Marjorie noted on Facebook that at Michael's memorial service yesterday one speaker had suggested that Michael had surely gone to heaven, where he was busy translating for all. A nice sentiment. But I would argue that Michael Heim had created a heaven here on earth—a kind of translated heaven—almost personally defeating the age-old curse of the Tower of Babel, as he brought forth communication in our everyday lives between speakers of numerous tongues. Through his struggles many cultures could finally communicate with one another and find shared values, a cultural peace.

---

*The central paragraph of that introduction reads, in the context of its 2003 publication date:

What has become increasingly apparent, in this horrible year of war, is the true need for such a series, the importance of helping English-language readers to know the writing and, by extension, the cultures of poets from around the world. In an interview with a Brazilian journal, I was recently asked to comment if I felt Americans knew of the poetry in other countries. My conclusion was a bleak one: most Americans don't even know a poet in this country, I quipped; and, perhaps even more disturbing, is my guess that most American poets could name, perhaps, 20 poets from other countries. I recounted the story of a poet friend, who is very interested in international writing, innocently asking me who was the poet whose book I held in my hands. The book was the collected poetry of Léopold Sédar Senghor, the great Senegalese poet, former President of the Republic of Senegal, and one of the founders of the Negritude movement of French-speaking Caribbean and African writers which utterly transformed Francophone writing in the 20th century. My fear is that precisely this lack of knowledge of the writing and experiences of other cultures underlies the American arrogance and belief that not only is our culture superior to others, but that it should be the culture of others. It is no accident, I suspect, that a president who had traveled very little before taking office could not comprehend that American values and methods of achieving those values were not shared by all others. I am not suggesting that poetry will change these conditions, but certainly it may help us comprehend a world which—despite its astounding ability to quickly communicate—seems to be splintering apart rather than sharing ideas.

LOS ANGELES, SEPTEMBER 8, 2012
Reprinted from *Green Integer Blog* (September 2012).

Center's Collapse

CÉSAR AIRA **VARAMO**, TRANSLATED FROM THE
SPANISH BY CHRIS ANDREWS (BARCELONA: EDITORIAL
ANAGRAMA, 2002 / NEW YORK: NEW DIRECTIONS, 2012)

THE FIFTH TRANSLATED BOOK I've now read of
Aira's is one of the most hilarious. An insignificant
Panamanian government employee, Varamo, is paid his
monthly salary, one day in 1923, in counterfeit money, money he recognizes as being false the moment it
is placed into his hands. This
law-abiding and fearful citizen
of Colón, accordingly, is faced
with an intense crisis for the
first time in his life.

If he attempts to cash the
money he is certain that he will
be arrested for counterfeiting
and, since Panama has had very
few cases of such a crime, will be

made an example of, the authorities creating new methods of punishment as an example to the populace. Yet how can he survive without money for another month? Although he lives modestly as a bachelor, he cares for a slightly mad mother, in addition to his own expenses. Moreover, just having the money on his person might endanger him. Were he to give it away, he is certain that he would be tracked down. Perhaps the counterfeit money itself is a kind of test. In short, Varamo is put into a kind of moral and even metaphysical predicament which requires all of his abilities to resolve.

Aira takes us through this first day and night of this man's horrifying situation, wherein he is threatened by forces larger than himself, and which all seem to implicate him in some grand plot of which he has no knowledge. On his way home from the Ministry he is accosted by a local madman who insists Varamo owes him money, and by a shady underground figure, Cigarro, who awards him the small winnings of his mother's gambling bet.

At home, even his personal objects, his shelves of food, his bed, and his mirror seem to accost him. His Chinese mother arrives in a state of near hysteria, having received, so she claims, a blackmail letter. Work on his hobby of embalming goes no better, and before he can stop her, his mother has cooked up the fish he painted with chemicals, serving it up for dinner.

In a near fever of dread, Varamo attempts to walk to the local bar, only to be confronted with what he describes as "the voices" speaking meaningless sentences to him, as they daily do.

Just as he is about to step into the street, he witnesses a car hit another automobile containing the country's Treasurer, who, in his newly announced role as Minister of the Interior, is determined to observe the country's "regularity rallies," "races" through the roads and highways where the goal is to keep to a slow, regularly-timed pace. The Treasurer/Minister is unconscious, and Varamo is forced by his driver (Cigarro in another role) to take him to a local house owned by two spinster sisters.

There, in the "lion's den," he discovers that the sisters know perfectly well who he is, that they have been working with the underground to sell golf clubs, carrying them as canes, one by one, from local ships with which they communicate in code through messages bounced off of the regular passerby Varamo, and which explains the mysterious voices he encounters night after night.

After another entanglement with Cigarro's girlfriend, the sisters' maid, Varamo is entrusted with the code book, and charged with scrambling up the codes before they fall into Cigarro's or others' hands.

When the dizzyingly confused Varamo finally escapes the sisters' house, he finds publishers at the bar, men who abuse Panama's lack of participation in the International Copyright Agreements, and who are interested in having him write a book about his embalming experiences, promising him an advance precisely of the amount of his counterfeited salary. Having never written a word before in his life, Varamo is skeptical, obviously, about such an undertaking, but has little choice: it is a perfect solution to his dilemma.

So, after a mind-releasing walk through late-night Colón, Varamo returns home to write:

> He sat down, and wrote the poem. It is true that the verb "to write" covers a wide range of practices. In this case the author simply copied out all the papers he had put in his pocket since leaving the Ministry that afternoon. He did this in a cumulative fashion, without punctuation or divisions, without rearrangement, in lines of irregular length (the idea of prose, a late refinement in old civilizations, was utterly foreign to him). The order was determined by chance. The code book provided a basic structure, and he alternated the keys with literal transcriptions of the other notes. He had the advantage of having received contradictory instructions, which he followed with providential diligence of a beginner: Caricias had told him to change the keys to make them unrecognizable, and the publishers had

advised him to leave the raw materials as they were.

The final work, *The Song of the Virgin Child*, Aira tells us at the beginning to the book, became the "celebrated masterpiece of modern Central American poetry," a work "drilled into the minds of schoolchildren or regularly chosen for recitation in poetry competitions."

In addition to Aira's hilarious spoof of how great experimental work is created, the author also plays with notions of genre, arguing that his own narrative, since it is "true," is not a *fiction* but a use of the third person to tell the "truth," as a journalist might. It is, after all, he insists, a story well known. And evident in the structure itself, like all highly modernist experiments, is a work that reveals its own reality.

Of course, Aira's work is not at all truthful, but an absurd series of "postmodern" lies pretending to represent reality. And the joy of *Varamo* lies in the fact that, as the fictional poet's world collapses about him, forcing him to build a new conception of his world, the reader gets to tag along, to play with the character and author in the creation of a new universe made up of the accidental and coincidental elements of an imagined life. And isn't that what the creative act is really all about?

LOS ANGELES, EASTER DAY, 2012
Reprinted from *Rain Taxi* (Summer 2012)

The Elements of Fiction

CÉSAR AIRA **LA COSTUERA Y EL VIENTO** (ROSARIO, ARGENTINA: BEATRIZ VITERBO EDITORIA, 1994), TRANSLATED BY ROSALIE KNECHT AS **THE SEAMSTRESS AND THE WIND** (NEW YORK: NEW DIRECTIONS, 2011)

THIS IS THE FIFTH English-language translation of Argentinean writer César Aira's over 80 publications of fiction. For devotees of his writing—and I now consider myself one of them—each new book is a must, different as they are from one another. For each of these slightly quirky fictions takes the reader into new territory where we feel that the author, like the greatest storytellers, is making it up as he goes along. These short volumes, accordingly, seem so fresh that if Aira were to begin the story over by repeating the first few pages, we might imagine the ending would be entirely different.

The Seamstress and the Wind begins, in fact, with the narrator revealing some of the author's methods. "Trapped" for a few weeks in France (the narrator

 proclaims he dislikes traveling), the narrator decides to write a fiction with two major elements: his central character must be a seamstress and the tale must include the wind. The narrator claims that he seeks through these two elements to write "a novel of successive adventures, full of anomalies and inventions." And he proceeds to do so, beginning with an autobiographical memory from his childhood in the Argentine suburb of Coronel Pringles, where one day he and a school friend decide to play a game of hide-and-seek within an open semi-truck parked near their houses.

As the friend draws near him, pretending to be a monster of sorts, the young narrator closes his eyes in horror. When he opens them, his friend has disappeared, and a few moments later he finds himself, almost as if he has fallen into a time warp, at his own kitchen table, startling his mother, who has been told he is missing and, unable to find him, is quietly pondering this predicament. It is his friend, in reality, who has gone missing, and after a search of the entire neighborhood, the mother, Delia, who works as a seamstress, becomes convinced, having begun to lose her sense of reality, that her son has been "stolen" by the neighborhood truck driver, Chiquito, now on his way to make a delivery of goods in Argentina's vast and empty Patagonia.

Scooping up the wedding dress upon which she is working, she hires one of the town's two taxi drivers to chase after the truck, and speeds away into the night.

Thus Aira whips up a kind of strange Keystone-Cop-like chase that results in a series of, just what he has determined his fiction should be: a story of odd adventures and inventions that removes this fiction from any sense of being a "novel," and transforms the work into a kind of absurdist fantasy. As the taxi and its occupants speed off into the desert, they suddenly crash, with enormous velocity, into the back of the huge truck, instantaneously killing the taxi driver and sending poor Delia into a kind of coma, as their small taxi is impaled into the back of the truck, without the truck driver having the least suspicion of the accident. He is in a hurry to reach his destination.

Meanwhile, Delia's husband, returning home from work, is told by the neighborly gossips that his wife has gone off, and he, in his own kind of madness, takes after her in the family car, followed by the small blue car of Delia's customer, determined to retrieve her wedding dress.

Part of the joy of reading Aira is the surprising series of strange events as they occur, so I will not reveal all of the amazing adventures that these figures endure. Let us just say that the remaining events of the fiction include Delia's husband's addiction to gambling, a strange gambling den in the middle of nowhere, the transformation of the woman who is to be married the next day, Delia's romance with the strong Patagonian wind, a mysterious "monster child" created out of a sort of atomic meltdown of the gambling den, and the rediscovery of a large Paleolithic armadillo shell. Few American writers, except perhaps for Mac Wellman, could whip up a story with these unlikely props. Aira makes it all seem easy, and, although it is thoroughly unbelievable—particularly for those steeped in realist traditions—the author somehow poetically combines them to create a credible sense of denouement. If the "scattered elements" of Aira's fable do not magically come together "at the end in one supreme moment," they magnetically click into place as the wind shuffles and deals each of these characters his or her fate.

LOS ANGELES, SEPTEMBER 16, 2011
Reprinted from *EXPLORING*fictions (September 2011).

Ruling Us

DUSTIN LANCE BLACK (SCREENPLAY), CLINT EAST-
WOOD (DIRECTOR) **J. EDGAR** / 2011

YOU HAVE TO ADMIRE Eastwood's Hoover biopic if
for no other reasons than because it has a remarkably
capable cast, authentic sets and costumes, and numerous well-edited and composed scenes. Eastwood is
an intelligent and sensitive director of the old Hollywood school who has presented us in this work with
a thoughtful and strangely touching piece about one
of the most powerful, irascible, and difficult men
in American politics—although I am sure Hoover
thought himself above and apart from the political
scene. He was in fact one of the most political animals
ever, and that ability is the reason behind his long survival through the governing of eight presidents. Both
Truman and Kennedy wanted to fire him, but, fearful
of the repercussions, did not act. Hoover primarily created the modern FBI, developed its sophisticated scien-

tific investigation techniques, and promoted the organization to the American public through films, comic books, and other media.

Eastwood steps carefully in revealing the less heroic side of this figure by allowing his Hoover (Leonardo DiCaprio in, perhaps, the best role of his career to date) to describe himself, or, to put it another way, to mythologize his concerns and actions in a long series of meetings with writers of a would-be FBI memoir. For anyone who knows about the FBI Director's activities over the years, it is fascinating, but also irritating, to watch and hear the chest-beating braggart strut his stuff. And the creaky plot structure that this device creates fills in a selective history, without moving the story forward.

Of course, by film's end, with Clyde Tolson's summary of the lies Hoover has promoted, we recognize that there is a logic to this structure, but with the focus on such a small selection of events, Eastwood and screenwriter Dustin Lance Black leave a highly inconclusive series of occasions that can hardly convey the scope of Hoover's vast pall over the whole of the American scene.

The film begins with the 1919 and 1920 so-called "Palmer Raids," headed by Hoover after mail-bomb attacks on several notable figures. The raids themselves rounded up few anarchists, but the result of these raids, and the fears raised by the FBI and other organizations, led to larger attacks against socialists, communists, and other groups whose principles did not accord with Hoover's and others' version of democracy. As the former head of The Enemy Aliens Registration Section, Hoover manipulated the system to have numerous figures such as Emma Goldman (the example used in the film) deported. Yet Hoover's fury was far more extensive than the one example *J. Edgar* names, for he later was behind the expulsion of notable figures such as Charlie Chaplin and numerous others, as well as influencing the little-discussed Mexican repatriation, ordered by Presidents Hoover in 1929 and Roosevelt in 1939, resulting in the return to Mexico of 35,000 American citizens who were originally born in that country. Indeed, *J. Edgar*, had Eastwood desired, could have had far greater resonance to the present than it does. As the film quotes one agent, Stokes, "The crimes we are investigating aren't crimes, they are ideas." And one might argue that, throughout his life, Hoover's actions were based more upon what he saw as dangerous ideas as opposed to actual threats, truly terrorist acts.

The second series of "selective" memories upon which the film focuses are the infamous FBI attacks on robbers and gangsters such as John Dillinger, Pretty Boy Floyd, and other criminal figures of the 1930s. By this time Hoover had developed a group of effective agents to serve him, but jealous of the attention his agents received, such as Melvin Purvis (who killed Dillinger), Hoover lashed out against the brightest of his own men, demoting or firing them. This almost maniacal demand for attention drove Hoover to several of his most ridiculous actions, and is revelatory of his desperation for power and popular approval. Certainly Eastwood's movie hints at this, but the few instances upon which it focuses make such conclusions fuzzy as opposed to telling a story that might more thoroughly reveal Hoover's contradictions.

Finally, the film gets terribly bogged down in the story of the Bruno Hauptmann kidnapping of the one-year-old son of American flying hero Charles Lindbergh. Hoover—and the film—detail the investigation quite thoroughly, demonstrating how Hoover's forensic developments led, finally, to Hauptmann's conviction and death. To me, the focus on this one event delimits so much else that the film might have revealed about Hoover and almost exonerates him in his leadership. What the film does not precisely depict is that even the governor of New Jersey doubted Hauptmann's guilt, and years later a large number of FBI files and other material were discovered in the governor's records that suggested some of the evidence was planted by FBI agents, bringing into further question several aspects of Hauptmann's guilt.

In short, by employing the device of Hoover's dictated memories, the film jumps and skips over some of the most egregious issues of Hoover's career. While we do see him developing private files, one containing a letter in which Eleanor Roosevelt addresses a lesbian lover, another containing information on John F. Kennedy's sexual encounter with a foreign agent, and a tape of Martin Luther King's illicit sexual encounter with a woman, these are sometimes so incidentally mentioned that anyone not immersed in the period may not comprehend their significance. The film glosses over Hoover's wiretapping, his extensive eavesdropping on thousands of American celebrities, and his involvement in the destruction of the lives of hundreds of individuals whose only crime was in questioning or disagreeing with his strong moralist and political stances—which included a kind of xenophobic view of the world, an abhorrence of all things sexual (particularly involving homosexuality), and a patriotism that might have made even Thomas Jefferson seem like a "commie." It seems almost comical that, had he not died, Hoover might have finally met his match in the equally righteous, but law-breaking Richard Nixon.

The film reveals the most in its fictionalized glimpses into Hoover's private moments. We cannot know precisely what Hoover's relationship was with his mother, but *J. Edgar* presents us with a claustrophobic home-life wherein it is hard to imagine how he was not smothered to death in love. Judi Dench brilliantly portrays a woman obviously doting on a young man whom she has molded through speaking lessons, moral homilies, and motherly affection. The film carefully tiptoes around the claims of Hoover's cross-dressing tendencies by showing him, upon his mother's death, in a fetish-like mania, donning her beads and dress.

When Hoover admits that he cannot bear to dance with women, she repeats the story of a childhood acquaintance who, dressing as a woman, was mocked by neighbor's through his nickname "Daffy" (for daffodil). Her concluding comment is one of the most horrific statements of the film: "I would rather have a dead son than a daffodil for a son." Afterwards, she puts her arms around him in an attempt to teach him how to dance.

Many of the critics whom I read seemed to suggest that Eastwood and Black barely touched upon the momentous hypocrisy of Hoover's life: his own possibly homosexual relationship with his assistant, Clyde Tolson. Yet I see this as, perhaps, the central focus of this work, or, at least, its most well-developed subject. From the moment he first meets Tolson (played by the immensely talented Armie Hammer*), Hoover goes into

heat, actually breaking out into a sweat when he interviews Tolson for a possible FBI job. The man is, at least in the terms that Hoover has laid out—total commitment to the organization, complete sobriety, and utter faith in him and the organization—unqualified for the position. Yet not only does Hoover hire him, but within a few months, he makes him second in charge. For the next 45 years the two dined with each other for lunch and dinner, and traveled together on vacations where the two shared bedrooms or adjoining suites. They worked every day at the office side by  side. The film suggests that, at least on a few occasions, they kissed; that Tolson was furious over Hoover's affair with Dorothy Lamour, and outraged at Hoover's suggestion that he might marry. Tolson, apparently, chose Hoover's suits and ties, and coached him on the niceties of societal behavior. Once Hoover met Tolson, although he had outlawed liquor for all FBI employees, he began increasingly to drink. Together the two gambled, went to the theater, and attended late-night clubs. Does that mean that the two were lovers?

Despite the long-time insistence of Washington, D.C. gays and political insiders (I lived in that city for 16 years during his tenure, and regularly was assured of Hoover's homosexuality), and the rumors that he had been seen at gay orgies in full drag with a bevy of blond-haired boys, I would side with the moderate views of this film. I suppose the question is whether a deep male camaraderie without sex might still be described as a homosexual relationship. There are plenty of couples, homosexual and heterosexual, I would argue, who seldom have sex. I can only understand a situation such as the one between these two men as being a kind of marriage, one of the dictionary definitions being "an intimate or close union." Indeed, more than anything else, it is apparent, Hoover craved love, and Tolson daily offered it up.

Hoover's grabs for power, which ultimately corrupted him and led him to hypocritical actions that are almost incomprehensible, grew evidently out of that need to be loved. Power, as every backyard bully and world leader come to comprehend, means the ability to influence and control others, particularly potential enemies. As Hoover himself said, "No one freely shares power in Washington, D.C." Year after year, like a king overseeing the election of new presidents, Hoover stood on the balcony of his FBI office, waving at the inaugural presidential parades. He had power, but in the process lost his sense of the very values that he imagined he was so carefully protecting. He, indeed, had become a kind of ruler, not a democrat.

---

*One of the ironies of the film is that Armie Hammer's great-grandfather, Armand, was a long-time target of Hoover, who questioned Hammer's close ties with the Soviet Union.

LOS ANGELES, DECEMBER 6, 2011
Reprinted from *Nth Position* (January 2012).

Sun Myong Moon and Me

I DO NOT celebrate anyone's death, and Sun Myong Moon's death, on September 3rd of this year, was no exception. Death is a sad occasion. One less person on the horizon—even if, unintentionally, Moon has long been someone I totally disagreed with. I am not religious, in any sense of that word, and quite thoroughly detested his Korean vision of multi-marriages and religious fanaticism. Perhaps I would have had no relationship to this absurd figure had I not, quite innocently, named my magazine and press Sun & Moon.

Seeking to imitate the wonderful John Ashbery journal, *Art and Literature*, I made a connection between those two wonderful genres by referring back to the great Austrian novelist—completely unknown by US readers—Albert-Paris Gütersloh, who was both a great surrealist artist and an important fiction writer, and who influenced many Austrian figures, most notably Hemito von Doderer, several of whose fictions I was to publish later on my Sun & Moon Press.

I bought the rights to Gütersloh's great fiction, *Sonne und
Mond*, asking the brilliant Ros-
marie Waldrop to translate it.
She had just discovered that she
had breast cancer, and suggested
that, given her health, she might
want to translate the work for
the fair price of $10,000. I had
no such funding, and had to pass.

The book never came to publication, although she did
translate a chapter to give me a sense of the work; it appeared to be just what I was seeking.

You must understand, I do not read German, but
I fell in love with this book in the long-gone Rizzoli
bookstore in Manhattan, where I asked several times—
as if asking for a special jewel—for them to take this
"masterpiece" out of the glass-enclosed case in which it
was embedded. Perhaps I perceived it as a masterpiece
because of the glass encasement, but something about
the book totally enchanted me—why I can't explain.
German publisher Klaus Wagenbach tried to convince
me that it was an archaic work—he, after all, had published Kafka and numerous other major psychological-
ly-based works that did not at all accord with the high
Austrian fantasist and romanticized works of figures
such as Albert-Paris Gütersloh.

I could not be dissuaded, however, and still today would have loved to have published his fiction. What I did instead was to name my magazine after his novel, *Sun & Moon: A Journal of Literature & Art*, recognizing the combination of two great planetary forces as a representation of literature and art. I could never have imagined that that phrase would suddenly put me into the camp of the religious fanatic, Sun Myong Moon. But that is what happened.

It began with seemingly friendly questions: are you connected with the Sun Myong Moon sect? No, I had nothing to do with that, I reacted. And soon, I just moved forward with great disdain for the religious connections. I would, I determined, create a Sun & Moon Press, despite the religious bigot who had become a thorn in my side. But at one American Booksellers Convention (now Book Expo) I was placed with religious presses, at another I was embedded in the section that contained mostly Korean, video-based publishers. Obviously, my customers could not find me in these odd isolationist spots, which has a great deal to do with my continued refusal to attend those large book fairs. Later, as the newspaper and magazine reviewers became more and more isolated themselves from comprehending serious literature, my press' name served as an anathema to their predilections, and reviews appeared less and less often. Sun & Moon was somewhat subliminally connected with Sun Myong Moon, who had bought up entire newspapers and other media networks to get out his religious perspective. It became clear to me that literary reviewers and their editors are not necessarily wise individuals who comprehend the intricacies of literary publishing. Today, they are even less inclined to comprehend what serious literature is, although I now publish under a less-loaded name, Green Integer—after all, they might ask, what is an integer (any number)? Am I a member of the Green Party?

So, I am sorry to say, I cannot exactly mourn this religious "messiah's" death. Sun & Moon Press was a delightful combination of major planetary forces, understood clearly in Asian countries and even in Europe. Americans, as usual, got confused. For nearly 30 years, that press provided a wide range of world poetry, fiction, and drama. Nothing to do with closed religious practices, and certainly uninterested in marrying throngs of young grooms and brides, but very much influenced by European and American modernism. Rest in

peace, Sun Myong Moon, my strange ghost of a name-sake. I will no longer have to deal with you, my own press having also gone, for other reasons, into the grave.

LOS ANGELES, OCTOBER 10, 2012
Reprinted from *Green Integer Blog* (October 2012).

A few days after writing about my Sun & Moon magazine and press in relationship to the death of Sun Myong Moon, I discovered among my files an essay I had written in 1976, the very year in which I published our first issue. I don't even recall penning this piece for the Maryland Arts Council, and I am quite startled by both its youthful enthusiasm and, at times, its insights ("A lifetime of frustration may result"). The concepts of "hot and cold type," "hot wax," and large paper purchases now seem something out of an ancient text, but were crucial issues of the day. And if my easy metaphor comparing publishing with a Broadway show production is glib and today somewhat embarrassing, it is appropriate for a young man who so loved theater throughout his youth. If my younger comments seem now blissfully absurd, I am, nonetheless, in admiration of that lost self for some of my insights and disparaging comments about my own impossible undertaking. Alas, most of my disparagement was merely bluff; I was already hooked and was ardently committed to literary publishing, as I remain today. If I had enough money (the problem with both endeavors), I'd probably still attempt to produce a play!

Sun & Moon: A Journal of Literature & Art— A Youthful Reflection

IF WE ARE to believe the motion picture industry, the national fantasy of the '30s and '40s was to produce and star in a Broadway show. Once Hollywood got hold of the idea, of course, it didn't matter whether such a fantasy had previously existed or not. It soon did. It was myth, and therefore it was truth. The ritual lines are still in our blood (at least in *my* blood): "Hey kids! I've got an idea! Let's get together and make a musical!"

I remember, as a child growing up in the '50s, living with that fantasy and acting it out in the form of "plays" in our basement, sometimes with others—a cousin or a shanghai'd brother or sister—more often alone. But by the 1960s, we had grown up, both as individuals, and, one hoped, as a nation, and we were interested in more "serious" things. And one of the most serious of all things was to begin a newspaper or a little magazine.

I won't call it a national fantasy, but from the evidence of those working around me, and from the statistical facts, there were certainly great numbers of individuals who actually said, "Let's start a journal." Of course, these were all sorts of little magazines, dealing with everything from politics to health food. The kind of journal that I was interested in, a literary magazine, may never have had such an impetus as in the middle and late '60s, although it had a long tradition, especially in this (20th) century. And I suspect that those of us with a "literary bent" dreamt of being editors simultaneously with producing Broadway shows.

The dangers of such manufactured fantasies are obvious. As we all know, most of these fantasies are unrealizable, and a lifetime of frustration may result; and, thus, I guess it was inevitable that I would eventually stop dreaming and act. My "fantasy" was finally realized a few months ago, at a time in my life when I have no more illusions about the simplicity of beginning a journal than I have about the possibility of a few friends getting together and opening a Broadway show. Working on the *Index to Periodical Fiction*,* both my co-editor, Howard Fox, and I studied the hundreds of small journals which yearly replace hundreds of others that couldn't survive. So we had no excuses. We knew the odds against the project on which we were about to embark. Moreover, neither of us had had any editorial experience, so we were in the strange position of not being blind, and yet being in the dark. I thought it might be interesting, therefore, to share some of what I learned from this unusual vantage point, so that others who can't shake their fantasies can bring their dreams, when and if they must, a little more easily to life.

It was late in May 1975 when Howard and I decided to pool our interests and begin a magazine of literature and art. We had thought out loud of the idea previously, but this was the first time that we took ourselves seriously. We had just been indexing a small journal, *The Floating Bear*, and we had seen in it an exciting magazine that had not been printed, but mimeographed. It was not that mimeographing appealed to us, but that it was affordable. By beginning with a mimeographed journal, we could publish immediately, and as we caught on—so our reasoning went—we could improve our format.

I suggested the title *Sun and Moon*, the title of a novel by the Austrian Albert-Paris Gütersloh. I'd never read *Sonne und Mond* (it has never been translated), but the title had appealed to me, and now it seemed to apply nicely to a quarterly that would try to embrace two different and yet related disciplines.

Later, we were to reconsider. We were afraid that it might sound too dated, as if it were something from the '60s like *The New Moon Trading Post*. For a while, we considered calling the journal *The Literature and Art Quarterly*, but that was too academic. *Eclipse* had too many negative connotations, although we felt it signified a dramatic event. Other titles were too provincial, too clever, too cute. When our friend Marjorie Perloff suggested we change the "and" to an ampersand, we found the journal's name stuck.

Now that we had a title, we immediately sent out letters to several of favorite authors and artists who had previously contributed to small magazines. Our letters were honest and personal; we made no large claims, pretended no exceptional experience. By late June and early July we received some responses. Far sooner than we had expected, manuscripts were arriving. Actually having the stories, poems, and artwork in our hands, we suddenly realized that we couldn't mimeograph. We both felt we owed it to our contributors (some of them noted figures) as well as to our egos to somehow afford a better format. Our first step, understandably, was to find out what else was available to us.

In the heat of late July and early August, I made the rounds of a few local printing centers, where I quickly learned a little about terms that had been previously vague, such as "letterpress," "cold type," "offset," and "type compositors."** At least I now knew that I was looking for a compositor on which I could rent time, and I was seeking an offset printer whom we could afford. That summer it seemed that no one except IBM had a compositor we could use, and it was beginning to look like we were doomed to the typewriter's unjustified margins, instead of set type.

Late in August, Merrill Leffler of Dryad Press mentioned the Print Center, Inc. in New York. However, to use the Print Center was impractical, especially since I hoped to be able to do our own typesetting (I am still a speed typist, and had worked as a typist in my one year in New York). To stay in New York for that length of time was not only unaffordable, it was impossible, since the classes I taught at the University of Maryland began in a week or so. Merrill also suggested we contact a place in Baltimore that we heard might be getting a composing machine. It was called The Maryland Writers Council.

No need to say what happened. Here I am writing for their newsletter, and anything I can say would only sound like an in-house testimonial. Let me just say that what the Council offered was perfect for a journal of our sort. But of course that hardly meant that every problem was solved, that now the issue could proceed without more ado. There was still type-size and style to choose, paper to select, and my own layout work to do.

The latter two problems were the difficult ones. The first was simply a matter of choice. The fact that we managed to add $50 to the $100 cost of typesetting by doing revisions after some manuscripts had already been set, and that an issue which we planned to be 80 pages long suddenly turned out to be 100 pages, I'll claim as commonplace mistakes beginning editors make. I suggest that future editors without experience should expect those kinds of problems; it is somehow inextricably linked up with an editor's education.

On paper, however, I can give advice. One should find a large paper company and helpful clerks, and one should ask to see everything the company has. The more different types of paper one can see, the more ably one can choose exactly what one wants. We chose a laid stock because we had developed certain aesthetic associations with it. But even laid papers differ, sometimes quite radically, and it took several weeks to choose the paper we liked and could afford.***

Doing the layout on the journal, that actual pasting-up of the pages, is where I learned the most about what a little magazine is all about. Some important considerations had begun to arise already in proofreading, and as I waxed each page, carefully aligned it, measured each line for evenness, and rolled the sheets into place, I reread it, wondering if, now that we had an issue, we truly had a magazine. Did the works we had chosen come together to say anything as a group, as a voice? For many weeks, after we had begun receiving manuscripts and had turned away from the mimeographed format, we had debated what we should be. We modeled ourselves, very vaguely, after magazines like John Ashbery's *Art and Literature*, a journal we felt to be superior. But, of course, we had not yet developed the friendships or taste of Ashbery, and we hadn't yet the attraction or the resources of his journal. Our contributors, for the most part we felt, were excellent, but were comparatively few. And, more importantly, we still hadn't—perhaps we still haven't—clearly established our own taste. Our solution has been eclecticism, but from those other journals with which we had worked we learned that eclecticism is not necessarily a hodgepodge of quality, styles, and tastes. Had *Sun & Moon* resolved those problems? I couldn't answer that question. I knew I would have to wait. No editor can be without these fears, and at no time are these fears more prominent, it seems to me, than when he is literally putting the journal into shape.****

Meanwhile, I had numbered wrong for perfect binding, I was having troubles without inserts, and, without my new glasses, I wasn't sure my lines were truly straight. But two weeks later I was finally finished.

Once again, good fortune saved the day. Long-experienced editors Pam and Charley Plymell***** working on their own journal had been on hand to give their expert pointers and advice.

Now the flyers have been mailed, subscriptions are being taken, the issue is at the binders, and I wait impatiently******. I have lost all objectivity, and I can no longer tell whether *Sun & Moon* will be the journal that I had once dreamt about. It doesn't really matter. For I have made something, and despite all the difficulties, I enjoyed doing it. Most importantly, I learned so much. Finally, I guess if I reconfirmed to myself that such fantasies are absurd, I also rediscovered the beauty and importance of those fantasies, especially when there is that urge to bring them to life. But please, please somebody stop me if I try to produce a Broadway show.

<hr>

*In 1974 through 1976 Howard Fox and I edited a 764-page volume of bibliographic listings of fiction published in hundreds of magazines and journals from 1965-1969. The book, published by Scarecrow Press in 1977, was meant to be a bibliographic annual, but the amount of work involved, and the numerous hours we spent in the Library of Congress and elsewhere compiling the information, discouraged us from continuing its publication.

**When we began our publishing, hot type, that is molten lead cast into letters and lines, was just beginning to give way to "cold type," type composed on computers. But the computers of the day, the one I worked on was called a Compugraphic compositor, were huge machines that looked more like giant organs inside of sleek laptops. The typesetter "composed" almost blindly, line by line, and transferred onto photographic paper, which then needed to be processed through a mix of deadly chemicals. The process was spotty at best; if, during the process, the chemicals were not perfectly blended, the work was destroyed. So too could the type become faded by simple exposure to daylight. Hot "wax" was applied to the underside of the sheets to allow them to be positioned onto large cardboard quartos that were later photographed for printing.

***Today, fortunately, most printing houses who do both the printing and binding also provide a selection of papers to be chosen from. In the early days of typesetting, however, the processes were often separate, requiring the editor to visit both a paper maker and a printing house.

****In fact, when I look back upon that first issue, we had not at all developed our aesthetic visions, and our selections did truly represent a vast array of poetic, fictional, and even artistic perspectives (although Howard continues to embrace the artists we began with today). It was not until the third or fourth issue that I began to perceive a poetic sensibility, and it was truly not until I began publishing books that I had defined my poetic and narrative sensibilities. If the journal helped me to do this, how can I complain?

*****Pamela Beach Plymell is the daughter of the renowned artist Mary Beach, who while working at City Lights discovered the poet Bob Kaufman, and later, under her own imprint, Beach Books, published William Burroughs; she is a distant cousin of the original publisher of Joyce's *Ulysses*, Sylvia Beach; Charley, involved early with the Beat Generation poets, lived for a while with Allen Ginsberg and Neal Cassady.

*****We received the completed first issue on February 14, 1976, Valentine's Day. *Sun & Moon: A Journal of Literature & Art*, published 11 volumes from 1976-1981, at which time the magazine was abandoned in order to publish only books, which had already begun in 1979. The issue displayed above is issue no. 8 (Fall 1979), featuring on its cover a piece by artist Robert Longo.

Reprinted from *The Supplement to the Bulletin of the Maryland Writers Council* (Special "Catch Up" issue, February-May 1976).

Celebrating Suppression

GEORGE CRAM COOK AND SUSAN GLASPELL **SUPPRESSED DESIRES** / PROVINCETOWN PLAYHOUSE, JULY 15, 1915

GEORGE CRAM COOK's and Susan Glaspell's satire on Freudian analysis was first produced in July of 1915, as the very second play performed by the Provincetown Playhouse. There is some question as to whether Cook and Glaspell arrived at Provincetown with the play in hand, or whether, naive as they were about theater, they presumed that, since they themselves were to be the major actors, they could simply ad lib the work. What that might mean for the character of Mabel, played in Provincetown by Lucy Huffaker, is not clear. But perhaps, since she was a close friend of Glaspell's, she knew the subject intimately.

Certainly the issues which the play satirized were well known throughout Greenwich Village, where psychoanalyst A. A. Brill had introduced Freud's and

Jung's theories, and numerous essays had been written and published, particularly Max Eastman's two-part article in June and July in *Everybody's Magazine*. Theater historian Jeff Kennedy argues that the playwright couple had obviously read Eastman's piece—which gives further credence to the idea that they were writing the play at the very time of the production—because of its reference to a Freudian case in which a woman had repressed feelings for her brother-in-law, and Eastman's mention of a quote from A. A. Brill about a woman who dreamt she was in a street with a flock of chickens.

Some critics argue that the performance occurred

before Glaspell actually wrote down most of the play's best lines, but the couple would have had to be brilliantly clever performers to ad lib some of the most hilarious of the psychoanalysts' interpretations, namely that the command Mabel hears, "Step hen," actually calls up her brother-in-law's first name, Stephen, and that the whole image of a hen derives from her sister-in-law's first name, Henrietta. And the play, although at times no more than a one-line joke about psychoanalysis, is overall far more sophisticated than its structure might suggest.

Henrietta may be laughed at for her complete immersion in and belief of Freud's and Jung's theories, but she is also presented as an intelligent, strong-willed, and freewheeling woman, able—even with great pain—to give up her husband if he truly feels walled in by their relationship. What she cannot endure is that her sister might also be in love with him and all too willing to run off with the man for whom the psychiatrist has convinced her she is repressing her love.

This short play is a long ways from almost any other work of its day in presenting a woman who is able to speak intelligently on psychology and even write layman essays on the subject. Although Henrietta is not trained as a psychologist, she is nearly as convincing in her interpretations of her sister's dream as the psychiatrist; and she is most perceptive in observing her husband's disenchantment with his life, part of which involves her compulsion to awaken him several times each night, demanding to hear his dreams. The situation reminds me of the incidents in Marianne Hauser's novel, *Dark Dominion*, a work which did not appear until 1947!

Even if Henrietta discovers that those around her have been suppressing desires that exclude her—she changes her entire viewpoint of the psychoanalytic world too quickly—the play still reveals that she is open-minded about life; and if both she and Stephen suggest that Mabel should suppress her desires, the irony of their statement is that they are not likely to celebrate suppression. For it is clear that the couple at the heart of the play will continue being quite forthright about their likes and dislikes.

If *Suppressed Desires* is not a great satire, seeming at times to be more a skit than a one-act play, it is an intelligent skit, witty and, in some ways, far ahead of its time.

LOS ANGELES, JUNE 24, 2011
Reprinted from *US Theater, Opera and Performance* (June 2011).

Celebrating Liberation

ERIC CROZIER (TEXT, BASED ON A STORY BY GUY DE MAUPASSANT), BENJAMIN BRITTEN (COMPOSER) **ALBERT HERRING** / LOS ANGELES, LA OPERA AT THE DOROTHY CHANDLER PAVILION / THE PERFORMANCE I SAW WAS ON MARCH 11, 2012

BENJAMIN BRITTEN'S comic opera, *Albert Herring*, as most critics have noted, is a rather light entertainment that, over the years, has been revealed to have darker and more profound messages beneath it. The excellent recent production of the LA Opera hints at a few of those more meaningful moments, but skims over some of the most important implications.

On the surface Britten's fourth operatic work reads a bit like a Ronald Firbank story or like other works of the British dialogue fictions, filled with typological figures. Lady Billows (Janis Kelly in the production I saw) is just what her title suggests, an elderly autocrat, who literally "bellows" to all those about, demanding virginal girls and normative behavior. Her housekeeper, Florence Pike (played by Ronnita Nicole Miller), is an uppity slacker who keeps a sacred diary of all the village of Loxford's goings-on, including the misbehaviors of nearly every young girl in town. Along with the head teacher, Miss Wordsworth (Stacey Tappan), the Mayor Mr. Gedge (Jonathan Michie), and the Police Superintendent Budd (Richard Bernstein), these figures attempt to maintain the traditional moral values—however they might be defined—for all Loxford citi-

zens, particularly the feminine sex, whose virtuous model is celebrated each year in the village's choice for May Queen.

The opera begins with the meeting of these important city figures attempting to decide upon which young woman they will bestow this year's award. As they run through each of their lists, however, it becomes apparent from Florence's diary that none of the village girls is above recrimination, even though some crimes are no more important than where they wear the hems of their dresses. Others have stayed out all night in barns, run off with boyfriends, or simply been gossiped about. In distress, the quintet struggles with their inability to

make a choice until one of their members suggests a May King, all ultimately agreeing that the only choice can be Albert Herring, a woman shopkeeper's son who has been carefully obedient to his mother. There is also a sizeable purse attached to the award, which pleases Albert's mother far more than him when the group announce their choice.

At first Albert is seen as simply a do-gooder, with no personality whatsoever. But by the second scene of Act I, we begin to see him question his allegiance to obedience, and, comparing himself with the fun-loving and sexually busy couple Sid and Nancy, realizing that he has nothing to show for remaining a mother's boy.

Putting Albert on display, the town leaders could care less about Albert's feelings or any reality he might be experiencing within, dressing him in white and awarding him an absurdly orange wreath, which he is forced to wear throughout the luncheon. But Sid has other plans for Albert, getting Nancy to spike Albert's lemonade with rum, an event which begins a series of adventures for our "hero" that ends, after another self-analysis of his life, with Albert going off into the evening to discover the life he has never before experienced.

Meanwhile, the village, having noted his absence, is in a tizzy about his whereabouts, the hypocritical quintet of village elders meeting to lament what appears to be his death. When Albert does reappear at the very moment that the others sing piously (and quite beautifully) about dying, he is shockingly filthy, having spent the night in at least two pubs and, after being thrown out of both, slept for some hours in the gutter. He has also been with two women and (more mysteriously) a man. The sexuality of those situations

is not quite established except for Albert's own admission that he has done everything of which he is accused "and worse," and that "it wasn't much fun." The audience's imagination is important here, for how one defines "worse" leads us to perceive how deep his rebellion against the Victorian notions of the community leaders has gone. Certainly he is no longer in thrall to any of them, particularly to his mother, as he virtually tosses the city leaders out of his shop so that he can get on with his business. Whatever that business may now be is uncertain; but it is clear that Albert has made a big transformation, as he rewards the children candies and graciously hands a peach to Nancy.

Conductor James Conlon argues that the exact

nature of his transgressions must remain vague. And probably that was what Britten also intended. But we must remember that, although he lived much of his life as an open homosexual, for Britten it might have been difficult to more thoroughly explore the issue in small-town life of 1947. Today, I, at least, would have liked a little more of the possibility of Arthur exploring homosexual experiences. For that might even have made him a kind of exceptional figure in Loxford history.

As it stands, Albert is simply a slow learner, a man who waited far too long to come to terms with any sexuality. Perhaps if we understood this as a truly exceptional sexual variance, we might be better able to explain Albert's slow awakening instead of merely explaining him as a kind of village simpleton or, as several characters describe him, not very bright. Let us hope at least that after his night of revelry he does not remain a greengrocer for the rest of his life!

LOS ANGELES, MARCH 13, 2012
Reprinted from *US Theater, Opera, and Performance* (March 2012).

Two Madams

The Blindfold

LUIGI ILLICA AND GIUSEPPE GIACOSA (LIBRETTO, BASED ON THE PLAY BY DAVID BELASCO AND THE STORY BY JOHN LUTHER LONG), GIACOMO PUCCINI (COMPOSER) **MADAMA BUTTERFLY** / THE PRODUCTION I SAW WAS A RE-BROADCAST IN HIGH DEFINITION OF THE METROPOLITAN OPERA PRODUCTION ON SATURDAY, MARCH 7, 2009 WITH PATRICIA RACETTE, MARIA ZIFCHAK, MARCELLO GIORDANI, AND DWAYNE CROFT

NEARLY ANYONE who has seen an opera knows the story of Puccini's *Madama Butterfly*. Having fallen in love with the dashing American Navy Lieutenant Pinkerton, the 15-year-old Cio-Cio-San marries him, despite the fact that in doing so she must give up her own family and friends. With Yankee haughtiness and a sense of superiority, Pinkerton scoffs at the American consul's warning that Cio-Cio-San is taking the marriage seriously, and, soon after, leaves her behind as he sails off to America and, ultimately, a "real" wife.

Cio-Cio-San sings her famed aria "Un bel dì vedremo," in which she describes one beautiful day when a ship will sail into the harbor, returning Pinkerton to her. Meanwhile, Cio-Cio, courted by local men such as the wealthy Prince Yamadori, refuses to give up her so-called "American" marriage, and ardently denies their insistence that Pinkerton has left her for good.

The consul, Sharpless, has been given the difficult task of reading a letter from Pinkerton to Cio-Cio reporting that he has been married and will not return, but she, so delighted to hear any word from her husband, cannot comprehend what he is attempting to tell her, and when Sharpless tries to explain the facts in a more outright manner, she produces her and Pinkerton's son, whom she is certain will draw Pinkerton back to her.

Pinkerton, in fact, has already returned to Nagasaki, and has no intention of visiting Cio-Cio. When he does hear of the child's existence, he, his wife, and Sharpless convince Cio-Cio's servant Suzuki to break the news that Pinkerton and his new wife will adopt the son.

Finally, Cio-Cio, who has been blinded throughout the entire opera to the truth, has her eyes opened, realizing, in horror, her delusional condition. She asks Pinkerton, a man so selfish that he has refused even to face her himself, to return so that she may offer up the child. But we also know that she intends to leave him her own body, committing ritual suicide. Who could not be moved by Patricia Racette's dramatically convincing performance? The Lithuanian-born American next to us—who had never before attended a Met video performance—was in tears, as were Howard and I.

David Belasco and the original playwright and storyteller John Luther Long, upon whose work Puccini based his opera, were quite prescient in this *fin de siècle* piece, establishing a type, the ugly American, which has remained in place for all those years since, particularly in the context of the Korean, Vietnam, Afghanistan, and Iraq wars. In Puccini's hands, the dichotomy between the all-consuming Yankee and the self-sacrificing Japanese maiden could not have been made clearer.

Yet, one can only recognize that Cio-Cio-San's propensity for self-sacrifice is as much a problem in

this relationship as has been Pinkerton's greed and disdain of her life. In her absurd innocence, she has not only been blinded to the impossibility that she could be recognized as an American wife, but has forgotten who she herself is and how her traditions and behavior conspire to permit the Pinkertons of the world to prey upon such youths.

Puccini poignantly points up this fact by having her son, whom she has sent out to play, wander into sight just as she is about to draw the knife. To protect him, she blindfolds the child, sending him on his way. But in doing this she merely reiterates her own condition all along. Singing of her hope that her son will remember her at the very moment that she is about to disappear from his life, we perceive that, were he to do so, it could only bring him great pain for the rest of his days. In Anthony Minghella's Metropolitan Opera production, the child, "Sorrow"/"Trouble," was played by a Bunraku-like puppet, manipulated by three hooded assistants, which visually restated the child's future sense of emptiness, his destiny, perhaps, to join the world of hollow bodies.

Accordingly, although the opera ends with a corpse upon the stage, we know that Cio-Cio-San is already a disappearing thing, representing as she does a way of living that will inevitably be replaced by the avaricious gluttony of the survivors.

LOS ANGELES, MARCH 28, 2009
Reprinted from *US Theater, Opera, and Performance* (March 2009).

Fin de Siècle

LUIGI ILLICA AND GIUSEPPE GIACOSA (LIBRETTO,
BASED ON THE PLAY BY DAVID BELASCO AND THE STORY
BY JOHN LUTHER LONG), GIACOMO PUCCINI (COM-
POSER) **MADAMA BUTTERFLY** / LOS ANGELES, LA OPERA
AT THE DOROTHY CHANDLER PAVILION / THE PRODUC-
TION I SAW WAS ON DECEMBER 9, 2012

ALTHOUGH THERE ARE many good things about this
LA Opera production, based on an earlier San Francisco Opera version—including the singing of Milena
Kitic as Suzuki, the ever-resilient bass-baritone of Eric
Owens (some of his tones lost, however, to the Dorothy Chandler Pavilion's unpredictable acoustics), and
the basically excellent performances of Oksana Dyka
(as Cio-Cio-San) and Brandon Jovanovich (as Pinkerton)—it would be simply unfair to compare this with
the brilliant Anthony Minghella Metropolitan Opera
production I saw in 2009. Although she has a strong
soprano voice, Dyka simply is not a good match for the

fragile, butterfly-like character. Singing at the top of her voice, one could certainly hear Dyka's lyrical tunings, but she hardly seemed like a humble, obedient 15-year-old, which Patricia Racette more thoroughly convinced us she was. I look forward to hearing, at some point, Dyka's *Aida* or *Tosca*.

The heavy reliance upon shifting screens may certainly be appropriate to the period, but the design has somehow aged, and the placement of Pinkerton's Westernized bed in the midst of this spare set was jarring. Jovanovich also has a fine, strong voice which he used to great purpose in the LA Opera production of *The Birds* in 2009. But here he seemed, at times, to be trying to sing out against his powerfully-voiced wife. However, these are surely quibbles about performances that the audience apparently quite enjoyed—as did Howard and I. I might just note that the usually "jump-up-to-applaud" Los Angeles audience remained mostly seated at opera's end.

What struck me most while watching this production was just how connected to the works of the *fin de siècle* is Puccini's 1904 opera. Beginning in the 1880s, writers such as Oscar Wilde, Joris-Karl Huysman, and Arthur Schnitzler openly challenged earlier moralities, and the characters of their works not only dismiss more conventional behavior, but reject previously moral values with clear hostility. Consider Bertha Garlan, the heroine of Schnitzler's book of the same name: Bertha, who has lived most of her life in quiet domesticity, becomes bored and impatient after the death of her husband, and—seemingly encouraged by a woman friend whom Bertha sees as an open-minded, slightly-libertine figure—attempts, on a trip to Vienna, to strike up a sexual relationship with a previous acquaintance, now a famous musician. The musician is all too ready to accept the sexual part of the relationship, but rejects any further commitment, leaving Bertha a nearly-destroyed woman who has suddenly behaved licentiously near the end of a life which she has previously lived with restraint and motherly affection. In Schnitzler's play *Hands Around*, men and women strike up brief affairs,

each figure moving on, in turn, to another, until the sexual interludes have gone full circle. Wilde's *The Importance of Being Ernest* proceeds out of a world dominated by lying (the major character participating in what he describes as "bunburying" his way through life) into a society where love seems to be based on one's first name. Huysman's Des Esseintes lives his entire life in the delectation of special foods and perfumes, reading obscure texts, and other sensate experiences.

So too does Puccini's "coffee-house girl," innocent though she may be, take up with an affair with a foreigner, delighted with his ultimate proposal of marriage. But Pinkerton, as we know, is a cad, not at all intending to keep his vow, and perceiving his Japanese wife of 15 years of age (it would be hard to imagine presenting such a child abuser on stage today) simply as something to be toyed with. As he tells the only truly moral figure of the opera, the consul Sharpless, someday he will have a "real" marriage with an American woman.

As callow as he appears today, Pinkerton was little different from almost any major *fin de siècle* figure, men and women willing to throw over everything for a life of sensual pleasures. Despite her utter innocence, so too is Cio-Cio-San willing to marry not only outside her culture, attempting to redefine herself in terms of what American men may like, but is insistent about abandoning her own religion and cultural values in order to explore the "pure joy" she feels from her love with Pinkerton—despite the ultimate rejection of her by all of her relatives including the powerful Bonze. Like Bertha Garlan, Madame Butterfly may have lived a life beyond reproach (much of that depends on how one defines a Geisha), but she is now determined to throw all that away for a man to whom she is immediately attracted (as she admits, she has fallen in love upon first sight). And although she describes herself as humble and modest, patient as she explains her real and symbolic climb up the hill to the house where Pinkerton intends to "install" her, she is also determined to live a better life, presumably in the United States, where she delusionally believes her husband will eventually take her and their son.

Puccini himself lived a sexually open life, rearing a son with his mistress, Elvira, while simultaneously having other affairs with younger women such as Corinna, trysts he described as "cultivating my little gardens." During the writing of *Madama Butterfly*, the jealous Elvira insisted he marry her, in response to which Corinna threatened to reveal his love letters to the world. In short, the composer was not so very different from his characters, particularly if one sees Corinna as a kind innocent in the whole affair.

In short, one of the reasons why the audience can emotionally bear the tragedy of Butterfly's death is not only because we know Butterfly lives in a world of denial—a world of how things *should be* instead of how they are—but because, despite how despicably Pinkerton has treated her, refusing to even admit his American marriage to her face, she too has been caught up in the liberating spirit of her age. And although all those around her insist that she face the truth, Butterfly stubbornly refuses to admit the consequences of her choices.

Based on a true-life figure, whose affair with Pinkerton probably occurred in 1892 or 1893, Butterfly herself was seeking experiences outside the range of normative moral behavior of the time, experiences which, the *fin de siècle* writers often advocated, but also warned, just as Sharpless warns Pinkerton, might lead to dangerous consequences. Unlike Wagner's heroes, whose pure love for one another is betrayed by others and the gods, Puccini's heroes have only their own desires, selfishness, and self-deceptions to blame for their fates.

LOS ANGELES, DECEMBER 10, 2012
Reprinted from *USTheater, Opera, and Performance* (December 2012).

Wasted on Youth

RICK ELICE (WRITER/DIRECTOR, BASED ON A FIC-
TION BY DAVE BARRY AND RIDLEY PEARSON) **PETER
AND THE STARCATCHER** / NEW YORK CITY, BROOKS
ATKINSON THEATRE / THE PERFORMANCE I SAW WAS
ON MAY 5, 2012

ON MAY 6, 2011 I attended Mabou Mines' *Peter and Wendy* at New York City's Victory Theatre, a delightful rendition of Barrie's Peter Pan story performed by actors and puppets. Quite by accident—although I now believe such "accidents" are "intentional coincidences"—almost one year to the date I attended, last evening, Rick Elice's amazingly theatrical prequel to Barrie's tale, *Peter and the Starcatcher*. Although I'm reluctant to compare it with the far less entertaining *Wicked*'s relationship to *The Wizard of Oz*, it stands in a similar position to the original.

Yet *Peter and the Starcatcher*, in many respects, is the polar opposite of Barrie's belovèd sweet bedtime

story etched into senior citizens' memories through Disney's cartoon transformation. Today's children—a number of whom were in attendance at the Saturday evening performance I witnessed—are quite obviously more sophisticated than I and my peers were growing up in the 1950s. For although the 7-year-old boy and his 13-year-old sister, sitting on booster seats in the row in front of me, could not have comprehended all of the witty linguistic confabulations of this play—much of it enveloped in camp humor and vaudeville-like risqué asides—they clearly understood and enjoyed a great deal of its multi-layered humor. That *Peter and the Starcatcher* is basically an adult comedy embracing all tried-and-true tricks of old-fashioned theatricality that still appeals to children and to the children-in-adults speaks volumes for the work's intelligence and sheer audacity. If I cannot truly describe this play as a great or even significant dramatic work, I have no difficulty in suggesting that it is a brilliant pastiche—which, given our time's disinterest in normative coherency, is perhaps a greater compliment.

This is a work, moreover, so different from most of Broadway's current theater offerings in that it thoroughly depends on its ensemble cast, as the actors transform themselves from sailors into pirates, mermen, and a strange band of Mollusk Island natives whose leader has suffered indignities as a servant in the home of a wealthy English family.

All of this play's figures perform delightfully, as one by one they get their individual turns to strut their stuff; but the clear "star" of this zany concoction is the dyslexic, spoonerism-spouting, "nancy-boy" pirate, Black Stache (Christian Borle)—an earlier manifestation of *Peter Pan*'s crocodile-hating Captain Hook—who discovers in the "boy" (who later changes his name to Peter and finally is awarded his last name, Pan) his perfect nemesis, a kind of kindred yin to his yearning yang. Even more delicious, when Stache prances forward to put his tongue upon the plank, is Smee (Kevin Del Aguila), close behind to correct those incomprehensible twists of tortured syntax.

Almost as enticing is the crowd-pleasing frivolity of Molly's sexually assertive nanny, Mrs. Bumbrake (Arnie Burton), and Fighting Prawn (Teddy Bergmann), who cling to one another, pushing and prodding from every possible position.

In contrast to these figures' shenanigans, Molly and the orphan boys, Peter, Alf, and the ever-starving Ted, are not nearly so much fun—although they might be forgiven when we consider that, by comparison with their orphan torments, Dickens' Oliver Twist might be said to have lived a life of luxury. They are, moreover, doomed to live in eternal adolescence as outsiders, perpetual kidnapped survivors of generations of temporary girl-moms. No wonder Peter, as he often announces, hates adults. Might he not simply be taken home to be petted and loved?

Evidently not, particularly after he has bathed in the star-laden waters that offer him whatever he might desire to become. And although he never really flies in this production he does occasionally soar with the rest of his friends. Fortunately, or unfortunately, depending on your point of view, he remains an innocent who, like most innocents and far too many children, is capable, competent, and serious-minded, while the adults around him all ridiculously blunder through their lives. One can only mutter at the end of this splendiferous caprice: "What a waste of youth!"

As I stood to leave, the young girl in front turned to announce, as if to confirm her own seriousness of intent: "I read the book"; while her equally sure-footed brother asserted: "I liked it, did you?"

ABOARD UNITED JET 1688 RETURNING FROM NEW YORK
TO LOS ANGELES, MAY 7, 2012
Reprinted from *US Theater, Opera, and Performance* (May 2012).

Finding Family

WES ANDERSON AND ROMAN COPPOLA (WRITERS),
WES ANDERSON (DIRECTOR) **MOONRISE KINGDOM** /
2012

OVER THE PAST several years there has been a spate of movies and plays devoted to and influenced by the tales of J. M. Barrie concerning Peter Pan. I reviewed two of those, Mabou Mines' *Peter and Wendy* (see *My Year 2011)* and, more recently, Rick Elice's *Peter and the Starcatcher* (above). Now we have Wes Anderson's *Moonrise Kingdom*, which, although it has no direct references to the Peter Pan story, clearly has relationships to it. I suppose that in a time when "centers collapse"—as I maintain in this year's cultural annual—we should be prepared for children striking out on their own, seeking worlds or attempting to create new worlds that parents have failed at; or, as my movie-going companion Thérèse Bachand put it, it is a time when children must parent the adults.

Anderson's films, as several critics have noted, have always occurred at the intersection of children's fantasies and adult lunacies, of which there can be no better example than Anderson's most recent film. Just as in his 2004 film, *The Life Aquatic with Steve Zissou* (see *My Year 2004*), Anderson's new film begins with a world in miniature, a representation of the sets we will soon encounter on a larger scale, which both underscores the theatricality that is so central to his art and suggests the toyland-like conceptions of Anderson's fantasies. Color, decoration, and costume dominate as he introduces, one by one, the cast of eccentric beings who are at the heart of this director's vision. Of course, this may be seen as coy and even fey to many moviegoers: both Bachand and my companion Howard found *Moonrise Kingdom* to be slightly irritating just on this account. Yet that is precisely why I so enjoy Anderson's art. From the very start, he makes clear that the story he will tell is "made up" out of a series of component parts, a tale spun by a storyteller who seems to be creating the work as he goes along.

Anderson makes that process clear by beginning his work with Benjamin Britten's well-known *Young Person's Guide to the Orchestra*, in which the composer, using a theme by Henry Purcell, takes apart the orchestra, instrument by instrument, and rejoins it to help his listeners perceive how a work of music comes together,

explaining how each instrument finds, metaphorically speaking, a role in the family of the whole. Anderson's metaphor is an important one, not only in representing his structural techniques, but in setting up his thematic concerns, since his heroine and hero, Suzy Bishop (Kara Hayward) and Sam Sakusky (Jared Gilman), have serious difficulties in finding their voices within familiar structures. Suzy is perceived as a troubled child— which she discovers through a guide her mother has left on the top of the refrigerator—desperate to escape the hostile environment of the Bishop house, wherein her lawyer mother, Laura (Frances McDormand)—escaping her life in a dreary affair with the local police captain (Bruce Willis)—is unhappily married to her lawyer husband Walt (Bill Murray), a man so disappointed with his lot in life that he wishes the impending storm would sweep him up and away, as if he might discover a new world similar to that which Dorothy encounters in Oz. Suzy is simply another sore issue in their failed relationship. When she goes missing, the two respond:

LAURA BISHOP: Does it concern you that your daughter has just run away from home?
WALT BISHOP: That's a loaded question.

Sam is an equally troubled boy, but his situation is even worse than Suzy's, for he has no family, both of his parents having mysteriously died, leaving him imprisoned in a large family of orphans in the Billingsley compound (certainly one of Anderson's private jokes, Barbara Billingsley having been the name of the actor who played June Cleaver in the utopia of American family life *Leave It to Beaver*). Notified of Sam's escape from an island scout camp, Mr. Billingsley reports that they cannot allow him to return the adoption home, to the shock and bewilderment of Police Captain Sharp and Scout Master Ward (Edward Norton). The precocious Sam has difficulty surviving not only in that home, filled with delinquents, but in the scout camp with his equally delinquent khaki-panted peers.

Sam and Suzy have met, quite by accident, one year earlier during a performance of Britten's children's opera, *Noye's Fludde* (see *My Year 2011*), based on the medieval mystery play. Showing us a flashback of their encounter and immediate attraction to one another, the director introduces yet more structural elements of his film, in particular the pairing of animals and humans and the threat of a disastrous flood, which, as the film's narrator (Bob Balaban) foretells, is about to strike the New Penzance Island of 1965. Together, using Sam's scouting skills and Suzy's imagination and pluck, the two trek across the island, attempting to outwit parents, police, scouts, and scouting master, as they seek a new paradise with one another in an isolated cove. For a short time they manage to elude  their would-be captors, escaping, like Peter and Wendy, into a kind of magical Neverland where they can explore life as intelligent and sexual beings, and hoping to establish the identities so rejected by all the others they have encountered before.

Ultimately, of course, they are tracked down and returned to a "civilization" that further demeans them, the Bishops enforcing tighter restrictions upon their daughter and the Billingsleys ousting Sam via correspondence from the only home he has known.

When the authorities receive a call from Social Services (hilariously performed by Tilda Swinton, dressed in a kind of Salvation Army-like blue garb), the Police Captain, Scout Master, and telephone operator are appalled by her cruel efficiency as she hints that the wayward boy may be sent to an orphanage or even given shock-therapy for his behavior.

Even the bullying scouts, startled to hear of these potential tortures in store for their former camp member, decide to get involved, helping Suzy to escape and bringing her to Sam, now locked away on a boat belonging to the Police Captain. This time, they all run off together, Suzy reading to the boys just as Wendy reads stories to The Lost Boys and Peter Pan.

Having now been abandoned by an entire scouting troop, the perplexed Scout Master Ward, Police Captain Sharp, and the Bishops again go in pursuit of the missing children, with the Social Services, Captain Hook and Crocodile-in-one, right behind them. For once, I will resist revealing the rest of this delicious plot, saying only that in the brewing storm lightning strikes thrice, and the adult world is devastated before the children are miraculously saved, Sam finding a home with the lonely Police Captain and Suzy returning to the "darling" Bishops' snug house. Just as Mrs. Bishop formerly snuck off for trysts with her Police Captain lover, so now does Captain Sharp bring his newfound son to the Bishop house so that Sam can secretly visit the young Suzy. Each has found a family, bringing their distinct voices into the orchestra of life.

Anderson cleverly repeats this theme once more in the credits, as Sam narrates the orchestral components of composer Alexandre Desplat's original score.

Corny? Perhaps. Obsessive? Obviously. Charming? I'll end with a quote from Anthony Lane's excellent review of this film from *The New Yorker*:

> Who knows, we may look back on Anderson's works as we do on the boxes of Joseph Cornell— formal troves of frippery, studded with nostalgic private jokes, that lodge inexplicably in the heart.

LOS ANGELES, JUNE 4, 2012
Reprinted from *Nth Position* (June 2012).

Mariachi to Merman

DAN GUERRERO (WRITER AND PERFORMER) ¡GAY-TINO! / EAST LOS ANGELES, EAST LOS ANGELES COMMUNITY COLLEGE, OCTOBER 4, 2012

ON MY COMPANION Howard's 66th birthday, we attended a performance of *¡Gaytino!* by performer and producer Dan Guerrero. The performance, which recounts much of Guerrero's life, was presented at East Los Angeles Community College in conjunction with a show of the Chicano artist Carlos Almaraz, who, as a close childhood friend of Guerrero's, played a large role in Guerrero's memories.

The two grew up together in East Los Angeles and moved, temporarily in Almaraz's case, to New York together, sharing for a while a small flat. Guerrero was gay and Almaraz, at least later in his life, was bisexual.

Guerrero's entertaining and somewhat self-satirizing show is subtitled "Mariachi to Merman, Sondheim to Cesar Chavez," and the range of those extremes are,

in part, his defining life experiences. To an audience of primarily Chicano students, Guerrero explained that he grew up without defining himself as anything but a second-generation American; although his parents were of Mexican background, he did not define himself in the 1940s and 1950s as either Chicano or Latino. Yet, without quite realizing it, he grew up at the very center of Mexican-American culture in that his father, Lalo Guerrero, was a famed mariachi composer-singer. In a recent interview, Guerrero recounted what he also reveals on stage:

> I was just a kid when Mom took me to see Dad perform at the Million Dollar Theatre in downtown Los Angeles, one of the great movie palaces built back in 1918. By the early 1950s, changing demographics kicked in and it became the cultural center for LA's Spanish-language community. You got a great black and white film from the Golden Age of Mexican cinema and a live variety show with the biggest names from Mexico and the biggest

Mexican names from this side of the border. Dad walked out on that stage and, when applause broke out, I knew he was special and not just a "regular" Dad like my friends' dads. He belonged to a bigger audience than just Mom and me. I knew it at that moment.

Late in his life, Lalo, who has been described as the "Father of Chicano Music," was named a National Folk Treasure by the Smithsonian Institution in 1980, and awarded a NEA National Heritage Fellowship in 1991. President Clinton presented him with the National Medal of Arts, the first Chicano to receive that award.

Yet, for much of his life, his son tried to dissociate himself from that music and that world. At one of his very first Broadway performances, Ethel Merman, singing "Some People" in the musical *Gypsy*, spoke what Guerrero felt was directed at him. He sings a few stanzas from that song in his performance with great Mermanian gusto.

In New York he took acting and dancing lessons, and tried out for dozens of roles, but, as he jokes, there weren't many roles for Latinos. Of course there was *West Side Story*, but, he admits, he wasn't the gang type. During these years he had to control what he now describes as an "expansive" nature; resist being what was then described as "light in your loafers." When Alma-

raz returned to Los Angeles and art school, Guerrero admits feeling utterly alone in the city he loved.

Although he did get several acting roles in summer stock companies—groups, he jokes, so sexually charged that he even had sex with a woman—he gradually realized that his dreams of being on the Broadway stage were growing fainter. Almost by accident, learning on the job, Guerrero began as an actor's agent, becoming very successful, casting numerous figures in works as

different as *A Chorus Line* and *Cats*. Among his several well-known clients was a very young girl who, however, was extremely wise as she sat in his office soliciting roles: Sarah Jessica Parker. Involved with the casting of the musical *Zoot Suit*, a musical about the 1940s Chicano community in Los Angeles, Guerrero's life suddenly came full circle as he re-encountered not only the music his father had created but actor friends such as Lupe Ontiveros and others he had known previously.

That event changed and reinvigorated him, encouraging him to return to Los Angeles, where he suddenly began to embrace all of the culture he had previously shunned. Previously working with everyone from Sondheim to Tommy Tune, Guerrero now cast mostly Chicano and Latino actors, and forged friendships with people who had known and respected his father, including the labor agitator Cesar Chavez, for whose funeral he organized the Chicano actors' contingent. Years before, Chavez had suggested to Guerrero's father where he might perform based on places at which Chavez planned to rally.

Of course he also reforged his friendship with the boy who as a child he'd known as "Charles," the now-renowned artist Carlos Almaraz, who tragically died of AIDS in 1989.

By turns campy actor, vaudevillian, and historian, Guerrero tells a remarkable tale in ¡*Gaytino!* that results in laughter and tears, engaging the younger audience in a cultural experience that it was clear many of them had never imagined might be part of their own heritage.

LOS ANGELES, OCTOBER 8, 2012
Reprinted from *US Theater, Opera, and Performance* (October 2012).

A few years later, on February 15, 2015, Howard and I were invited to Dan Guerrero's West Hollywood condominium for what he described as his first "salon." With noted artists John M. Valadez, long associated with the Chicano art movement, Patssi Valdez, a noted figure of the Asco artists, and Los Angeles Times *critic Carolina Miranda and her companion Ed, we dined on a delicious meal cooked by Guerrero.*

The afternoon was a truly joyous one, in which Dan, John, and Patssi reminisced about their pleasant—and sometimes not so pleasant—memories of the 1970s and later. Valadez, who had recently returned from an excit-

ing art commission in Bordeaux, France, took pleasure in describing the beauty, food, and wine of the place.

Patssi, who brought a beautiful flower, embedded in a hand-designed pot, spoke of her current problems with severe shoulder pain—the result of years and years of art-making. She also spoke of the difficultly, at times, of dealing with the "old" days of Asco, remarking on the charismatic domination of the group by Gronk, and revealing another, parallel, life she led during the same period, when, on some evenings, she joined amazingly fashionable young Chicana women wearing Saint Laurent and other designers' gowns at the clubs, many of whom she had documented with photographs which were now being evaluated by curators at the Hammer Museum of Art. I *suggested meeting her to further discuss this rather unreported aspect of Los Angeles Chicano culture, and Dan argued that it would make a great movie.*

Dan and I also discussed our kinship in loving Broadway musicals, he suggesting that his favorite composer was Cole Porter, about whom I have written below. I had long ago chosen to pair that essay with my piece on Dan's 2012 performance.

LOS ANGELES, FEBRUARY 16, 2015

On Sunday, September 17, 2017, I attended yet another reincarnation of Daniel Guerrero's ¡Gaytino! This clearly revised version was performed in connection with Howard's Carlos Almaraz show, Playing with Fire, *at the Los Angeles County Museum of Art's Bing Theater. And instead of performing for a young audience who would know little of Guerrero's several theatrical and cultural references, the mostly sold-out 600-some-seat Bing Theater was filled with many people who not only knew the performer but had known him throughout his life.*

Consequently, their fondness for the performer permeated the theater, and Guerrero came alive, embracing all of his natural performative abilities—singing, dancing (which he describes as "movement"), dramatic storytelling, and just plain joie de vive. *Although his story* may be a little tattered these days after his endless re-tellings, his seemingly endless energy and panache made it a remarkably pleasant afternoon in which Guerrero could strut-his-stuff, relive his own life, and retell incidents from his long friendship with Almaraz.

His sad recounting of the final day before Almaraz's death of AIDS, when he imitated a child's farewell to Almaraz as he left his hospital room, "Goodbye, old friend," seems almost too perfect to be real, although I don't doubt its authenticity, it could itself be played out as a theatrical tableau. And the scene in which he describes when, while attending the funeral of Cesar Chavez, he pushed the Chicano actors and artists he had brought to the event to the front, next to Ethel Kennedy and other celebrities, is almost heroic. Finally, he argues, "we took our proper place."

Always flamboyant and, yes, always somewhat self-centric, Guerrero is nonetheless always equally entertaining.

LOS ANGELES, SEPTEMBER 30, 2017

Pure Poetry

P. G. WODEHOUSE AND GUY BOLTON, REVISED BY HOWARD LINDSAY AND RUSSELL CROUSE, REVISED AGAIN BY TIMOTHY CROUSE AND JOHN WEIDMAN (BOOK), COLE PORTER (MUSIC AND LYRICS) **ANYTHING GOES** / LOS ANGELES, AHMANSON THEATRE / THE PRODUCTION I SAW WAS ON DECEMBER 1, 2012

THE MUSICAL *ANYTHING GOES* has been rewritten so many times, adding Porter's songs from other musicals while subtracting several of the original songs, that one might almost describe what I witnessed the other day as a shadow of its first conception, even if, arguably, the layering revisions have burnished it into a better work. Most of the changes, however, have been to the story, but since the silly couplings and un-couplings of the work hardly matter, it is hard to be interested in the "ur-text." I will be glad to accept Timothy Crouse's and John Weidman's assurances that they were "purists," "but only to a point." What is important is that they

restored as much of Porter's score as they could, adding only three wonderful Porter songs: "Friendship," "It's De-Lovely," and "Goodbye, Little Dream, Goodbye."

The story, in fact, pretty much lives up to the musical's title, the characters almost changing partners willy-nilly. This time round, nightclub singer (former evangelist?) Reno loves Billy, Billy loves Hope, Hope pretends to love Lord Evelyn Oakleigh but really loves Billy, Lord Evelyn loves Reno, Elisha Whitney loves Evangeline Harcourt, and Erma loves everybody. Enough said. The book—whatever version you choose—makes soap operas, by comparison, look like grand operas. "Frothy" is the appropriate word.

Yet this chestnut has been immensely popular

since its 1934 opening in New York, running 420 performances even during the Great Depression, and reappearing in successful productions in England and New York in 1935 (261 performances), 1962, 1987 (784 performances), 1989, and 2011 (521 performances). What I saw was a sold-out performance of the touring version of the 2011 production. Why has it succeeded again and again?

The answer, quite obviously, is not just a cast of talented singers and dancers (a requirement of course!) but Cole Porter, who in this and other works turns what might have been Tin-Pan ditties into pure American poetry. Sure, the music itself is sprightly and often borders on a kind of regularized jazz. But those words! No one, not even Stephen Sondheim, can write as wittily idiomatic lyrics while pulling his audiences into a kind of licentious world that hints of everything from adultery and drug addiction to sexual orgies and open homosexuality, with his characters simultaneously hoofing up innocent-seeming line dances across the stage.

The fun begins with this show's very first song, "I Get a Kick Out of You," where Broadway libertine Reno Sweeney (the talented Rachel York) tells Billy about her frigidity concerning everyday life:

I get no kick from champagne.

Mere alcohol doesn't thrill me at all,
So tell me why should it be true
That I get a kick out of you?

Some get a kick from cocaine.
I'm sure that if I took even one sniff
That would bore me terrific'ly too
Yet I get a kick out of you.

The whole idea of sexual excitement being likened to the "kick," of champagne and cocaine would be unimaginable in Irving Berlin's near-Puritanized romances. Berlin could be funny, even witty, but he couldn't be funny, witty, and naughty at the same time. When Berlin's characters said they loved someone they meant it, for all time. For Reno and numerous other characters of Porter's world, love may haunt one, even torture one, but it is seldom seen as permanent and can even be an everyday occurrence, something to traffic in, something someone might want to "buy"— just like champagne and cocaine.

Or consider the wonderful shifts in the notion of "friendship" in the song titled that. It begins as a song of spirited support of one being for another, in this case the musical's two major "hustlers," Reno and Moonface Martin (the 13th most wanted criminal):

If you're ever in a jam, here I am
If you're ever in a mess, S.O.S.
If you're so happy, you land in jail, I'm your bail.

Gradually as they each try to outdo one another in imagining life-saving necessities, the song becomes a kind of contest which reveals that underneath their "perfect friendship" there is not only an open competitiveness but a true hostility:

If they ever black your eyes, put me wise.
If they ever cook your goose, turn me loose.
If they ever put a bullet through your brain, I'll
complain.

The lyrics grow even more outlandish as they imagine the worst for one another:

If you ever lose your mind, I'll be kind.
And if you ever lose your shirt, I'll be hurt.
If you ever in a mill get sawed in half, I won't
laugh.

It finally ends with imagining each other being eaten

by cannibals, in which the second half answers, "Invite me."

These are not the words of supportive human beings, but of criminals who might turn on each other in a minute. Plumbing the unconscious depths of Americans' fascination with violence—notably present in the entertainments of the 1930s—Porter has created almost a paean to the macabre, a world wherein people wind up in jail, put bullets through brains, lose their minds, get sawed in half, and are consumed by cannibals, lines somewhat reminiscent of William Carlos Williams' observation, "the pure products of America / go crazy," and Allen Ginsberg's opening line in *Howl*, "I saw the best minds of my generation destroyed by madness, starving hysterical naked...."

Hearing once more the musical's title song, "Anything Goes," I realized that, again, the most important thing about this work is its lyrics—which unfortunately, in the quick-paced rhythms, got somewhat lost in York's rendition; suddenly it became clear to me that the original Reno, played by Ethel Merman, with her emphatic pronunciations of every word, may have been the perfect Porter interpreter—ensuring that the audiences heard every one of Porter's quips.

Like the peeved reactions of conservative parents throughout the mid 1960s, Porter presciently reiterates the very same issues of change in his opening refrain:

Times have changed,
And we've often rewound the clock
Since the Puritans got a shock
When they landed on Plymouth Rock.
If today,
Any shock they should try to stem,
'Stead of landing on Plymouth Rock,
Plymouth Rock would land on them.

The song goes on to explain the topsy-turvy morality of the contemporary world:

The world has gone mad today
And good's bad today,
And black's white today,
And day's night today,
When most guys today
That women prize today
Are just silly gigolos

Porter might almost have added: "Or are gay today." Indeed, Porter does add himself, indirectly, to that list:

Good authors too who once knew better words,
Now only use four letter words
Writing prose, anything goes.

The incessant repetition of the word "today" simply reiterates the inescapable contemporaneity of it all, the insistence of this song's presentness without past or future. Porter's world—at least in this musical—is without guilt or consequence, a godless place where "grandmas who are eighty" sit in nightclubs getting "matey with gigolos," where "mothers pack and leave poor fathers" to become "tennis pros," and "The set that's smart / Is intruding in nudist parties in studios." It is a world we all imagine we live in or, at least, might like to have

lived in, even if the truth is something far different; and for that reason, the elderly audience with whom I sat at the matinee performance, instead of being even slightly taken aback, leaned forward with complete enthusiasm, as the cast tap-tap-tapped.

In such an "anything goes" atmosphere Porter was freed up to even question the normal structure of his songs, to query and challenge the standard introductory lead-ins and normalized language of Broadway music:

[HOPE]
I feel a sudden urge to sing

The kind of ditty that invokes the spring.

[BILLY]
I'll control my desire to curse
While you crucify the verse.

[HOPE]
This verse I started seems to me
The Tin-Pantithesis of a melody.

[BILLY]
So spare us all the pain,
 Just skip the darn thing and sing the refrain...

Of course, what they sing is "delightful, delicious, de-lovey, delirious" in its de-construction of the English language, letting themselves go in a thrilling drilling (de-de-de-de) of words that suggests being out of control.

Porter's lyrics almost always seem to be slightly over the top, about to spill over into pure ridiculousness as they finally do in "You're the Top," where the same couple, Reno and Billy, again in an attempt to outdo one another, compare each other with almost anything that comes to mind, from the Louvre Museum, to a symphony by Strauss, to a Shakespeare sonnet, and even Mickey Mouse, blithely jumping across the bodies of outstanding individuals, expensive drinks, glorious visions of nature, national institutions, celebrity salaries, and marvelous industrial creations, moving across the whole society as if it were all of one piece—not unlike Williams in his *Spring and All.* *

> You're the top!
> You're Mahatma Gandhi.
> You're the top!
> You're Napoleon Brandy.
> You're the purple light
> Of a summer night in Spain.
> You're the National Gallery.
> You're Garbo's salary.
> You're cellophane.**

Never has the simple metaphor been used to such an extreme! At one grand moment the couple compare each other to the great romantic poets only to suddenly drop into the most banal of American consumer products—

> You're Keats.
> You're Shelley.
> You're Ovaltine.

—hinting at the purist poetry possible!

*Compare, for example, these lines from Williams' *Spring and All* from 1923:

O "Kiki"
O Miss Margaret Jarvis
The backhandspring

I: clean
    clean
    clean: yes...New York

Wrigley's, appendicitis, James Marin:
Skyscraper soup—

Either that or a bullet!

**Surely it is not coincidental that in the very same year as the Broadway production of *Anything Goes*, 1934, *Four Saints in Three Acts*, Gertrude Stein's and Virgil Thomson's noted opera, premiered in Hartford, Connecticut, the set festooned with cellophane. The opera had been previously performed in Ann Arbor in a concert version in 1933.

LOS ANGELES, DECEMBER 4, 2012
Reprinted from *US Theater, Opera, and Performance* (December 2012).

Mothers

in memory of Celeste Holm

PEDRO ALMODÓVAR (WRITER AND DIRECTOR)
TODO SOBRE MI MADRE (ALL ABOUT MY MOTHER) /
1999

AFTER HEARING OF the great actress Celeste Holm's death yesterday, I reached for, in of our numerous shelves of DVDs, the film *All About Eve*, just to watch her excellent performance in that work. Not so long ago, I'd reviewed *Gentleman's Agreement*, so I felt *Eve* would be a nice addition to my ongoing film discussions (I'd written a short piece about it, in a work about the fate of women actors, some time before). Alas, I discovered that we evidently do not own that movie, although I have seen it on dozens of occasions. Next to where it might have stood, however, was our copy of Almodóvar's *All About My Mother*, a movie I hadn't seen for a long while, and which I instinctually felt might be a good alternative.

In fact, I had forgotten that the Almodóvar film begins with the young son, Esteban (Eloy Azorín), watching the scene from *All About Eve* in which the Holm character introduces Anne Baxter to Bette Davis. Soon after, in the Almodóvar film, Esteban's mother gives him a birthday gift of Truman Capote's *Music for Chameleons*, and by the next scene the two, mother and son, are attending a production of Tennessee Williams' play *A Streetcar Named Desire*. Although the stylized production from which Almodóvar shows us scenes looks quite moribund as a theatrical event, it is clear that the starring actress, Huma Rojo (Marisa Paredes), and the play are favorites of the young Esteban, evidently a budding young gay boy. So enamored with

Huma is Esteban that he waits in the alley after the play, hoping to get her autograph, and when her car speeds by without acknowledging his request, he chases after. Moments later he is hit and killed by another car.

So begins the tragic series of events that might be defined as following the trail of "blood on the ground" of his mother Manuela's life. She has told Esteban nothing of his father, but had promised him she would reveal that information the next day. It is now too late, and, in mourning, Manuela follows her son's donated body parts to the new recipient, then follows the tracks of her life back to Barcelona, from where she has originally come. As in many an Almodóvar film, it is the journey that leads to self-perception and, in this case, reconciliation with an outré past that Manuela has tried to put behind her in order to build a more normative life for herself and her young boy—a past that includes prostitution, drugs, lesbianism, transvestitism, and AIDS.

We realize in the very first scenes in Barcelona just how different is Manuela's past from the productive life she lives in Madrid as a nurse-teacher, helping her fellow employees learn how to obtain permission

from victims' families to donate their loved ones' body parts. Taking a taxi to an isolated circle round filled with drag queens, transvestites, and whores, Manuela discovers an old friend, the transvestite Agrado (Antonia San Juan), being robbed and beaten. With Manuela's help, Agrado is freed, and the two turn to a local nun to seek employment, but mostly in order to get Agrado off the streets. The nun, Hermana Rosa (Penélope Cruz), tries to find employment for them in her mother's house, but her mother, a harsh critic of Hermana's activities and her friends, refuses. A few days later, however, the tables are turned, as Hermana, realizing she is pregnant, begs for a room in Manuela's newly rented apartment.

As anyone who has seen an Almodóvar movie might suspect, coincidences abound: we soon discover that the father of her child is Lola (Toni Cantó), the father also of Manuela's Esteban, Lola being a transvestite who has continued to practice heterosexual acts and who has also been Agrado's roommate. As Manuela summarizes the bizarre sexual situation: "How could anyone act so macho with a pair of tits like that?"

Attending a Barcelona performance of the Williams play she and her son saw the night of his death, Manuela insinuates herself into the life of Huma and her drugged-out actress lover, Nina, who plays Stella in the drama. When Nina fails to show for one performance, Manuela, who has played the role in amateur productions as a young woman, goes on for her, creating even closer bonds between Huma and herself. Ultimately, Agrado takes over Manuela's role as Huma's secretary, while Manuela turns her attention to Hermana, who has now discovered that through Lola she has been infected with HIV.

In short, Almodóvar creates in *All About My Mother* a strangely interrelated group who stand against the normality of the world, but serve each other almost as a tightly-knit family—substitutes, perhaps, for their own failed family ties. When Hermana dies in childbirth, Manuela adopts the child, caring for it in the very house from which Hermana's mother had originally rejected her. But when the mother observes Manuela showing the child to a transvestite, the returned Lola, she is outraged. With the patience and forbearance that Manuel has displayed throughout, she explains that the man-woman is the child's father. Hermana's mother is horrified, afraid even to touch the child for fear of contracting AIDS. Even the forgiving Manuela perceives the situation; as she puts it to Lola, "You are not a human being...Lola. You are an epidemic."

Once more, accordingly, Manuela leaves Barcelona without saying goodbye, but returns two years later for an AIDS conference where she reveals that the baby is now completely AIDS free.

In the end, of course, we have discovered nearly everything we need to know about Esteban's mother, but where is Esteban in all this? Dead, of course, having learned nothing of the truth the viewer has received. Lola, finally told of Esteban's existence, also dies soon after, so that we can only wonder where the center of perception has shifted. Obviously, it is Manuela, through her memories of her first son and the process of raising the second, for whom the encounters in the film have any true meaning. What she has been seek-

ing throughout the film by revisiting Barcelona and her bizarre past is not Lola and her old friends but herself, that part of herself she has destroyed in order to move forward. By film's end, moreover, the "my mother" of the title is not so much about Esteban's mother as it is *any* mother and the truths and lies mothers share with daughters and sons. The director brings these various loose threads together when he equates, in a dedication, the various great actresses of films and plays with all women, all mothers, his own mother:

> To all actresses who have played actresses. To all women who act. To men who act and become women. To all the people who want to be mothers. To my mother.

That link, in turn, strangely interconnected this film with my own previous discussion of *All About Eve* (see my essay "Life upon the Wicked Stage" in *My Year 2002*), a film about a world in which women rarely come to any good.

LOS ANGELES, JULY 16, 2012.
Reprinted from *World Cinema Review* (July 2012).

The Wrong Girl

MOSS HART (SCREENPLAY, BASED ON A NOVEL BY LAURA Z. HOBSON), ELIA KAZAN (DIRECTOR) **GENTLEMAN'S AGREEMENT** / 1947

I HAVE WATCHED the film *Gentleman's Agreement* more than a dozen times in my life, and have come to feel that it is one of my favorites. It brings out all my missionary zeal, and, following my parents' feelings, I have an intense hatred of anti-Semitism.

Watching it more carefully this past week, however, I realized, despite its overall excellence, that the film has a great many flaws, some of them perhaps negative in their effects. The most obvious, of course, is the positioning of Philip Schuyler Green (Gregory Peck)—one cannot imagine a more waspish middle name—as its "hero." Green, assigned to write on anti-Semitism by magazine publisher John Minify (Albert Dekker), decides, after great skepticism about the piece, to "become" Jewish by ridding himself of his middle name and simply declaring that he is Jewish, Phil Green.

PHIL GREEN: Ma, listen, I've even got the title, "I was Jewish for Six Months."

MRS. GREEN: It's right, Phil.

PHIL GREEN: Ma, it's like this click just happened inside me. It won't be the same, sure, but it'll be close. I can just tell them I'm Jewish and see what happens.... Dark hair, dark eyes. Just like Dave [his long-time Jewish friend]. Just like a lot of guys who aren't Jewish. No accent, no mannerisms. Neither has Dave.

Like journalist John Howard Griffin, who in the 1960s chemically darkened his skin to pass as a black man, writing of his experiences riding the buses throughout the racially tense US South in *Black Like Me*, so Green "becomes" Jewish, as if it were only a matter of declaration. And before he can even tell his girlfriend, Minify's divorced niece, Kathy Lacey (Dorothy McGuire), he begins to experience racial and social tensions. Before long he is suffering feelings, as he describes to Dave Goldman (John Garfield), he has never encountered before: "I've been saying I'm Jewish.... It works too well. I've been having my nose rubbed in it, and I don't like the smell."

At one time in my early years, seeking for some-

thing I didn't have in my own family life, I wanted to convert to Judaism, but after about a day of thinking, I realized what I was most searching for, family traditions, a sense of community perhaps, had already passed me by, and what I would be left with was only the religion, the faith—which I find hard to maintain in any religious context.

Yet here, it is as if Phil Green can comprehend everything with very little experience. Except for a racial attack by other boys on his son, Tommy (Dean Stockwell), it is, in fact, the *little* things that most attract his attention. While Dave cannot even find a home for his family in New York, Phil goes about the city fighting mostly with his fiancée for having qualms about his decision, and raging against his secretary—who he discovers is herself Jewish—for her disparagement of "the wrong Jews." The most serious thing that occurs to him personally is that he is turned away, when he enquires whether the hotel takes only Gentiles, from the famed Flume Inn, where he was to have spent his honeymoon with Kathy. While these offences, along with whispers and slurs, are certainly offensive and destructive, it is clearly Dave who has the real perspective.

> DAVE GOLDMAN: You're not insulated yet, Phil.
> The impact must be quite a business on you.
> PHIL GREEN: You mean you get indifferent to it in
> time?
> DAVE GOLDMAN: No, but you're concentrating a
> lifetime into a few weeks. You're not changing
> the facts, you're just making them hurt more.

Perhaps it is his utter humorlessness that betrays that Phil is not Jewish most. At a party given by fellow journalist Anne Dettrey (Celeste Holm), Professor Fred Lieberman (Sam Jaffe in a stand-in role like Einstein) answers the question about anti-Semitism in a manner that Phil could never comprehend:

> PROFESSOR FRED LIEBERMAN: Millions of peo-

ple nowadays are religious only in the vaguest sense. I've often wondered why the Jews among them still go on calling themselves Jews. Do you know, Mr. Green?

PHIL GREEN: No, but I'd like to.

PROFESSOR FRED LIEBERMAN: Because the world still makes it an advantage not to be one. Thus it becomes a matter of pride to go on calling ourselves Jews.

Accordingly, *Gentleman's Agreement*, in some senses, is doomed by its own righteousness. I suppose the nation would learn nothing if the information Phil Green shares in his magazine article came from the

pen of a Jewish person himself, but that *is*, after all, the whole problem. No one is willing to listen from the other side. Like Griffin's acts and book, there is something inevitably paternalistic about an outsider revealing to the world what "insiders," the sufferers, have so long complained about.

Is it any wonder that both *in* the film and *in* reality, film producers such as Samuel Goldwyn and others attempted to discourage Darryl Zanuck from making the movie? Would it change anything? Certainly they, as Jews, had not previously been heard. It might actually cause harm.

The most serious flaw in this film, however, is not that the hero is a crusading outsider hero, but the fact that he cannot evidently see that a man like himself, who supposedly has grown up under the guidance of a wise and saintly mother (the wonderful Anne Revere), is doomed by his infatuation with Kathy—an intelligent, but also rich, snobbish, and self-deceiving woman of great beauty. There is something always "pinched" about McGuire's acting, as if it hurts her to open up to others. That was certainly true in *A Tree Grows in Brooklyn*, where she played a hard-working mother inured to life's difficulties, but unable to enjoy the humor and zest of her musician husband. Later roles such as those in *Three Coins in a Fountain* and *Friendly Persuasion* continued to cast her as half-spinster and half-shrew, or at least "a scold." In *Gentleman's Agreement* she is perhaps softer, and she smiles quite sweetly from time to time. But inside we still sense something unutterably cold. Her prejudice by silence is at the center of Phil's discoveries:

KATHY LACEY: You think I'm an anti-Semite.

PHIL GREEN: No, I don't. But I've come to see lots of nice people who hate it and deplore it and protest their own innocence, then help it along and wonder why it grows. People who would never beat up a Jew. People who think anti-Semitism is far away in some dark place with low-class morons. That's the biggest discovery I've made. The good people. The nice people.

As opposed to Kathy's cold and meek "niceness," Moss Hart focuses on Phil's colleague, fashion editor Anne Dettrey, who, through Celeste Holm's striking performance, comes alive as a vibrant, witty, fun, *and* intelligent figure.

ANNE DETTREY: Mirror, mirror, on the wall. who's the most brilliant of them all?

PHIL GREEN: And what does the mirror say?

ANNE DETTREY: Well, that mirror ain't no gentleman.

The viewer instinctively feels that she, who recognizes what a gentleman is or isn't, is the equal of Phil Green, someone who would fight for the right causes with him. Dettrey portrays this time and again, and even reveals her spunk by, as she puts it, "laying her cards on the table" in an almost "catty" attack on Kathy and all she and her family stand for. I was convinced, and will continue to be, by her arguments. Moreover, the very idea that Phil Green, his mother, and son would

 be comfortable in Kathy's impeccably designed Darrien cottage is inconceivable. There is absolutely no way that "Atlas," as Phil has been nick-named early in the film—carrying the world on his shoulders, rushing this way and that, and stepping on everyone's toes—could for one moment sit comfortably in that fragile house!

Equally unbelievable is Kathy's sudden self-discovery, after a conversation with Dave, that her refusal to leave or comment when a dinner-table guest tells a disgusting anti-Semitic joke is at the heart of the problem. Clearly it has taken her the whole film to comprehend what Phil has explained to her again and again.

At least, in allowing Dave and his family to live for a year in her Darrien house while she moves in with her sister next door—in order to make sure the neighbors treat them correctly—Kathy will be out of Phil's life for a short while, and the Goldmans will be near their friends the Greens. Yet the story seems to indicate that Phil and Kathy will ultimately marry and settle into Shangri-La. Of course that will mean Phil's demise. Atlas can at last shrug.

For all that, the movie is still powerful and moving. Elia Kazan won an Academy Award for Best Director, and the film won for Best Picture. So powerful was its message that the nefarious House Un-American Activities Committee called Zanuck, Kazan, Garfield, and Revere to testify. Revere refused, and both she and Garfield were placed on the *Red Channels* of the Hollywood Blacklist.

LOS ANGELES, AUGUST 15, 2011
Reprinted from *World Cinema Review* (August 2011).

Everybody's Opera

JEREMY SAMS (WRITER AND CONCEIVER), WITH
MUSIC BY GEORGE FRIDERIC HANDEL, ANTONIO VIV-
ALDI, JEAN-PHILIPPE RAMEAU, AND NUMEROUS OTHERS
THE ENCHANTED ISLAND / NEW YORK, METROPOLI-
TAN OPERA / THE PRODUCTION I SAW WAS A LIVE HD
BROADCAST ON JANUARY 21, 2012

PERHAPS for the first time since the days of Baroque opera, an opera company, in this case New York's Metropolitan, performed a pastiche, a mix of operatic works assembled and woven into a new story. As several critics noted, this might have been a disastrous mishmash of music and story, but with the encouragement of the Met's general manager, Peter Gelb, and Jeremy Sams' selections intertwined with elements of the plots of Shakespeare's *The Tempest* and *A Midsummer Night's Dream*, the opera community has a charming new work that threatens to become a standard in opera houses. Certainly I would go back for another visit to

this quite satisfying piece.

Prospero (David Daniels), having taken over the "enchanted" island of the opera's title, has at first loved and then abandoned Sycorax (Joyce DiDonato), a sorceress banned to the dark side of the kingdom, and furious about the results. Prospero and his daughter Miranda, having stolen away Sycorax's spirit servant, Ariel (Danielle de Niese), spend most of their days reading books filled with the formulas of potions and magic spells, attended by Caliban, Sycorax's dunder-headed and brutish son. He should be the inheritor of the island, she argues, using him to gain entry back into Prospero's sight. Yet, it is clear, Caliban has little talent to rule anything.

Passing by this isolated island is a ship bearing Prince Ferdinand, a likely suitor for Miranda's hand. Determined to marry her off to Ferdinand, Prospero plans to summon up a storm that will bring the Prince to his island and into the arms of his beloved daughter. Ariel, who is charged to carry out the spell, however, chooses—in part because of the influence of Sycorax— the wrong ship, and sets the storm upon a boat carrying four Athenian lovers, who wind up on the island instead of Ferdinand. Confusing the two males of the foursome with Ferdinand, Ariel serves them a magic potion, which brings all those involved—Miranda, Helena (Layla Claire), Hermia (Elizabeth DeShong), Demetrius (Paul Appleby), and Lysander (Elliot Madore)—into a confusing series of mismatches, each falling in love with the others, until it is difficult to know who is madly in love with whom.

Indeed, as in *Così fan tutte*, it doesn't seem to matter—one by one they feel betrayed, confused by the vagaries of the heart, while Caliban cooks up his own scheme to be loved by one and all, men, women, animals, and demons from the dark.

As in Baroque opera, each figure gets his or her own say in a series of beautiful arias, some well-known, others long forgotten.

It is only by calling up Neptune (Plácido Domingo), at first furious for the interruption, then magnanimous in his help, that order is restored: Miranda is married to Ferdinand, Sycorax restored to her proper

position, and the Athenian foursome paired with whomever they might at the moment desire.

The frothy results are a delight, but would not have been so amazing without the wonderful costumes and sets of Phelim McDermott and his team (who previously put together the sets and costumes for *Satyagraha*). Every moment of this splendid work is underlined with their splendiferous wit.

In a post-postmodern culture such as ours, it is only fitting that pastiche might come back into fashion; and if *The Enchanted Island* is any sign of its pleasures, bring it on! As the opera closes, even its performers seem enchanted by the experience joyously singing "Now a bright new day is dawning." Bringing together numerous composers, this is everybody's opera and an opera for everyone.

LOS ANGELES, MARCH 16, 2012
Reprinted from *US Theater, Opera, and Performance* (March 2012).

Anybody's Opera

MICHEL LEIRIS **OPERRATICS** (LOS ANGELES: GREEN INTEGER, 2001)

FRENCH AUTHOR Michel Leiris (1901-1990) was a central figure in French culture for much of his life. Early on, he became interested in poetry and jazz, and—through his introduction to numerous writers and artists—Max Jacob, Jean Dubuffet, Robert Desnos, Georges Bataille, and Leiris' so-called "mentor" André Masson among them—was involved in the Surrealist movement, writing for its magazines and publishing several Surrealist-based works, including the fiction *Aurora* (1927-1928). In 1926 he married Louise Gordon, Picasso's art dealer Daniel-Henry Kahnwiler's stepdaughter.

Three years later Leiris had a falling-out with surrealist leader André Breton, contributing to several anti-surrealist publications before involving himself with essays on art and creating ethnographical and sociological works, including the seminal study *L'Afrique fantôme*, a work that argued, along with Claude Lévi-Strauss, for an anthropological perspective for such studies. Leiris later became known for his insightful autobiographical works such as *L'Age d'homme* (*Manhood*) of 1939.

As the publisher of Sun & Moon Press and, later, Green Integer, I had read and known of several of Leiris' writings, but was quite surprised when my then-typographer and brilliant translator Guy Bennett brought me in 1998 his English-language version of one of Leiris' major unpublished works, *Operatiques*, a quirky collection of short pieces Leiris had penned on his secret love, opera. As Leiris declared in his outline to this small, but densely-written work, he perceived his "impertinent" and even "naïve" collection of "fragments" on opera as an attempt to bring his views of the genre to the reader, neither from a musician nor a man of

the theater, but from "a writer who deals" openly with "aesthetic issues," combining the concept of "opera" with the "erratic," as in something deviating from the conventional or customary course, a kind of

"wandering" through his beloved subject.

For a lover of opera, with only a rudimentary knowledge of music (I sang throughout college in choral groups and in musical theater), Leiris' *Operratics*, as we came to title it in English, was a perfect book for a press, Green Integer, that had declared itself open to publishing works of "pataphysics and pedantry," in particular *belles-lettres* that combined erudition with exploratory writing. Leiris suggests his own approach to the subject quite coherently in his short comparison of "Nietzsche and Wagner," wherein he describes Nietzsche as an "aphorist," and therefore a more modern thinker, as opposed to the "grandiose, fluid lyricism" of Wagner, which helped to make him a Romantic interested in the effacement of structure.

Leiris himself is a kind of aphorist in these opera pieces, which consist of a combination of precise ideas, categorizations, observations, and what he has described elsewhere as "brisées," metaphorically speaking, "broken branches," the remnants or perhaps buds of new thought—as opposed to essays or structured critical commentary.

In such works there is a strong implication, helped by his own demurral and the very brevity of the pieces, that these works might have been penned by *anyone*, at least by any intelligent, occasional opera-goer. In truth, of course, Leiris' comments are extremely well-informed. Who else amongst us might suggest, as he does in his short piece "*Die Zauberflöte*," the relationship of Mozart's characters to Eastern antiquity, and speak of the libretto's "racial hierarchies," or describe Monteverdi (in "Discovery of Monteverdi") as having "expressionistic" qualities that reached their zenith in Puccini?

Yet it is the appearance of his sleight-of-hand observations that make his works seem so unpretentious, linking his work more to a popular guide of literary and historical ideas about opera than to the erudite commentaries of opera critics and musicologists. While grounding his aphoristic commentaries in philosophically-based perceptions, Leiris, nonetheless, makes it all seem easy, encouraging any intelligent opera-goer to feel that he or she might gather his or her comments about the subject.

That seems important, somehow, within the context of today's HD-live Met broadcasts and the seemingly increasing popularity of opera in general. In just the past few months I have attended not only several of the Met broadcasts and LA Opera productions, but recently saw a small new Los Angeles-based company, the Pacific Opera Project, perform a delightful rendition of Leonard Bernstein's *Trouble in Tahiti* in a theater space in a Santa Monica public park; heard a network news report of the recent "hyperopera" production of a new work, *Crescent City*, in a rented art space in Atwater Crossing (near Los Angeles) where attendees had their choice of sitting on regular chairs, hunkering down on beanbags, or standing and wandering about; watched a YouTube recording of Mayo Thompson's opera *Victorine*, performed (with Felix Bernstein and Gabe Rubin) in the Whitney Museum of Art Biennial in New York; and happened upon a free New York Symphony Space production of Ned Rorem's *Three Sisters Who are Not Sisters*, with text by Gertrude Stein.

Had Leiris lived to partake of these new opera-going opportunities, I am certain he would have embraced the transformative changes they represent. Once the domain primarily of devotees, claques, and wealthy patrons, opera has opened up to everyday theater- and filmgoers who rush to and gush over these new experiences. I know hundreds of purists might wish me into the lower depths of the Rhine, but wouldn't it be wonderful if there we were to discover a new ring—of blogs by Leiris-inspired, amateur opera-goers, tweeting away about their newest encounters?

LOS ANGELES, MAY 13, 2012

Growing Horns

EUGÈNE IONESCO **RHINOCEROS** / PERFORMED BY
THE THÉÂTRE DE LA VILLE-PARIS, ROYCE HALL, UNI-
VERSITY OF CALIFORNIA, LOS ANGELES / THE PERFOR-
MANCE I SAW WAS ON SEPTEMBER 22, 2012

ALTHOUGH I READ Ionesco's acclaimed play when it
was first published in English in the early 1960s, I had
never seen a theatrical production of the work (and
only clips from the 1974 American film), so I jumped
at the chance of attending the performance at UCLA's
Royce Hall by the Théâtre de la Ville-Paris in French
(with English-language subtitles).

Yet, I left the theater, despite having finally seen
one of the best plays by one of my favorite playwrights,
slightly disappointed. That sometimes happens, even at
brilliant productions: one is tired or slightly distracted
for reasons other than the play one is observing. Here,
part of the problem simply lay in the fact that the distance between the translation board and the stage was

vast enough that it was hard to follow the stage action and still read the English, and the constant vertical motion of the eyes often distracted me.

More importantly, however, is that Ionesco's play, often touted as his best, is a parable that, once it has asserted its major premise, has little place else to go. *Los Angeles Times* critic Charles McNulty quoted Kenneth Tynan: Ionesco is "a brilliant, anarchic sprinter unfitted by temperament for the steady, provident mountaineering of the three-act form." Also, having seen this production, I now wonder whether other plays such as his early short works (including the unforgettable *The Chairs*) and later works (such as *The Killer* and *Exit the King*)are not simply more profound. At the heart of *Rhinoceros* is an important but quite simple warning of cultural conformity, and in the wake of World War II (the play was written, we must remember, just over a decade after the end of the war) Ionesco's rhinoceri—whether two horned or one—perfectly encapsulated the cultural betrayal of everyday citizens who suddenly embraced Fascism and Nazism.

But there are deeper problems with director Emmanuel Demarcy-Mota's production of the Ionesco play. His version is absolutely brilliant when it comes to the ensemble scenes. For example, the second act scene in the local, small-town newspaper office, where characters react en masse to the increasing gossip about the beasts roaming the city and, soon after, despite Botard's (Jauris Casanova) argument that there can be no such animal in France, discover that another employee, Boeuf (so his wife reports), has become a rhinoceros and is threatening to stampede their very offices. The marvelous mass movements of the characters, as their desks, chairs, and bodies go spinning with the charges of the beast, are evidence of this company's brilliant group acting.

And there are numerous other moments of excellent performance, particularly in Bérenger's speeches and the logician's perfectly absurd discussion of the difference between African and Asian rhinoceri. Yet, in perhaps the most important scene of the play, as the

sensitive Jean (Hugues Quester in this production)—completely opposed to the rhinoceri transformations—gradually is transformed into just such a beast, the work loses focus because he is transformed behind a plastic door where we see only the outlines of his facial shifts. As I mentioned previously, I did not see Zero Mostel's 1961 rendition of Jean, but in the movie and in descriptions of his New York performance I recognize significant differences which made this early interpretation a true theatrical wonder. In a fascinating article in *The Jewish Daily Forward* by Mostel's nephew, Raphael Mostel describes the events behind the Broadway production:

The scene Z is most remembered for in this play is the one in which he transformed into a rhinoceros. Ionesco had envisioned the transformation happening behind a curtain, and the actor bursting through with a rhino mask. But Z could perform the most astonishing physical feats—whether reducing Johnny Carson to hysterics by placing a proffered cigarette on his brow and somehow getting it to roll all around his face until it fell into his mouth like a pinball machine, or doing a Dada-like imitation of a coffee percolator. And he wanted to make the frightening transformation with his face and body in full view of the audience.

As reviewer Jack Kroll wrote of that performance in *Newsweek*: "Something unbelievable happened. A fat comedian named Zero Mostel gave a performance that was even more astonishing than [Laurence] Olivier's" (Olivier had performed the role in London).

Just such an "astonishing" individual performance is what is missing in this otherwise capable French rendition. One might even suggest that few companies could have better portrayed the kind of mass hysteria which is at the heart of Ionesco's play. But, as Bérenger himself ponders, it is not just the masses wherein these transformations are taking place, but in the individual hearts. Jean stands against the rhinoceros invasion at the very moment he begins to grow, in his very reasonableness, more and more lenient. Even while attacking the beasts he grows more and more sympathetic to their plight, to their odd differences. And in that very allowance of human empathy he is himself destroyed. That is perhaps a more frightening statement than the fact that some individuals have turned into beasts: the idea that one cannot ever permit the thought that there may be some good in these transformations because it actually allows the transformations to take place. And seeing that struggle up close and in person is crucial to the structure of the play.

In the end Bérenger is left alone, like Miles Bennell in *Invasion of the Body Snatchers*, with no one to tell his tale to except, perhaps, the audience. And it is we who must determine, accordingly, whether he is mad or sane.

Demarcy-Mota's production focused more on the chorus, all of whom allowed the transformation to occur, than on that man set apart. But then, that is part of the problem with Ionesco's engaging parable: it is more fun to watch a pack of charging rhinoceri than a non-capitulating loner shouting abuses at them.

LOS ANGELES, OCTOBER 5, 2012
Reprinted from *US Theater, Opera, and Performance* (October 2012).

IMAGINARY MOVIES

Music for Dead Asses

SALVADOR DALÍ AND LUIS BUÑUEL (SCENARIO),
LUIS BUÑUEL (DIRECTOR) **UN CHIEN ANDALOU** / 1929

THE WELL-KNOWN 1929 experimental short film, *Un chien Andalou*, might almost be described as a purposeful shocker. Eschewing most normative narrative devices, and purposefully selecting disconnected scenes based on dreams involving "no idea or image that might lend itself to a rational explanation," the film's two creators, Dalí and Buñuel—so legend has it—turned up on opening night with rocks in their pockets, expecting the audience to negatively react. When the audience responded rather calmly, the artists were disappointed. In fact the film's run, planned for only a limited period, had to be extended to eight months!

The growing popularity of Freudian psychology as well as the innate conservatism of Surrealism, which I

have commented on elsewhere, probably accounted for the film's success. And more than anything else, what the film does show us is that the human brain will instinctively attempt to link everything to narrative, even if the work of art does not pretend to tell a story. We think in narrative, even when we encounter something seemingly disjunctive, and particularly when it comes to dream imagery—the brain struggles against the notion of unrelated images to bring them into more coherent patterns.

Rather than restating the sequence of this 16-minute film's events—this is a film that demands to be seen more than to be talked about—I shall recount the *kind* of events that occur in this film to explain what I mean. One might suggest that the scenes in this picture fall into at least six categories, some images relating to more than one: religion, social or cultural institutions, sex (both heterosexual and homosexual, including variations of gender), nature, violence, and death.

The film begins, indeed, with what appears to be a violent act, a man (Luis Buñuel) cutting a woman's eye with a razor. Later, another man (Pierre Batchef) attempts to attack the same woman (Simone Marueil),

after he has been sexu-
ally aroused by strok-
ing her breasts, in an
attempt to rape her.
A woman who has
found a severed hand
in the middle of the
street is run over by
an automobile. Later

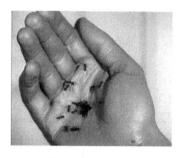

a third man (Robert Homent) appears to chastise and
punish the second man for wearing a nun's habit over
his male clothing. The man he chastises ultimately
shoots him with magically-appearing pistols. The man
falls dead in the middle of a meadow. The film ends
with a couple buried up to their waists in sand.

In the religious category is the man bicycling down
the street with the nun's habit over his suit. When he
is later prevented from attacking the young woman, he
picks up a rope to which are tied stone plates of the Ten
Commandments and two grand pianos containing the
corpses of dead donkeys, all hooked up to two shocked
Seminarists (Dalí and Jaume Miravitilles). One might
even describe the very first scene, with the influence of
the full moon, as suggesting an archetypal religious/
sacrificial event.

Social and cultural forces are represented by the
reading material left by the young woman when she ris-

es to look out the window: a reproduction of Vermeer's "The Lacemaker." The grand pianos also fall nicely into the cultural forces at work in this film. The police who keep the crowds away from the young woman poking the severed arm are obvious social forces. And even the scolding man who forces his "friend" to remove the nun's clothing appears to be representing social and cultural norms, the friend's punishment being evidently, like some schoolboy, to stand in the corner.

 Natural imagery appears in the very first scene in the image of the moon, and reappears several times when the young male lover's hand becomes infested with ants. A death-head's moth prevails over some of the final scenes, as does the idyllic meadow in which a man dies, and the final stroll of a seemingly happy couple by the sea. Even their embedment in sand suggests the forces of nature.

Sexuality, with which a great many of the film's images are concerned, seems to link up many of these seemingly random occurrences. Certainly the violent cutting of the eye in the very first scene also seems connected to sex, a stealing of the woman's proper vision.

And, throughout the film, sex is implied in a series of
gender confusions: the man dressed in a nun's habit, the
woman on the street looking very much like a transvestite. The man who comes back to life attempts to feel
the young woman's breasts and struggles to get nearer
to her as he is transformed almost into a werewolf,
blood dripping from his mouth. The young man who
comes to chastise the man dressed as a nun appears to
not only be correcting his ways, but in his intense stares
and emotional involvement with the other man appears
to have some very deep relationship with him; perhaps
the two have been lovers. When another man arrives,
he wipes his mouth with his hand as the young woman

applies lipstick, sticking out her tongue at the would-be suitor. Certainly the last stroll by the sea suggests that the young couple have finally found true love, even if that love ends up in Spring (the season for lovers) with their being half-buried.

Death of course is the end of many of these events. The ants plaguing the hand of the man who has fallen from his bicycle certainly suggest a burial. The woman who is struck by the automobile apparently dies. So too does the man whom the cross-dressed man shoots, his death being more thoroughly revealed in his second collapse in a meadow. The death-head's moth clearly calls up the skull of a dead man. And the half-buried couple suggests a kind of perfect Beckettian endgame.

That these various categories are interrelated are often self-evident. The attempt to rape the woman is held back by the culture and the church, representing so many stubborn taboos which must be destroyed before the man can act. Love leads, again and again, to violence. Violence, symbolized by the severed hand, leads ultimately to death. Bit by bit, accordingly, each viewer ends up with a series of inter-causal relationships between these seemingly disjunctive images that creates a kind of poetic narrative, the kind of narrative without plot that American poet David Antin argues for in his "talk-poems."

We might even go so far as to describe *Un chien Andalou* as being a kind of imaginary movie, a film less interested in defining the genre of cinema as it is in creating a large mulligan stew of the subterranean relationships between sex, culture, religion, society, nature, and death. It is no accident that Buñuel called for Wagner's finale to *Tristan and Isolde* and a variation of a tango as the music to accompany this love-and-death-dominated work of art.

LOS ANGELES, AUGUST 1, 2012
Reprinted from *World Cinema Review* (August 2012).

The Ultimate Conformist

WOODY ALLEN (WRITER AND DIRECTOR) **ZELIG** / 1983

ONE OF WOODY ALLEN's most likeable and fascinating films, *Zelig,* presents, in documentary style, the story of Leonard Zelig (Allen), a man who gradually begins to develop the strange malady of becoming one with the people around him: turning black among Negro jazz players, turning Chinese in Chinatown, becoming a gangster among mafia folk, etc. Even talking to fat men makes him fat. Attending the opera he becomes Pagliacci; attending a baseball game he is suddenly seen in a baseball uniform waiting to bat. By itself this clever "device" might become tiresome, but director Allen envelopes this "Zelig phenomenon" within a broader tale of a doctor and patient relationship and, most importantly, weaves his narrative with language attributed to writers such as F. Scott Fitzgerald, singers such as Fanny Brice, and current celebrity commentators such as Bruno Bettelheim, Susan Sontag, Saul Bellow, Bricktop, Irving Howe, and others, who comment, in color, on this fictional  black-and-white being as if he were a historical fact.

Beyond this is Allen's fascinating psychological metaphor about the desire for assimilation, which, in part, has been the desire of nearly all immigrant groups, particularly Jewish immigrants who had been so shunned, hated, and forced to leave their previous homelands. The central desire of Zelig, "to be liked" (he was hated by his father and mother, they hated by their neighbors, etc.), is the wish of many, from bullied children to alienated adults—in short nearly everyone. Allen, accordingly, creates in Zelig a kind of exaggerated folk hero, a figure who not only, like a chameleon, blends in with his background, but actually *becomes* those with whom he associates.

Such a figure is naturally loveable, by both the audience and the psychiatrist attempting to cure him, played beautifully by Mia Farrow. Indeed, in Allen's fiction the whole nation temporarily embraces Zelig, the movie's composer and choreographer creating wonderfully authentic songs and dances of the late 1920s and 1930s in celebration of this human chameleon. Show-

ering him with un-
conditional love, Far-
row's character finally
discovers the man be-
hind his transforma-
tional mania, while in
the same moment figures from his past, some of whom
he has married or hurt through his various pretenses,
turn the morally aghast country against him.

Allen further darkens his tale, as Zelig, discovered
in Germany, is seen in deep regression, having become
a Nazi attending one of Hitler's rallies. Not so very different than the central character, Marcello Clerici, in
Bernardo Bertolucci's *The Conformist*, Zelig—in his
need to blend in, to be seen as "normal," even when
normality actually becomes abnormal—is, as Bettelheim muses, "the ultimate conformist." So does Allen's
seemingly comic mockumentary become something
far more profound and, in its metaphoric ripples, represent a substantial statement about desire and power.

The director—long before the computer technolo-
gies which make such transformations far easier—has
also created a marvel of cinematic magic, cooking up
a sense of reality for his imaginary movie by inserting
Zelig's image into various historical photographs and
old film clips. Using, at times, the very cameras of older
eras, at other times scratching and crinkling the film,

Allen and his crew wondrously recreate a believable world that further legitimizes the sincere sounding observations and assessments of his contemporary celebrity intellectuals.

Because in *Zelig* Allen takes his art so seriously, at film's end we see the work less as a comic gesture than as a kind of reality, despite the implausibility of events, that *could* have existed, and that has more seeming "reality" behind it than many more emotionally manipulative documentaries. So while Allen's work is certainly an "imaginary" movie, a movie that is more about its creation than what it ultimately represents, it is, in some respects, utterly believable. Zelig may not exist in a single individual, but he certainly exists in our collective consciousness and hearts.

LOS ANGELES, MARCH 1, 2013
Reprinted from *World Cinema Review* (March 2013).

Disappearing from History

ELEANOR ANTIN (SCREENPLAY AND DIRECTOR)
THE MAN WITHOUT A WORLD / 1991

YET ANOTHER OF Eleanor Antin's personae, Yevgeny Antinov was supposedly a Russian-Jewish filmmaker whose films, thought to be lost, were rediscovered in Soviet archives. His two major silent films, *The Last Night of Rasputin* and the shtetl-based *The Man Without a World*, fill the gaps in Russian cinema, giving us a view of what should have been depicted, even if it was not. In a prologue to the film, Antin tells us that having gotten into trouble with Stalin, Antinov fled to Poland, where, in Cracow, he encountered a couple of affluent American entrepreneurs who were willing to back a film on shtetl life for the "Jewish nostalgia market" back home. She notes, "For a secular urban Jew, doing a Yiddish shtetl film must have presented something of a problem." *The Man Without a World* appears as if it actually were created in the late 1920s, a mix of cinematic styles that uses the tropes of figures from Yevgeni Bauer to Sergei Eisenstein. And the screenplay mixes elements of Isaac Babel, Sholem Aleichem, and other Jewish writers.

Indeed, Antin's film is so convincing that it is hard not to imagine it as a real document. But, of course, it was not filmed by a Russian-Jewish filmmaker of the early 20th century, but by a sophisticated woman artist well aware of the century's film tradition, with unusual tips of the hat to Bergman and Fellini! And in that sense, this is only an "imaginary" film, even if it feels like a work that should have existed.

For all that, however, Antin's film is a splendid piece of cinema-making, a remarkable piece that, while pretending to be something it is not, is in itself special.

The story is a simple one: a beautiful country girl, Rukhele (Christine Berry), is in love with a local boy, Zevi (Pier Marton). But before the couple can even express their love to each other, a group of performing gypsies arrives in town, including a handsome Magician (James Scott Kerwin), a Gypsy fortuneteller (played as a transvestite by Sabato Fiorello), a Strongman (Nicolai Lennox), and a beautiful Ballerina (Eleanor Antin). The latter immediately attracts the eye of Zevi, who soon joins the group in the local bar with "the Intellectuals": a Zionist, a Socialist, a Cynic, and later two strange women, a sexy Anarchist and a bomber. Rukhele is quickly forgotten until she appears at the bar to tell Zevi that his mother is dying and desperately wants to see her wayward son for one last time.

Zevi's sister, Sooreleh, was gang raped as a young girl by Polish boys, and is now mad. And the old woman curses her bad luck as the Angel of Death jumps onto her belly, putting the woman out of her misery.

After the funeral, Zevi is briefly reunited with Rukhele, realizing her worth and seducing her. The girl soon finds herself pregnant, but by that time Zevi has returned to the Ballerina and the bar, performing his poetic dramas to the locals. Perceiving that her daughter is with child, Rukhele's mother quickly plans to marry her off to the local Butcher, whom the daughter finds ignorant and coarse. But she has no choice.

When the village fanatics, however, kidnap Sooreleh in order to perform an exorcism upon her, Rukhele again encounters Zevi, who eventually discovers that his one-time lover is pregnant with his baby and determines to mend his ways. Despite the fact that wedding contracts have been signed with the Butcher, Zevi marries Rukhele instead. Going to work for his future father-in-law, a tailor, Zevi clumsily tries to take up the new trade, without much success.

Meanwhile, the women celebrate the upcoming wedding at the house and at the ritual wedding bath. The couple are married, and the women again gather over the bride for the traditional cutting of her hair and shaving of her head. While waiting for Rukhele, however, Zevi and others encounter the drunken Butcher, who attempts to kill Zevi; pulling the knife away from him, Zevi stabs his enemy to death just as his new wife returns to the celebration.

Determined to run away with her new husband, Rukhele is dissuaded by the Gypsy ballerina, who explains that Zevi and she will be living without money in a small, cold, basement apartment, predicting that Rukhele's milk will dry up and their baby will die, that Zevi, a poet after all, will be associated with dangerous men and be arrested, etc. A country girl, Rukhele, it is clear, will be unable to survive in Warsaw.

> "Zevi is a poet. He would write. You would starve. There is no help for it."

Realizing the truth of the prediction, Rukhele remains behind while the Gypsies and Zevi walk, suitcases in hand, down the road to Warsaw, the Angel of Death following after. A final crawl of sentences occurs on the screen, restating one of the major themes of this lovely film, that this world will soon be disappearing from history.

> In April, 1939, Germany invaded Poland.

In 1941, the deportation of the Jews began.

By 1943, the shtetl world had disappeared.

The story, fitting the pattern of numerous such tales, might almost have been written by Isaac B. Singer. But the great wonder of this film lies in its images, several of which are particularly evocative: the first Gypsy episode, where the Magician magically produces eggs, one by one, handing them to the Egg Seller (Page du-Bois); Sooreleh's mad "dance of death" with the dead women at the cemetery; the Rabbi (Jerome Rothenberg) dancing in his attempts to lure the dybbuk from Sooreleh's body; the hilarious chase through Rukhele's house, particularly by her mother, as they try to recapture the fowl that the Butcher has brought his love; Rukhele's ritual bath whereat two young girls embrace in an impassioned kiss, trying out their love for one another before they encounter the opposite sex; the bald Rukhele, tears running from her eyes, as she is about to lose Zevi; and the final Bergmanesque walk down the road by the Gypsies and their new cohort, Zevi, followed by the Angel of Death. Even the very first scene, where an old Hassid builds up the market through a series of stills with magical claps of his hands, presents us with a wonderfully magical sense of filmmaking.

These images and others are unforgettable, and help to transform Antin's imaginary movie into something beyond what might have been, in other hands, a kind of academic exercise in imitation.

If there was never actually a filmmaker like Yevgeny Antinov, we, nonetheless, desire his existence! And my only regret is that he did not leave more films behind at his death.*

———

*Antin did attempt to make more films, but could not get funding.

LOS ANGELES, MARCH 19, 2012
Reprinted from *World Cinema Review* (March 2012).

In 2000 my publishing house, Green Integer, published the screenplay of Antin's film. In one of the early showings of this film, I sat at the Cinefamily theater in Los Angeles next to Marcia Goodman, Eleanor's sister, who played Rukhele's mother in the film.

The Problem with Glass

GEORGE TOLES AND GUY MADDIN (WRITERS, BASED
ON A STORY BY KAZUO ISHIGURO), GUY MADDIN (DI-
RECTOR) **THE SADDEST MUSIC IN THE WORLD** / 2003,
USA 2004

BEGINNING IN LATE 2011 and more increasingly in
2012, I began to have problems falling upon getting
up in the middle of the night to go to the bathroom,
suddenly blacking out for a few seconds to find myself on the floor, often in great pain. The problem was,
apparently, my drugs for high blood pressure. One in
particular, Clonidine, reported complications, at least
three times in its list of possible "side effects," of "dizziness." One such fall was into a glass mirrored closet, facing our bed. Although the wall itself was backed with
sticky paper to prevent the glass from falling out *en
masse*, numerous small pieces of glass embedded themselves in my back and, for days, appeared upon our carpet floor. The following morning I was scheduled for

an endoscopy, which was cancelled—might anyone be surprised—because of high blood pressure. The anesthesiologist suggested I get rid of the Clonidine, which my doctor and I did, after weeks of trying to discover another successful mix of pills to protect me from high blood pressure. We were successful, although many of my new drugs also warn of "dizziness" (like Diovan, one of my major pills).

The point is, I have come to fear falling (I recently fell again, turning my cheek into a good resemblance of Batman's "The Joker"—terrifying given it happened on the same day when John Holmes, identifying himself as The Joker, murdered 12 people in a Colorado movie theater). And I am now terrified by the effects of glass.*

Back in February of 2012, accordingly, I wrote a poem titled "The Problem with Glass," which I've reprinted below:

"The Problem with Glass"

The problem with glass
                              —it breaks
it striates a wrist, the back
shattering shards
sever almost everything in sight.
The heart is made up of tissue
the brain corrugated mass.

Glass is recomposed sand.
People who live in stones
 should not throw ice.

For the ordinary or even casual reader of cinema reviews, all of this introductory information may seem entirely beside the point—and I might agree—except that Guy Maddin's film does not behave as an "ordinary" film might. Maddin's movie, like its own structure, seems at times to engulf everything, crying out for viewer collaboration. Filmed in black-and-white, with the slightly out-of-sync sound of films of the 1930s (the film is set in 1933 Winnipeg, Canada), this work is a perfect example of a participatory aesthetic. It uses various film formats (regular, Super 8, Super 16, pale-blue-salmon-colored two-strip Technicolor) and numerous old-fashioned camera tricks (forced perspective, multiple exposures, and rear projection) that evoke the films of Fritz Lang (*Metropolis*), James Whale (*Frankenstein*), Tod Browning (*Freaks*), G. W. Pabst, Erich von Stroheim, and numerous others, including—since *The Saddest Music in the World* is also a musical—the films of Busby Berkeley, while allying itself with more contemporary cinema such as Jack Smith's *Flaming Creatures* and, in its serial contest format, Christopher Guest's *Best in Show* and *A Mighty Wind*. Maddin not only relied on the considerable talents of his cinematographer,

Luc Montpellier, but armed many of his cast members with hand-held cameras to add to the immediacy of several scenes. In short, to call this film pastiche is almost beside the point; it is like a carpet woven of a knowledgeable filmgoers memories, a veritable encyclopedia of clips and frames from film history. And in that sense, Maddin's film, at its heart, is an imaginary one, a film that dreams about film.

To say that is not to declare the director's work unoriginal, however one defines that. For there is perhaps no movie quite like *The Saddest Music in the World*, no film ever made that wholeheartedly embraces the serious musical, camp humor, melodramatic, sexual, and just plain comic tropes that this work does.

For the fourth year in a row, Winnipeg has been named by the London *Times* as "the world capital of sorrow," and Lady Helen Port-Huntley (Isabella Rossellini), the wealthy beer heiress, is determined to raise Prohibition-free Winnipeg's beer sales by sponsoring an international contest, with a $25,000 dollar prize, to determine which country has the saddest music in the world.

By coincidence, the hard-hearted, easy-going,

Broadway producer Chester Kent (Mark McKinney) has just happened to arrive in town, down on his luck and accompanied by his current girlfriend, Narcissa (Maria de Mediros). When asked, "Are you an American?" she replies, "No, I'm not an American. I'm a nymphomaniac."). When he hears of the prize money, he quickly pays a visit to Lady Helen Port-Huntley, attempting to become the entry from the US.

He and Port-Huntley, we gradually discover, once had a relationship or, perhaps I should say, a series of unfortunate encounters, beginning with their meeting through Chester's father Fyodor (David Fox), who, after the death of his wife, first fell in love with the young Port-Huntley. Cuckolded by his son, the former doctor grows alcoholic and—one night while the son is driving with Port-Huntley fellating him and temporarily obscuring his view—crashes into their car, pinning one of the girl's legs under the overturned vehicle. Before Chester can prevent him, the drunken Fyodor amputates the leg in order to save her; however, he saws off the wrong one, and before the evening is over, Port-Huntley is legless. Despite that horrific event, however, the bitter Port-Huntley still harbors deep love for Chester, and permits him to be the US representative. Fyodor, still eager to mend his relationship with Port-Huntley, begs to be Canada's representative.

In a twist of the plot, Serbia's representative, the

© 2004 IFC Films

morose and hypochondriac cellist Gravillo the Great, is actually, so we discover, Chester's brother, Roderick, whose son has died and whose wife has disappeared. This unholy trinity duke it out in a series of contests with Mexican, Thai, Spanish, Cameroon, Indian, Scottish, and other world entries, each proclaiming their music to be the saddest. Overseeing this absurd sequence of musical numbers are two commentators who glibly speak of the various national types in a manner that Fred Willard perfected in Guest's film about the National Dog Show: "No one can beat the Siamese when it comes to dignity, cats, or twins."

Fyodor's sad rendition of "Red Maple Leaves" is quickly eliminated, but the two brothers—Chester

dishing out razzle-dazzle spectaculars such as "Swing Low, Sweet Chariot," and Roderick dolefully sawing away at Jerome Kern's and Oscar Hammerstein II's "The Song is You"—come closer and closer to a stand-off between their offstage fights. When it turns out the mysterious Narcissa is also Roderick's missing wife, the battle grows even more intense, until finally their mutual disgust for one another boils over.

Underlying all these hilarious shenanigans is a darker tale of a world encased in glass. A short listing of events concerning glass might even summarize the finale of the story. The Winnipeg that Maddin has whipped up is covered with ice; in the streets hockey players spin out of control as perpetual skaters glide by. One of the central slogans of Port-Huntley's beer company repeats the refrain "have another glass," and throughout the film, drinkers raise their glasses as they down the brew. Knowing that Port-Huntley is allergic to both leather and metal, Fyodor has carefully created a pair of glass legs for her—filled with beer! When the Baroness is delighted with her new bright and glittering legs but still rejects her former suitor, Fyodor quickly consumes

the beer from earlier incarnations of the glass legs and, in a stupor, falls through a glass ceiling over the contest arena to his death. Encountering Narcissa once again, Roderick drops the glass bottle containing his dead son's heart, which, as it shatters, implants a shard into the heart itself. In the midst of the final performances between Roderick and Chester, the soulful chords of Roderick's cello playing shatter Port-Huntley's new legs at the very moment she herself goes on stage in Chester's grand retelling of an Eskimo kayak tragedy. In revenge for his thoughtless behavior, she stabs Chester in the stomach with a shard of the glass legs which had given her so much pleasure.

Smoking one last cigar before he goes to hell, Chester plays on the piano perhaps the saddest song of all as the whole arena goes up in flames.

So, in the end, you see, my little poem seems appropriately participatory in a work that has employed so many thousands of collaborating images.

---

*I had had an even more dreadful encounter with glass back in the early 1990s. Coming home from a trip abroad, I arrived at my office to realize that I had locked my keys away in the suitcase I had left inside. Only my assistant editor had another set of keys, but she was not scheduled to appear until hours later in the day. Attempting to push open a loosely locked French door, I suddenly discovered that my left hand had gone through a glass panel. Blood suddenly spurted out, forcing me to run to a nearby doctor's office to have it bound up. At the hospital where they ultimately sent me, I was told I had nearly severed my thumb and had a deep cut across my wrist. I have both of those scars still today.

LOS ANGELES, JULY 22, 2012
Reprinted from *World Cinema Review* (July 2012).

Film Effects

ABBAS KIAROSTAMI'S 2008 film, *Shirin*, might be described as a film without a film, or a work of "film effects." Throughout this almost two-hour movie, we see nothing but an audience of mostly women, head on, as they watch and react to a film on the screen which we never see but can hear.

The story, a kind of melodramatic version of *Tristan and Isolde*, concerns a 12th-century Armenian princess and later queen, Shirin, who falls in love with a Persian prince, Khosrow. He is equally in love with her, but in order to save his kingdom he must ally with the Romans, marrying a Roman woman. Each time the would-be lovers come close to one another, something happens to keep them apart; finally Shirin even gives up her kingdom in order to live in Persia, although her love can never be consummated, and she and Khos-

row die without ever knowing each other's love.

This is what we might call, in the US, a "woman's pic," and we observe several of the dozens of women watching it in tears or, at the very least, with their faces in great consternation. Almost all of them, except French actress Juliette Binoche, are Iranian women, and Kiarostami presents us with several types, each of whose reactions is somewhat different from the others.

Strangely, even without being able to view this film—or perhaps one should say *because* we are unable to view the film—we must imagine it, perhaps, as a splendiferous color spectacle, laced with Persian miniatures. The only things we have to work with are the dialogue, the music (a historical film score by Morteza Hananeh and Hossein Dehlavi), and visual clues from the faces of the audience members.

In some respects, the central characters' love for each other is not unlike our own relationship with the missing images; we desire to see the missing film, and so must create it for ourselves, crafting it in our own image of that desire.

Apparently, Kiarostami filmed these women (some say in his own home) by simply asking them to gaze at a series of dots above his camera. Even he had no idea what movie he might pretend they were watching, and only at the last moment chose the famous 12th-century tale.

It reminds me of what the Iranian-born sculptor Siah Armajani once told me about his childhood film-going experiences. A local theater owner in Tehran would gather pieces of American and British cinema that had been cut from the films for purposes of censorship. He'd then link these pieces together in a loop and, while showing them, create a dense narrative for his mostly youthful audiences about the evils of the West. "Never before or since," Siah sighed, "has film been so immersive and exciting. We had to imagine those narrative connections which these strange 'forbidden' images only hinted at."

In a sense, Kiarostami's work requires the same sort of process, while even further cleansing his art of images, as if to explore how to make art without the actual art. And in this manner, the filmmaker has perhaps made one of the purist and most theoretical works of cinema ever, forcing the audience to become directors of his story.

LOS ANGELES, NEW YEAR'S EVE, 2016
Reprinted from *World Cinema Review* (December 2016).

Quicksand

MICHAEL HAZANAVICIUS (WRITER AND DIRECTOR)
THE ARTIST / 2011

GEORGE HAZANAVICIUS' *The Artist* may not be the most original film of the year, but it is certainly one of the most enjoyable. Echoing dozens of films which relate to acting and filmmaking, *The Artist* steals its situation from *A Star is Born*, with a story that, like the Judy Garland/James Mason work, centers around a young up-and-coming actress falling in love with a matinee hero whose career is about to collapse, the former star sinking into alcoholism and suicide. *The Artist*'s focus on the quick shift from silent films to talkies is parallel with much of *Singing in the Rain*. And the film's obvious love affair with silent-film acting demonstrates connections to *Sunset Boulevard*. But while those great films told their story through their characters' words and songs, Hazanavicius does it without a peep—well, not quite! The music—popular songs of the day, the

poignant Bernard Herrmann love theme from *Vertigo*, and original music by Ludovic Bource—is crucial to the film. And, although I doubt this will happen, the sound man should receive a major award. Despite the characters' silence, sound does play important roles throughout.

The story is almost insignificant. A noted actor (Jean Dujardin as George Valentin) accidentally bumps into a wannabe chorus girl (Bérénice Bejo as Peppy Miller), he (trapped in an unhappy marriage) falling for her, she already in love. Peppy gets a small dancing role in his next movie which intensifies their relationship. But before anything can happen between them, the advent of talking films changes everything:

Peppy is suddenly asked to star in a new film, while George is fired.

Using his own money and directing himself, George attempts a comeback, a silent film that ends, quite ridiculously, with the hero being swallowed up in quicksand, just as his life has been swallowed up by the new medium in which Peppy is featured. Both films are scheduled to open the same night!

Peppy is one of the few members of the audience for George's disaster, while her own film is mobbed. Suddenly, as the fan magazines might put it, she is "everyone's favorite," while George's wife leaves him, demanding that he clear out of their house. The stock market crash leaves him reeling. Spiraling into alcoholism, he is forced even to pawn his tux. He fires is loyal driver-butler (James Cromwell) and puts his few possessions that remain up for auction, Peppy secretly buying them.

The rest of *The Artist* is an artful seesaw between the two, as time and again Peppy—a nearly unstoppable force—attempts to create a deeper relationship, George, out of stubborn pride and self-pity, pulling away, until he finally tries to burn down his apartment with himself in it. His amazing pet dog, Uggy, races to a nearby policeman, who pulls George to safety. Peppy, rushing to his side, finds him lying in a hospital in a near coma, and takes him home to her new mansion. She even blackmails the studio head (John Goodman) into featuring George in a talking picture. But when George gets wind of her good deeds and discovers her purchase of his mementos, he once again returns to his burned-out hovel, taking out a hidden gun with the intent of killing himself. When Peppy discovers his absence, she calls out for her driver, Clifton (the former driver for George, whom she has hired), but when he does not appear, she impatiently takes the wheel herself, despite the fact, as it quickly becomes apparent, that she cannot drive. The tension between the possibility that she will kill herself in an automobile crash and George's slow fiddling with his gun is an exciting near-end for this melodrama.

I don't think it will ruin the film to tell what anyone who understands this work as a comedy will have already figured out. She hits a tree, but safely arrives; and although an intertitle shouts "BANG," George does not shoot the gun.

The final scene is a joyful filming of them dancing, a là Astaire and Rogers. The pair, as the director declares, are sensational! With so much talent, one wonders why George has not previously attempted to act in talking films. Asked by the director to repeat the scene, George says he'd be glad to—with the heavy French accent, of course, of Jean Dujardin!

It has all been great fun! But *The Artist* is not really

about its clichéd plot. Rather, its concerns are silent and sound filmmaking. How does film mean? And how does film narrative get conveyed? It's not just that Hazanavicius' film is a valentine to silent pictures, it is a kind of imaginary silent film that should/could have been made, had that era had all the technical abilities that we have today. And in that sense *The Artist* is a sort of wonderful fraud, just like forged art that looks like an original until you discover that the paint did not exist during the artist's life, or that the canvas upon which the work has been painted was made years after the artist died.

I do not mean that Hazanavicius is attempting to fool anyone, and, in fact, the audience has joined in the pretense from the beginning. He makes his act of "forgery" quite obvious, and it is these obvious "clues" that make this work so interesting. When George first discovers the existence of talking films, for example, suddenly a brush and comb are alive with sounds, a jar scratches across the table, the whole chattering world is blown in through his window. The noise is unbearable!

Later, in a moment of utter drunkeness, George

suddenly sees minia-
ture versions of him-
self and fellow cast
members. He is about
to wipe them off the
bar counter before
he falls stone drunk
to the floor, as if in destroying his visions of himself,
he has himself died. When the dog soundlessly barks
at the policeman, the officer at first seems impervious
to his calls for help. Is the dog barking or pretending to
bark? If a tree falls in the forest without a witness, does
it make noise?

These inherent cinematic conundrums and numerous others enrich this work and transform it from a
mere exercise in recreating an older form into a questioning of that form and of film in general. By film's
end the director has publicly investigated the role of
the artist, director, editor, composer, and actor. And, in
doing so, Hazanavicius has truly brought some of the
past back to life...or, more correctly, stolen some of our
present to bring back into the past.

LOS ANGELES, DECEMBER 14, 2011
Reprinted from *Nth Position* (January 2012).

Although I first saw Guy Maddin's 2011 film in 2014, I realized that it was very appropriate to the essays I have written above on "imaginary movies," and, accordingly, have included the film, which received general US release in 2012.

Redecorating a Haunted House

GUY MADDIN AND GEORGE TOLES (SCREENPLAY), GUY MADDIN (DIRECTOR) **KEYHOLE** / 2011, US GENERAL RELEASE 2012

AFTER AN INTENSE SHOOTOUT, a gang of hoodlums regroups within the living room of an old house, trying to determine which of their members are dead. The gang's temporary leader, Big Ed (David Enright), demands that the living line up against the wall facing

 out, the dead ghosts should face in. They are forced to leave the house, where the police will surely gather them and send them to the morgue. So

begins this seemingly zany mash-up of the gangster movie, the haunted-house horror film, and a meta-physical speculation by Canadian film-maker Guy Maddin.

And from this scene on, we enter a strange surrealist-like world where ghosts mingle with the living, sometimes even while they are engaged in sex, and figures like Calypso (Louis Negin) and Ulysses (Jason Patric) are intertwined with other cartoon-like figures such as Johnny Chang and the forever masturbating, Yahtzee-playing Brucie, Ulysses' now-dead son. And for a few moments, before Ulysses finally shows up carrying the body of a nearly-dead woman named Denny (Brooke Palsson), we almost feel that this cacophony of genres and character types will result in nothing but a campy pastiche. Yet anyone who has seen a Maddin movie knows that the director is absolutely brilliant in his ability to juggle various opposing elements, weaving them ultimately into a kind pattern that Penelope herself might have envied.

Ulysses' wife, however, is here called Hyacinth (Isabella Rossellini), and it is her love and the homelife with his three boys, Ned, Brucie, and Manners (the lat-

ter of whom the gangsters have captured, tied up, and bound) that this Ulysses has returned to claim. In order to recover that past, he is forced to go through the house, room by room, gradually calling up through ghostly visions the other-worldly emanations of Denny, and getting a recharging jolt from the electric chair created by his son Manners, a figure he pulls with him throughout his journey.

In Greek myth, Hyacinth was a beautiful young male, beloved by Apollo, who, was killed while playing discus when the jealous Zephyr blew the stone into Hyacinth's body. Loved also by the Thracian singer Thamyris, Hyacinth represents one of the first examples of homosexuality in Greek mythological storytelling. But in Maddin's mythology, Hyacinth is simply a beautifully sorrowful flower whose father Calypso is chained to her bed, and whose current lover Johnny

Chang controls her every move. Since her children and husband have all been killed off, she has few alternatives, and is clearly

bitter about her situation—although she also is fascinated and frightened by the possibility that Ulysses might somehow be able to reach her room.

As loony as it sometimes seems, Maddin's tale is a kind of Proustian story in which Ulysses orders interior decorators to return the haunted house to the beautiful home it had once been, at that same time as he, room by room, attempts to remember the whole of his past life. With the help of the drowned Denny, of his son Manners, who once loved Denny, and of the jolt of electricity, he gradually reclaims time, and with Manners' help puts everything back in its precise spot, freeing Calypso (whose bonds Hyacinth has already severed) and Hyacinth at the same moment he destroys Chang. And, if at first, the film seems dense and incomprehensible, it gradually, scene by scene, begins to make narrative sense. If, in his lifetime, Ulysses has ignored, squandered, and destroyed his near-perfect homelife, by *Keyhole*'s end, most of his gangster friends have been eliminated, and he and his family have returned to their former lives. Time past has not only been restored but reclaimed.

But, of course, we know it's only in fiction and

film—expressions of the imagination—that such things actually happen; and, in that sense, Maddin's movie becomes a sort of rumination on the restorative power of film itself. If gangster and horror films dole out the bloody dead, so too can cinema retake its past, undoing that pattern, like the Penelope of Homer's myth, weaving and unweaving a pattern of life and death until it again becomes a blank space on which to reinvent history. Through the keyhole, Ulysses may only be able to glimpse fragments of the life once lived, but by opening the doors to every room he can finally cleanse the haunted house of its ghosts.

LOS ANGELES, APRIL 19, 2014
Reprinted from *World Cinema Review* (April 2014).

On Credit

ELEANOR ANTIN **BEFORE THE REVOLUTION**, HAM-
MER MUSEUM, LOS ANGELES, JANUARY 29, 2012 / I SAW
THE MATINEE PERFORMANCE OF THIS WORK

OF ALL of artist Eleanor Antin's numerous personae, Eleanora Antinova, the black American dancer attempting to be a leading ballerina in Diaghilev's famed Ballets Russes, is the most endearing. Somehow the very idea of the somewhat short, dark-complexioned Antin—a woman who makes no claim to being able to dance in "real" life, and certainly has not trained for ballet—joining the tall "all-white machine" of Diaghilev's company goes beyond absurdity into the world of a touching fantasy. Antin as Antinova plays out her several *Eleanora Antinova Plays*, performances enacted by the artist from the mid-1970s through the next decade, works that my own Sun & Moon Press collected into a book in 1994.

Of these works, perhaps the most significant was

the 1979 *Before the Revolution*, in which, performing numerous characters—from Antinova, Diaghilev, Stravinsky, and Nijinsky, to balletic beings such as Marie Antoinette and Louis XVI—Antin develops her "Historical Prophecy and an Interlude and an Interruption." Although I saw most of Antin's performances when they first appeared, I did not witness the 1979 premiere of *Before the Revolution* at The Kitchen in New York and its later manifestation at the Santa Barbara Museum of Art. So I was delighted to be able to attend what she described as a "re-performance" of the piece, this time with several actors, on January 29, 2012.

The work is divided into six sections: I. The Lesson, II. The Argument, III. The Vision, IV. The Rehearsal, V. The Interruption, and VI. The Truth, each loosely connected with the actions conveyed in their titles. The overall arc of this disjunctive narrative is Antinova's insistence that she dance a major role in the Ballets Russes (instead of playing merely ancillary and exotic figures such as Pocahontas, etc.), her insistence on choreographing her own ballet (wherein she plays a ridiculously overstated Marie Antoinette), her rehearsals for that performance, and her personal relationships with other figures of the company, particularly the disturbed Nijinsky.

At the heart of this work, however, is Antin's personal "Interruption," wherein Antin states the major themes of her piece, and argues for an art that not only "borrows" or builds upon the past but, in a Brechtian manner, creates a space between the artist and the figure she portrays that must be joined through the imaginations of the audience. Beginning with a discussion of Diaghilev, accused by many as being a borrower, Antin brings several of these issues together in a monologue that might almost be stated as a manifesto of her art:

> And who is not a borrower? Didn't we get our face and our name from our parents, the words in our mouths from our country, the way we say them from the children on our block, our dreams and images from the books and pictures other people wrote, painted, filmed? We take from here, from there and give back—whatever we give back. And we cover what we give back with our name: John Smith, Eleanora Antinova, Tamara Karsavina, Sergei Pavlovitch Diaghilev, and somewhere each one of us stands behind that name, sort of.
>
> Sometimes there is a space between a person and her name. I can't always reach my name. Between me and Eleanor Antin sometimes there is a

space. No, that's not true. Between me and Eleanor Antin there is always a space. I act as if there isn't. I make believe it isn't there. Recently, the Bank of America refused to cash one of my checks. My signature was unreadable, the bank manager said. "It is the signature of an important person," I shouted. "You do not read the signature of an important person, you recognize it." That's as close as I can get to my name. And I was right, too. Because the bank continues to cash my checks. That idiosyncratic and illegible scrawl has credit there. This space between me and my name has to be filled with credit.

What of me and Antinova? I borrow her dark skin, her reputation, her name, which is very much like mine anyway. She borrowed the name from the Russians, from Diaghilev. I borrow her aspirations to be a classical ballerina. She wants to dance the white ballets. What an impossible eccentric! A black ballerina dancing *Les Sylphides*, *Giselle*, *Swan Lake*. She would be a "black face in a snow bank"! The classical ballet is a white machine. Nobody must be noticed out of turn. The slightest eccentricity stands out and Grigoriev hands out stiff fines to the luckless leg higher than the rest. So Antinova designs her own classical ballet. She will dance the white queen Marie Antoinette. She invests the space between herself and the white queen with faith....

This profound statement of the separation of art and the artist, who must be given credit by both herself and the viewer to make meaning, is at the heart of Antin's *oeuvre*, which, like a Kierkegaardian leap into faith, transforms simple desire into an almost sacramental act.

The "Interruption" was even more poignant at the Hammer Museum performance I witnessed because Antin read these words on a small iPad whose images disappeared as she spoke them, forcing her to ask her son Blaise to help her recover the message she was attempting to repeat.

It was also interesting to have Eleanor Antinova played throughout by a black actress (Danièle Watts), who certainly freed Antin from being seen as a white actress in black face, which some critics accused her of being the first time round.

Actor Jonathan Le Billion was also very effective as the slightly mad Nijinsky, railing against Diaghilev, as the great dancer did in real life. But overall, the acting was mixed, with some figures unable to completely realize their roles. In part, that was simply due to the fact that in life these personali-

ties were exaggerated, and that Antin's work is not, at heart, a drama. To say what *Before the Revolution*, exactly, is difficult. Perhaps it is easier to say what it isn't: it is not truly a play, a historical performance, a monological statement, a ballet-in-the-making, or a personal encounter with a black ballerina. In its radical genre-bending elements, it is so much more!

Although, as I mentioned previously, I did not see the original, it seems to me it is essentially a work for one person. Eleanor may not have been the greatest of actresses in that original, but, given the "credit" we must grant to bring her art to life, the slightly mad ramblings of a single person (sometimes hiding behind cut-outs of her characters) seem the most appropriate rendering of this fascinating performance. Despite the separation of name and character, Antin *becomes* Antinova, *becomes* even the figures inhabiting Antinova's imagination in the original, and that, it seems to me, is the true miracle of this art. What we witness is a kind of madness like Nijinsky's being transformed into something of significance. The artist in this work is almost like a child, a child so intent upon imagining other existences that she truly creates them, bringing viable others into that envelope between the creator and the creation. If that act demands credit, it reflects back upon the audience for their commitment to the creative act, coming as a kind of unexpected reward for their faith.

Art, for Antin, is almost always—despite its seeming focus on the various aspects of self—a communal act. Her King of Solana Beach could never have been a king without willing (even if unknowing) subjects. Antin's Nurse Eleanor Nightingale could not have survived the Crimean War without her imaginary patients. So too did the audience of *Before the Revolution* enthusiastically applaud this dramatic presentation of the dilemmas of Antinova's life.

I was at Eleanor Antin's side after the 1981 performance of *Recollections of My Life with Diaghilev* at the Museum of Modern Art when an enthusiastic attendee, with great reverence and respect, gushed, "Tell me, being so close to Diaghilev, what was it really like?" Eleanor was a bit abashed; she would have had to be in her mid-70s (she was then in her 40s) to have actually performed with Diaghilev's company. Yet I perceived that never before had "credit" been so innocently and completely proffered!

LOS ANGELES, MARCH 15, 2012
Reprinted from *USTheater* (March 2012).

The Man Who Talks to His Shoes

HENNING CARLSEN AND PETER SEEBERG (SCREEN-
PLAY, BASED ON THE NOVEL BY KNUT HAMSUN), HEN-
NING CARLSEN (DIRECTOR) **SULT** (**HUNGER**) / 1966

IT MUST HAVE seemed like an act of moxie that director Henning Carlsen took on a film adaptation of
Knut Hamsun's great novel of 1890, *Sult* (*Hunger*). For
one thing, Carlsen is Danish, while the events occur
in Kristiania (Oslo, Norway). The languages of these
two friendly Scandinavian countries are quite similar,
but there are just enough differences, I am sure, to dis-
tract the Norwegian viewers of the film, like the film's
Danish title, *Svält*. More importantly, in Hamsun's narrative very little actually happens. His work is a piece
of internal language, a conversation with the self that
the unnamed character carries on as, starving, out of
work, and homeless, he wanders the streets of Kristiania. Only a few things actually "happen" to him: he

writes an article and attempts to place it with a publisher; he observes a lovely and slightly flirtatious woman whom he dubs Ylajali (Gunnel  Lindblom); although we cannot be certain, since many of the events are those of his imagination, he may actually visit Ylajali and contemplate having sex; he stares in the windows of the various stores and encounters some of his friends from the past; he is kicked out of his rooming house and briefly finds another (for one night), only to be ousted the next day by a boarder whom he observes having sex with the landlady; and he sits on park benches, sometimes talking to his worn-out shoes as if they could understand and converse with him. In short, there is no traditional story attached to this work; it is merely a series of psychological incidents played out upon a realist setting, the Oslo of 1890. That is, in part, why Hamsun's fiction was so innovative and groundbreaking. Without any of the gewgaws of plot, Hamsun created a character so amazing that he stands alongside the memorable figures of Dostoevsky, Kafka, Camus, and others.

Miraculously, the film has come through remarkably well, and, although different in many ways from the literary work, is true to its essence. Of course, most of the praise must go to *Hunger*'s brilliant director, Henning Carlsen, who filmed in black and white (and sometimes sepia), more closely linking his film to silent pictures. There are occasional conversations in the film, as well as the noises of the street—the clip-clop of horses, the drum of the feet of workers and ladies out for a stroll—but for all that it may as well be described as a silent film. And Carlsen and cinematographer Henning Kristiansen have used their camera to catch the smallest of facial and bodily nuances, the grimaces of disgust on the faces of the bourgeois citizens of Kristiania as they pass the beggar-like hero, a dog's violent gnawing of a bone (which our hero would love to share), the scuttle of a rat, the blinks of Ylajali's large eyes. All of these help to make the film come alive and replace what might have ordinarily been told in dialogue.

But a large part of the film's success must be accorded to the actor Per Oscarsson, who plays the hero (Pontus, as he is called in the film) with all the aplomb of Chaplin and Keaton combined. Oscarsson won the Best Actor Award at the 1966 Cannes Film Festival, well deserved surely. From the very first scene, as Pontus stands with his back to us on a bridge, the actor completely enthralls us with his every movement. In this scene he seems to be doing something that we cannot quite interpret, yet it appears to be something slightly

obscene, a regular
movement of the
hands. Is he mas-
turbating in public?
When the camera
finally moves in, re-
vealing his actions, we humorously recognize that he *is*,
metaphorically speaking, masturbating. He is attempting to write with a pencil upon a slip of paper. Yet he
seems to be getting nowhere, repeating again and again
a date, circling empty words, etc. Writing is not an easy
task in the open air.

Pontus, as I have mentioned above, has not eaten
for several days, and when he finishes his attempts to
write, he rips off a small bit of paper and stuffs it into
his mouth, simply to chew on something. Oscarsson's
lean, unshaven face is perfect for the role. We can see
that he is handsome even in his haunting decay. If
only...will someone in this society come his rescue?
Yet by the film's end we know that would be impossible. This is a proud and self-destructive man, a kind
of hunger-artist, determined to get by on almost nothing. He awards even his bedding to another unfortunate. Time and again, at the editor's offices and when
he encounters friends who ask if he needs a small advance or to join them in a meal, Pontus lies to hide his
penniless situation. When he is accidently overpaid at

a grocer's whom he has visited to purchase a candle, he throws the coins into the hands of a woman beggar and returns to the grocer to upbraid his inattention. When he finally is able to buy a little soup, he discovers he can longer stomach it. As played by Oscarsson, Pontus is a 19th-century dandy in the dress of a fool; a man—one is tempted to say, much like the author—who, despite the turmoil and terrors of the upcoming century, wants to remain a romantic.

And, in that sense, he, and only he, is responsible for his fate. Despite Hamsun's dour and unforgiving portrayal of the Kristiania bourgeoisie (Carlsen portraying them at moments a bit like the figures in some of the paintings of Edvard Munch), it is Pontus' inability to recognize his own suicidal tendencies that is his undoing. He has talent, it is clear, but he has no idea how to reveal it. The only solution to his condition—as he has been previously told by his landlady—is to leave, to return to the country or go elsewhere. At the very last moment that a ship is about to leave port, the hero signs on. Where he is headed no one knows, not even, apparently, the character. But it does not matter to someone who talks to his shoes. It will be a better place by far, and finally he can learn again how to eat.

LOS ANGELES, JANUARY 21, 2012
Reprinted from *World Cinema Review* (January 2012).

In 1986 or 1987, I met Henning Carlsen, introduced to me by my friend Martin Nakell, who had met Carlsen some time earlier. I was, of course, a great admirer of Knut Hamsun, and had written about him for years before I met Carlsen. I treasured the director's film version of Hunger, *so I am certain that the meeting was a kind of love fest, I stating my admiration for the Danish director.*

Unfortunately, I now remember little of our meeting. Yet Carlsen did later give me permission to reuse one of his images for the cover of our publication of Paul Auster's The Art of Hunger; *but he had also met Paul long before, so that was not a testament to our brief relationship. I do recall how pleasant and personal our meeting was. What each of us said has disappeared from my memory, as I'm certain our whole meeting has been swept away by time in Carlsen's own memory. But it was a fortuitous event, as I went on to teach his* Hunger *at the UCLA Scandinavian Department and view the film numerous times over the years.*

Pulling Down the Roof

JOHN ARDEN **SERJEANT MUSGRAVE'S DANCE** IN
JOHN ARDEN PLAYS: 1 (LONDON: METHUEN PUBLISHING,
1994)

WITH THE DEATH of British playwright John Arden
on March 28, 2012, I decided to read his most well-
received play, *Serjeant Musgrave's Dance*. Productions
of this work have been rare in the US, so I'd never had
the opportunity to see the play, and this was my first
reading—although I'd read several reviews of the play
when it first appeared at the Royal Court Theatre in
October 1959.

The Brechtian-like work, complete with songs
(music by Dudley Moore), is a cry for passivism in a
time when British and American societies were moving
full-blown into more and more international conflicts.
The incidents which sparked Arden's play occurred in
1958 when British soldiers killed five innocent people
in Cyprus. By placing his play in a period of pre-Kipling,

Redcoat soldiery, however, Arden shifted the theme of *Serjeant Musgrave's Dance* into a timeless statement of anti-war sentiment.

The four soldiers—murderers, robbers, and deserters—descend upon a small Northern English town with vague motives. The locals, none too happy for their appearance, are in the midst of a mine strike, and are fearful that the soldiers have been placed in their town to keep order should their negotiations break down into a riot. The local authorities (The Parson,  The Constable, and The Mayor) see their arrival as a chance to get rid of the mining agitators, if only Musgrave and his men can get them to volunteer into the army.

For his part, Musgrave keeps his motives much to himself. Although the three other men with him know that he is vaguely planning to spring his anti-war sentiments upon the populace, they cannot foretell his method. Sparky, Hurst, and Attercliffe are simpler men who enjoy drinking, sex with the local whore; and, although they share Musgrave's regrets about their military past, they are not at all ashamed by their murderous duties.

The first half of the play is taken up with the local's suspicions and the military men's attempt to allay them. But Musgrave is not at all easy with  his own intentions to create anarchy. A highly religious man, he believes still in duty—even if that sense of duty has shifted to disobedience. Most importantly, he is man of conscience, horrified by the death of a young friend from the very town which they are visiting, a soldier whose skeleton is among their possessions.

In this atmosphere of suspicion and opportunism, things do not at all go right. The soldiers waver in their obedience to the man they have nicknamed "God." And their own desires, particularly their admiration for a local "soldiers' whore," Annie, get in the way of Musgrave's mission. Although Hurst and Attercliffe spurn Annie's sexual attentions, the younger Private Sparky lusts after her, and is even willing, so it appears, to desert the deserters, asking Annie to hide him until they might run off together. The other two, overhearing his intentions, try to prevent him, accidently killing him on the point of his own bayonet.

Trying to cover the "accident" up, Musgrave hurriedly calls for a town celebration, with bunting, flowers, speeches, and all, hoping to waylay any further doubts by the townfolk. After the usual banal speeches of the Mayor and Parson, Musgrave begins his "dance," unveiling the weaponry available to murder innocent folk, setting it out, piece by piece, so that he might, indeed, kill his very audience. To everyone's surprise, he slowly starts the tale of his soldier's duties, which involved, after the murder of the local boy, pulling innocent people from their houses into the streets and slaughtering them. The town gentry, Mayor, Parson, and Constable are horrified by the shift of his speech. The local miners are confused; while they want little to do with the soldiers and are perhaps ready to go to battle for their jobs, they cannot conceive of the anarchy against the government that Musgrave is proposing.

Hanging the local boy Billy's skeleton from a lamp post, Musgrave tries, with weapons at the ready, to find volunteers for his anti-army. Annie, however, reveals the murder of one of their own, as Musgrave's lofty intentions begin to crumble, Hurst shouting at him: "You've pulled your own roof down!" Suddenly loyal dragoons, called for in case of a riot, appear, arresting the deserters.

The last scene reveals the imprisoned men, who are scolded by the innkeeper Mrs. Hitchcock for their lack of understanding. The men's only hope is that when they are hung, a seed from their actions will begin an

orchard, that something might grow out of their ineffective but well-meaning words.

In many respects, Arden's play is a brilliant statement locked away in its own level-minded cynicism. The values it declares are perhaps admirable—a complete shake-up of the militaristic British world—but its hero, Serjeant Musgrave, still a product of that world, is not strong enough in intelligence and will to transform it. Arden may argue for a revolt against the class system, but such a revolt can never occur, he reveals, through the principles on which that system is based—God, duty, honor. Musgrave presents himself only as another kind of God, not a true alternative to the system which destroyed his own faith.

LOS ANGELES, APRIL 14, 2012
Reprinted from *US Theater, Opera, and Performance* (April 2012).

Count Down

FRANCESCO MARIA PIAVE (LIBRETTO, AFTER THE
PLAY *LA DAME AUX CAMELLIAS* BY ALEXANDRE DUMAS
FILS), GIUSEPPE VERDI (MUSIC) **LA TRAVIATA** / THE
PRODUCTION I SAW WAS THE METROPOLITAN OPERA
HD LIVE BROADCAST ON APRIL 14, 2012

IN THIS Willy Decker / Wolfgang Gussman production of Verdi's standard, there is no consumptive
coughing, no overdressed men and women attending
the red-plumaged Violetta. Bringing the story into a
more contemporary period, the director and designer
have established from the outset—through the presence of a gigantic, surrealist-like clock—that the consumptive courtesan's time is short. The entire set, in
fact, looks like a giant waiting room with a long, curv-
ing, cement-like embankment and an elliptical mezzanine, where the choruses, a bit like observing doctors,
can look down upon the theater of operation, Violetta's
"apartment," wherein she plays out the short life she has

yet to live.

In some respects, this expressionistic set overstates everything. It certainly does not allow any dramatic tension to interfere with the inevitability of the plot. But it does free up the characters to symbolically enact a ritual (which, after all, is not about story anyway) centered on the intense musical relationships of the three major characters: Violetta (Natalie Dessay), Alfredo (Matthew Polenzani), and his father Giorgio (Dimitri Hvorostovsky).

Dessay, a trained actress, begins the opera as a performer about to go on stage, appearing the way many have described Judy Garland offstage just before her entry, her small frame suddenly rising into a figure slightly larger than life. Violetta, having recovered from a recent consumptive attack, is weak, not at all sure she will be able to attend the party she is throwing that night. But bit by bit she pulls herself together, transforming herself into the party girl in a short red dress her guests—men and women all dressed in black and white suits—have come to expect. This "bacchanal," however, is closer to a mimed performance of Baz Luhrmann's *Moulin Rouge* than it is to Verdi's original salon party.

The champagne they drink is from empty glasses, the camellia obviously a silk flower. Dessay has not only to sing of "Sempre libera degg'io," but, raised and lowered on a red couch, must balance herself and dance upon the prop. She is, in short, less a consumptive woman confined to a couch than a jumping, singing acrobat. And any joys she may have in her party-life seem more like those that come from a successful theatrical performance than a lust for life. If Dessay was contrite, during the intermission, for having missed one of her high notes, it was easy for her appreciative audience to forgive her, given her otherwise beautiful singing during her energetic apologia to the "good life."

It is little wonder that we find her, in the second act, having capitulated, escaping with Alfredo to the country. In the flower-laden landscape of Alfredo's world, Violetta becomes almost young again, wrapped in a flower-patterned housecoat, playing hide-and-seek among the flower-covered couches. Indeed, she becomes one with the couches, becomes something and someone other than her former self. In this production it is immediately apparent why Violetta has given up her Parisian life; even the dreadful clock, ticking down the hours left to her, is half-covered in the same pattern, and the elliptical mezzanine has become a kind of garden. The snake creeps into this paradisiacal world with her servant's revelation that Violetta is selling her

Paris belongings to support her country life. Alfred is determined to rectify the situation, rushing off to Paris, allowing the more horrific Satan, Alfredo's bourgeois father Giorgio, time to destroy her momentary joy in life.

For Giorgio, Violetta is, at first, nothing more than a selfish courtesan out to steal his son's money and affection. Gradually, however, when that vision proves difficult to sustain, he employs the usual tricks of men who cannot escape the petty limitations of a societally controlled life: his beautiful daughter will lose her fiancé if Alberto does not return home. Crueler yet, Giorgio tells Violetta of her own destiny, her loss of beauty and betrayal, perhaps, by Alfredo. As Violetta

notes, the punishment for her libertine lifestyle comes not from God but from man. Even Giorgio, however, finally comes to recognize Violetta's sacrifice, singing in a beautiful aria (Hvorostovsky at the top of his form) of her love and generosity.

So pure is Violetta's love that she agrees, most reluctantly, to give up Alfredo and return to Paris, knowing now that her fate will be an early death. Accepting an invitation to her friend Flora's costume ball, she pretends to take up once more with her former protector Baron Bouphol.

While in Verdi's original the costume ball was replete with gypsies and bullfighters, the new Met version has mixed in the costumed partygoers, along with a male dressed as Violetta in mockery of her return to their world. If the whole scene is a kind of confusing mish-mash at times, it still makes more sense than the presence of the Verdi "types" at the grand ball, and the partygoers' taunting tales only reiterate what we know: Violetta's life as a grand courtesan is over. The clock itself is now transformed into a gambling table where Alfredo, who in revenge has rushed back to Paris, wins, tossing his winnings at and stuffing them into Violetta's orifices in what is clearly a kind of capitalist rape. Even Giorgio, having followed his son to the party, is shocked by Alfredo's behavior; but then, propriety is at the heart of his torturous demands.

The partygoers, now carnival celebrants, reenter the cold waiting room once again, this time with another women, clad in a red dress, strapped to the clock. Violetta is no longer the life of the party; she has almost been drained of life.

Sick and suffering, with just a few hours to live, she awaits the return of Alfredo, who, having survived his duel with the Baron, has discovered the truth of Violetta's abandonment and has written of his determination to see her once again. As in any grand opera, the lovers reunite to imagine the life they could have had, a reunification that the audience has known is impossible from the start. For a second, just before her death, the courtesan is relieved of all pain and age, until she faints away, leaving both Alfredo and Giorgio to face their own failures of faith in her love.

Some of the subtlety of this opera may have been lost in the symbolic posturings of Decker's and Gussman's vision, but the overall dramatic impact, particularly in Dessay's powerful performance, remains, and *La Traviata* seldom wavers in its musical splendor as this grand courtesan had in her past.

LOS ANGELES, MARCH 15, 2012
Reprinted from *Green Integer Blog* (April 2012).

The Dreamer and His Critic

JOSÉ MARIA DE EÇA DE QUEIRÓS **CORRESPONDEN-CIA DE FRADIQUE MENDES**, TRANSLATED BY GREGORY RABASSA AS **THE CORRESPONDENCE OF FRADIQUE MENDES** (DARTMOUTH, MASSACHUSETTS: TAGUS PRESS / UMASS DARTMOUTH, 2011)

FRADIQUE MENDES, originally conceived of as a Pessoa-like heteronym, was created by the great Portuguese writer Eça de Queirós and two friends in 1869 in a newspaper, to poke fun at their fellow countrymen. The poet, Carlos Fradique Mendes, wrote poems in a kind of satanic Baudelaire manner, which was an affectation of many younger Portuguese poets whom Eça de Queirós felt needed to be satirized.

The figure and his writing so engaged him, however, that he continued to write through the pseudonym from 1888 onward, revising the work into a comical biography and collection of letters published in 1900, the year of Eça's death. In many respects this work can-

not be separated from his great fiction, published in 1901, *The City and the Mountains*. Both works swing between two extremes, between a kind of dandyish figure living in the center of Portuguese culture and a more retiring version of the same figure, returning to the quiet isolation and nostalgic innocence of a previous time. In the later book, the protagonist Jacinto begins as a believer in change, embracing the most progressive developments of the late 19th and early 20th centuries, a man who, when that world falls apart, retreats to his home in the mountains, where he rediscovers the quietude and order of an agricultural tradition.

So too does Fradique Mendes begin by being a man of the world, living in France and traveling to exciting exotic locales such as Arab countries and Brazil. Yet, like Jacinto, Fradique Mendes, whose great love fails him, gradually reverts to more conservative-based realities, often scolding his correspondents for their desire to become involved in urban life and their lack of religious values. Fradique Mendes finally "disappears," traveling, as he describes it, "on a very long and distant journey," which, he declares, is no longer out of curiosity, "for there are no longer curiosities left, but to put an end in a most worthy and beautiful way to a relationship like ours."

The letters of Fradique Mendes' fiction are fascinating for their swings between worldly knowledge and peasant pleasures, for their alternation between a cultivated artistic sensibility and a craving for the simplicities of the past. In the end, because of this oscillation of values, Fradique Mendes is a grand failure, a made-up man who fails in life primarily because of his vicissitudes. The difference is that, in *The Correspondence of Fradique Mendes*, Eça forces us to compare this failed dreamer with an academic critic who is so slavishly attracted to the "ecstasy" of Fradique Mendes' earlier poetic dabblings that he cannot see the failures of the man. Presenting his subject in metaphors even more romantically inspired than the poet's later life, the critic of the fiction ridiculously drops names—from Ponce de León to Mozart and Beethoven, from Voltaire to Klopstock and Immanuel Kant—that reveal even more confused notions of reality. Here's a sample:

> Here I fell back, wide-eyes. Victor Hugo (everyone still remembers), exiled at the time on Guernsey, held for us idealists and democrats of 1867 the sublime and legendary proportions of a Saint John

on Patmos. And I drew back in protest, eyes in-flamed, so much it seemed to me beyond the realm of possibilities that a Portuguese, a Mendes, could have held in his the august hand that had written *The Legend of the Centuries*! Corresponding with Mazzini, camaraderie with Garibaldi, that was all very well! But a sojourn on the sacred isle, to the sound of the waves from the Channel, strolling, chatting, pondering with the same of *Les Misérables*, looked to me like the impudent exaggerations of the Azorean islander who was trying to put one over on me....

If there was ever an example of literary hero-worship, this critic says it all. Fradique Mendes is great because he associates with the great!

At times, this comic lavishing of metaphors and comparisons wears on one—as it is meant to. And *The Correspondence of Fradique Mendes* is, overall, not quite the masterwork that is *The City and the Mountains*. But the fiction remains a wonderful send-up of Portuguese cultural pretensions, and perhaps, to a certain degree, a revelation of the cultural tensions in Eça's own life. Given the depths of his literary contributions, however, it is well worth reading through this satiric work.

LOS ANGELES, MARCH 13, 2012
Reprinted from *Rain Taxi* (online edition, Summer 2012).

Separating Language from Meaning

CONSTANCE DEJONG (VOCAL TEXT), CONSTANCE
DEJONG AND PHILIP GLASS (LIBRETTO), PHILIP GLASS
(MUSIC) **SATYAGRAHA** / THE PRODUCTION I SAW WAS
AN HD LIVE BROADCAST FROM THE METROPOLITAN
OPERA IN NEW YORK ON NOVEMBER 19, 2011

IN MANY RESPECTS Philip Glass' pageant opera, *Satyagraha*, is one of the most frustrating of all opera experiences. It is not that the work isn't, at times, musically splendiferous and even powerful—at least in the Met high-definition live broadcast I saw in 2011. But Glass takes away so much of what opera is really about—drama, language, and, at times, musical comprehension—that it is difficult to get one's bearings.

I don't mean that the opera itself is difficult. The plot, if it can be said to have one, is quite apparent if you have a program. The seven scenes in three acts of the work represent significant moments in the early

career of M. K. Gandhi, as he transformed himself in
South Africa from a Western-dressed lawyer to a political advocate for the poor and suffering. Beginning with
an imagined scene from the battlefield of the *Bhagavad
Gita* (The Kuru Field of Justice), Glass and his co-libret-
tist, Constance DeJong, take us from 1910 to 1913 in
Gandhi's life, exploring his attempts at collective farm-
ing on his Tolstoy Farm (named after the great author
and social experimenter), through the "vows" of South
African Indians to resist registration, and Gandhi's return to South Africa, greeted with violence. We see his
newspaper activities on *Indian Opinion*, in which he
first expressed his concepts of "satyagraha" ("insistence
on truth"), the 1908 protest against the Black Act, in
which his supporters burned their government certifi-

cates, and his final strike-march to the Transvaal border, where many were arrested.

Each of Glass' acts are overseen, furthermore, by a historical figure who influenced Gandhi or over whom he would have an influence. From the past, we see Leo Tolstoy; from the present, Gandhi's close friend, the Nobel Prize-winning Indian poet Rabindranath Tagore; and from the future, Martin Luther King.

The program notes explain in some detail what we are experiencing. However, the experience itself is much less lucid. As Richard Croft (playing Gandhi) explained in an intermission interview, it is a difficult role to act because what is occurring is happening inside, not in the actual drama on the stage. The chorus and, more importantly, the Skills Ensemble often play out—in a highly imaginative use of masks, puppets, and staged acts—what is symbolically occurring, but the actors, somewhat like those of Wagner, are allowed little movement. Yet, unlike Wagner's figures, the major actors here are not even communicating with the audience in a language they can comprehend, since they sing the entire opera in Sanskrit, quoting spiritual fragments of the *Bhagavad Gita*.

I am sure that when Glass first got the idea to use the language and images from this book which Gandhi knew intimately, it must have seemed a brilliant concept to separate language from meaning. But it

ultimately cuts us off from true communication and, more importantly, given Glass' minimalist repetitions, presents us with long passages in which we only have a vague idea of what is happening—not that it would help to know, at any moment, that Gandhi, for example, is reaffirming his ideals...or whatever. We sense the emotional impact, and Glass' simmering music often seduces us, but, nonetheless, it is sometimes a long endurance test, particularly in the last act, when Glass almost sentimentally links Gandhi with the future American racial revolutionary Martin Luther King Jr.—over and over again, so that eventually we must ask whether Gandhi or what he has wrought is something other than American-based.

The most successful act of this opera is Act II, when puppets, chorus, and major singers all come together to create the horror of the wealthy Dutch landowners, the busy industry of putting together the newspaper, and the dramatic bonfire of government-issued certificates.

The cast, including Croft, Rachelle Durkin as his secretary, Miss Schlesen, Kim Josephson as a supporter, Mr. Kennenbach, and Alfred Walker as Parsi Rustomji, were all quite adept; and the Met chorus was absolutely stunning in its ability to learn the Sanskrit score while counting Glass' tricky rhythms. The costumes and settings by Julian Crouch and Kevin Pollard, as well as the stage direction of Phelim McDermott and conducting of Dante Anzolini were all spectacular.

The Met audience seemed thoroughly charmed by the opera, remaining throughout the entire series of applause. Yet, for me, that was just the problem: long on charm, the opera was too short on substance, despite focusing on such a substantial historical figure. But then it is difficult, if not impossible, to think without language.

LOS ANGELES, NOVEMBER 20, 2011
Reprinted from *Green Integer Blog* (November 2011).

Medea's Last Dance

TENNESSEE WILLIAMS **IN MASKS OUTRAGEOUS AND AUSTERE** / NEW YORK CITY, CULTURE PROJECT / THE PERFORMANCE I SAW WAS A MATINEE ON SUNDAY, MAY 6, 2012

ON SUNDAY, MAY 6, I attended, with Charles Bernstein and Susan Bee, the premiere of Tennessee Williams' last play, *In Masks Outrageous and Austere*—uncompleted at the time of his death—at Bleecker Street's Culture Project. Despite rather dismissive reviews—David Finkel in *The Huffington Post*, for example, describing it as a "turgid" and "ludicrous" cauldron of "picked-over Williams obsessions" and Ben Brantley of the *New York Times* summarizing it as inhabiting a "tepid, in-between realm" that permits neither "audacious sincerity" nor the permission to "go ahead and laugh"—I found the play and production utterly fascinating and far less problematic than almost all the reviewers had determined. Williams himself, while still working on the text (which he continued to do up until his 1983 death), described it as "important," "extremely funny," and "bizarre as hell." It is, in my estimation, all three  of those assessments—but then, one might describe almost any Williams play in the same way.

Although the Culture Project's production suffered a bit from their attempts to encourage the "over-the-top" sensibility of Williams' text with LED flat screens, video renditions of telephone conversations with the central character's advisor and doctor (distorted images and voices of Buck Henry and Austin Pendleton), banks of white, red, and blue lights, and eerie musical interludes by Dan Moses Schreier, this production did conjure up a sense of dreadful foreboding of a world on the edge of the apocalypse, a Key West-like Babylon that might, at any moment, sink (or even be burned up) into the ocean waters so detested by the major figure of the play, Clarissa "Babe" Foxworth (Shirley Knight).

True, with the exception of Knight and Alison Fraser's absurdly comic Mrs. Gorse-Bracken (channeling a slightly hysterical version of Bernadette Peters), most of the young actors of the cast have not yet mastered the sort of anti-naturalistic unmelodramatically-driven voices so necessary to properly perform Williams' lines (a problem as well for the language-driven playwrights such as Mac Wellman, Len Jenkin, Jeffrey Jones, Richard Foreman, and numerous other contemporary playwrights). But then, except for Babe and Gorse-Bracken, none of the characters truly matter, their roles serving merely as examples of sexual variations upon which Babe and, occasionally, her spiritual opposite, Gorse-Bracken, comment.

Despite many critics' assertions that *In Masks Outrageous and Austere* was simply a restatement of all of Williams' previous themes, I'd argue that he took them much further, almost laying all his cards on the table, so to speak, creating a far more straightforward and, yes, *honest* statement of his sexual obsessions than he previously had.

There's no question that behind every Williams male and many of his females is a homosexual, lesbian, or "perverse"—by the general societal standards—sexual being! It is hard to think of the few "normal" individuals (although no such word is truly possible in Williams' canon, since it is those who believe themselves "normal" who are the most abnormal beings): Stella perhaps, the gentleman visitor of *The Glass Menagerie* maybe. After that, it gets difficult. Even the Big Dad-

dys and Big Mommas of Williams' world have suffered incomparable torments in their sexual relationships. But in most of Williams' works, up until his final short and longer plays, these figures were kept somewhat in the shadows, their true sexual identities exposed, certainly, but just so ever slightly blurred that they could escape the deficient attentions of many middle-class Americans and even the harsh lights of Hollywood movies. Most viewers certainly comprehended that in the motion-picture version of *Cat on a Hot Tin Roof*, for example, Brick's real problem was his homosexual attraction to his high-school football companion Skipper; but people like my parents and their friends, had they even ventured out to that film (they were not adventurers), might have easily believed Burl Ives' assertion that his son's problem was immaturity, an inability to grow up and out of his idealized friendship with his former "buddy." They might even have convinced themselves that Blanche was a subject of small-town gossip and was just terribly misunderstood.

Such brain-washing slips of the imagination are quite impossible, however, in this last Williams work. Babe, full-face to the audience, announces one by one the sexual peccadilloes of nearly every figure in the cast: from her gay—and in this Williams play, it is "gay," not "homosexual" behavior, that is the proper description of the characters' acts—husband Billy's (Robert Beitzel) abandonment of her bed for his ship-board dalliances with his Harvard-bred "secretary" Jerry (Sam Underwood), to her own lesbian past (which she characterizes, humorously, in the old-fashioned expression of "acts of Bilitis"). She, a pure sensualist, determined to "gratify everything in me as the luna moth dies at dusk," announces to us that, as the wealthiest woman in the world, she has purchased her current love-interest to fulfill her needs. But he has failed her, just as her endless cocktails of vodka and champagne have failed her, her dying father has failed her, her nerves have failed her, and, now, even her guardians, the nefarious Gideons— a security force made up of mentally-loving gay boys hired by the Kudzu-Clem corporation watching over her wealth—have seemingly failed her. She, in short, is the perfect exemplar of Mick Jagger's and Keith Richard's lyrical wail: "I Can't Get No Satisfaction." So too does she announce, in case the audience has turned a blind eye, that her neighbor Mrs. Gorse-Bracken, living in an invisible nearby house, is obviously engaged in an incestuous relationship with her forever-masturbating son, Playboy; that her maid, Peg Foyle (Pamela Shaw), is a slut; and her estimation that Peg's current boyfriend, Joey (Christopher Halladay)—whom Peg has met in a local church—is a stud worthy of her attention. Babe, in short, is the Chorus to Williams' ridiculous Greek-like tragedy, where the masks fall from the characters' faces as quickly as they might attempt to attach them. Despite its lugubrious title, there are, in fact, no "outrageous masks" possible given Babe's revelatory announcements.

If nothing else—and there is a great deal else to be said about this play—Babe's drunken pronouncements, which Knight delivers in a kind of stammering delight, at times appearing as if the overwrought actress has almost forgotten her lines, are like a slap in the face, an outrageous howl of sensual disappointment. The fact that she, along with her slim-waisted and mentally wasted husband, has been abducted and deposited into this seaside hellhole, in a manner similar to the Church of Scientology's alleged imprisonments of their own doubting adherents, only ratchets up Babe's vengeful dance of truth-telling, until finally, exhausted, she disappears into the strangely lit-up aurora-borealis-like sunset to swim in a sea she has so boisterously admitted she abhors. In her absence, her current objects of disappointment are destroyed, murdered, leaving her free to move on, like the Capitalistic world she symbolizes, devouring others in her desperate search for love.

As a comedic-romantic Williams has always se-

cretly equated love with suffocation, desire with greed, the sexual act itself with self-immolation; and in this play, all these tropes become quite visibly apparent. Pumped up on drugs, perhaps satiated beyond his capability to accept any further love, Williams created in Babe a startling rendition of Medea's dance of death, a song of vengeance for all those who so disappointed this man's, and every man's like him, insatiable desires. For Williams' last lover, the play's director David Schweizer, the recreation of this text can only have been a painfully poignant reconstruction, one I, at least, felt honored to have experienced.

LOS ANGELES, MAY 10, 2012
Reprinted from *USTheater, Opera, and Performance* (May 2012).

The Making of Blanche Dubois

TENNESSEE WILLIAMS **THE ECCENTRICITIES OF A NIGHTINGALE** / FILMED VERSION ON TELEVISION SHOW *GREAT PERFORMANCES*, JUNE 16, 1976, DIRECTED BY GLENN JORDAN

THE OTHER DAY I watched a filmed version of a production of Williams' little-known play *The Eccentricities of a Nightingale* (based on a production at either the Actors Theatre of Louisville or The Old Globe in San Diego—both are named at different sites). *The Eccentricities* is a rewrite of his *Summer and Smoke*, but the characters behave quite differently than they do in the latter play and the tone is completely different, as Williams himself noted, far less melodramatic and certainly less symbolic than *Summer and Smoke*, first performed a year after his great *A Streetcar Named Desire*.

One recognizes immediately, in fact, this play's close relationship with *Streetcar*. The central character, Alma Winemiller (Blythe Danner), shares many simi-

larities with Blanche Dubois, and perhaps gives us a glimpse of some of the forces behind the over-the-top figure of Williams' earlier play (*Summer and Smoke*, in earlier versions, however, predated *A Streetcar*).

Alma, the daughter of the Glorious Hill, Mississippi Episcopalian minister, is a fragile being, as we recognize from the very first scene where she is frightened over and over by the fireworks going off around her on the 4th of July. She has been singing, and describes herself as being overwrought because she feels the songs so strongly. Also, she perceives her next-door neighbor, John Buchanan, Jr. (Frank Langella)—a young doctor who has been away at school at Johns Hopkins University—staring at her as she sits with her father (Tim O'Connor) and mother (Louise Latham) in the square.

The mother, who we soon discover is insane, is quickly whisked away, as she is throughout much of the play. Buchanan comes over to speak with Alma, but he too is soon taken off by his mother (Neva Patterson), who insists that he pay a doctorly visit to a patient that his father is too tired to attend to. Thus Williams immediately sets up the situation: Alma is clearly aflutter in the presence of Buchanan, and Buchanan is obviously dominated and controlled by his mother.

What is also apparent is that the still-beautiful but virginal Alma is—in a word the play itself uses to describe her—almost hysterical, using any reason to swallow down the small white pills the doctor has prescribed for her (probably just placebos). Her father, in fact, attempts to have a heart-to-heart talk with her in the very next scene, now Christmas, about her fluttering hands, her exaggerated gestures and speech, and—the most comical of accusations—her penchant for feeding birds in the town square. She is getting the reputation of an "eccentric." Despite her father's stern warnings, however, Alma stands up for her own behavior quite strongly, in contrast to her usual role of a supporting daughter. Yet she is hurt, feels shunned by the local community, particularly when local carolers visit the Buchanan house but turn away from the Winemiller home. Alma seeks solace in a small gathering of would-be intellectuals, odd people who mostly have inflated egos, confusing Blake with Rimbaud, and writing endlessly long verse plays. Only Alma, of the group, seems to know anything about poetry or literature.

She invites Buchanan—who has again returned for a stay in Glorious Hill—to the gathering which ends in unpleasant bickering among the group and, once more, the young doctor's being led off by his mother, who has a very different view of whom her beloved son will marry.

The scene with the two of them, mother and son, in the Buchanan home is as close to a love scene as the young doctor ever gets. Mrs. Buchanan clearly is the smothering type, who continues to control his life. Yet despite his mother's interference, he has managed to make a date with Alma, whom he admires for her intelligence and the shifting alternations of personality that run across her face. Her very eccentricities, he observes, are what make her so special, so different from all the other women he has met, certainly setting her apart from any woman his mother might wish him to marry.

Langella plays this scene, as well as others, with a kind of gentle passivity that almost angered me: why doesn't he speak out, speak up for what he sees in Alma? Why can't he show some anger at his mother's bourgeois visions for his future life? Instead he merely answers with quiet irony and, we later perceive, coded phrases that make him appear detached.

Alma is fearful when evening arrives for their date that he won't show; and when he does, she is almost overwhelmed with a kind of energized force, telling him after the movie of her life-long love for him. She even suggests that they go someplace for sex, to which he demurs. Alma admits that she does not expect this friendship to go any further, but if only she might have one night, a whole evening to remember.... Again he demurs, but finally agrees to take her to a hotel that specializes in just such encounters. Once there, however, it becomes apparent that nothing will happen. What doesn't get said is quite obvious: the young doctor is gay, uninterested in sex with a woman. Alma perceives the situation immediately. And in the last scene of the play, described as an epilogue, we see her seated on the same park bench where she sat early in the play. She has aged. When she encounters a young salesman, she begins a conversation, suggesting that they visit the same hotel. Apparently, she has now found regular companions for the one-night encounters she had sought out.

This might almost be a reincarnation or glimpse of an earlier Blanche Dubois, the young woman of entitlement given to romantic notions of the world, but also desirous of the pleasures of sex. Like Blanche, her first love turns out to be a homosexual, unable to give her what she desires. Alma has already begun on the long downward spiral where Blanche ends, in the arms of a teenage boy in a similar seedy hotel.

Danner's performance as Alma is splendid, and her stunning portrayal of Williams' "eccentric nightingale" brings this play to life in a way that *Summer and Smoke*, with its smoldering old maid at the center, never achieves. I might even go so far, after watching this excellent TV production, as to suggest that *The Eccentricities of a Nightingale* is one of Williams' best works.

LOS ANGELES, OCTOBER 6, 2012
Reprinted from *US Theater, Opera, and Performance* (October 2012).

Two Films by Chris Marker

Memory of Death

CHRIS MARKER (WRITER AND DIRECTOR) **LA JETÉE**
(**THE JETTY**) / 1962

THE DEATH of filmmaker Chris Marker on June 29 of
this year provoked me into seeing two of his most beloved films, *La Jetée* and *Sans soleil*. The French director,
a member of what was often described as the Left Bank
group (including Alain Resnais, Agnès Varda, and Armand Gatti—the latter of whom I have published), was
born Christian François Bouche-Villeneuve, changing
his name to Marker because of his love of marking pens.
Marker kept his life rather mysterious, claiming to have
been born in Ulan Bator, Mongolia; most sources name
the Paris suburb of Neuilly-sur-Seine as his birthplace.

This first of his better received films is built upon a
series of still photographs, some depicting the ruins of
European cities after World War II in a manner that is

reminiscent of Resnais' *Hiroshima, Mon Amor*. In this work, however, the events supposedly occur in the future, after World War III, which thoroughly destroyed Paris and other international cities. A young boy, visiting the pier of Orly Airport to watch the planes, observes a beautiful woman (Hélène Chatelain) at the end of the jetty at the very moment that he observes a man being killed, relating it in his mind with the beginning of the war.

Surviving as a prisoner below ground in the Palais de Chaillot galleries, the now-grown man (Davos Hanich), so we are told by the narrator (Jean Négroni), becomes obsessed with the vision of this woman. The world now facing the survivors is in near destruction, and, in order to attempt a survival, authorities are ex-

perimenting on several of the prisoners with time travel, attempting to take them to the past and the future so that they can discover how to cope. Most of the subjects die or become insane after the experiments.

Because of his obsession, the man is chosen to be the next subject, and he fears that it will end in death. But his ability to focus on that long-ago event permits him to return to the past, where he re-encounters the beautiful woman and, after several more returns, begins a relationship with her in which they casually tour the then-beautiful city, enjoying each other's company, without, it appears, her questioning the long absences between their visits to the Grande Galerie de l'Évolution, the Jardin du Luxembourg, and elsewhere. The relationship between the Man and the mysterious woman becomes so intense that, at one point, the still photos that we have been observing spring into motion, as the sleeping woman's eyes flutter into wakefulness.

Without actually understanding the consequences, the Man is told that he will now be sent into the future, his visits to the beautiful woman suspended.

In the future he meets up with a passive group of men and women who seem to have switches implanted into their foreheads—perhaps hinting at a more robotized or electronically-linked survival of the species. At first they are suspicious of him and reject him, but gradually they accept him, offering him the possibility of regenerating his own dying society.

Upon his return, having accomplished his task, he discovers that he will now be executed. Daring to visit the future in his own dreams, he is offered escape from his world, but chooses rather to return to the moment when he first perceived the lovely woman on the Orly jetty. Arriving again on the pier, he perceives the woman, but in running to her also spots one of his jailers, an agent determined to kill him. Suddenly he perceives that the incident which he witnessed in his childhood was his own death.

The haunting passages of Marker's film obliquely discuss physical and philosophical issues concerning the relationship of the past and future to the present, suggesting that what we think we know of the past may have been shaped by the future, and what we think are the past and future may be living out as a kind of present. Marker seems to be fascinated with the question of what memory actually is. Is the beautiful woman, we can only wonder, possibly the boy's own mother; and, if so, is his later relationship with her a projection of his desire or a strangely incestuous obsession not unlike Oedipus'? Marker makes no attempt to even pose these questions, let alone answer them. Yet his dream-like images and the poetic handling of his cinema encourage us to find our own links. Certainly, the film suggests what we believe to be impossible, the memory of one's own death. Do we dream after death of death itself?

In this sense, what might have been a simple science-fiction drama blossoms into a kind of muted tragedy, a speculation not only on the death of a single man, but the death of nations and the human species itself, issuing from, perhaps, an inability to link past, present, and future, presenting us with the specter of a culture's failure to recall the disasters of the past in order to save itself for its future.

LOS ANGELES, AUGUST 8, 2012
Reprinted from *World Cinema Review* (August 2012).

The Loss of Forgetting

CHRIS MARKER (WRITER AND DIRECTOR) **SANS SOLEIL (SUNLESS)** / 1983

OSTENSIBLY a documentary performed as a kind of random travelogue—scenes were filmed in Japan, Guinea-Bissau, Iceland, Paris, and San Francisco—Chris Marker's *Sunless* is a collage of images from Japanese films and television, stock footage, and newly filmed scenes from a silent film camera as an exercise, in part, to juxtapose behavior by playing time against place. Indeed the film opens with two quotes, the first by Racine, "The distance between countries compensates somewhat for the excessive closeness of time," and a quotation from T. S. Eliot's *Ash Wednesday*, "Because I know that time is always time / And place is always and only place / And what is actual only for one time / And only for one place."

Marker's film, accordingly, is a kind of melancholic and slightly nostalgic study of time and memory (the title is taken from a song cycle by the Russian composer Modest Mussorgsky).

As the film's narrator relates the travels of fictitious cameraman Sandor Krasna, he emphasizes the dilemmas of being unable to remember:

> I will have spent my life trying to understand the function of remembering, which is not the opposite of forgetting, but rather its lining. We do not remember. We rewrite memory much as history is rewritten. How can one remember thirst?

Without memory, moreover, how can we understand and comprehend global histories; how can we come to know our fellow man? The traveler's method, therefore, is not to explore what we think we know, but the banal aspects of life.

> He liked the fragility of those moments suspended in time. Those memories whose only function had been to leave behind nothing but memories. He wrote: I've been around the world several times and now only banality still interests me. On this trip I've tracked it with the relentlessness of a bounty hunter. At dawn we'll be in Tokyo.

The result of this search for banality often produces fascinating information and connections as the

 film focuses on the beauty of children on an Iceland road, on the powerful women of Guinea-Bissau, and on a shrine for cats in Japan. Some of the narrator's comments are in fact quite profound and succeed in revealing new layers of the disparate cultures the film explores.

At other times, however, Marker's narrative reminds me a bit of the often hackneyed and clichéd notions of culture that we have seen from French theorists who talk of the entire US in terms of Los Angeles and Las Vegas in vague overstatements that have little to do with the reality of those places,  let alone the whole country. In short, Marker's narrator often finds profound ideas in what might be quite meaningless to the cultures themselves, reminding me also of late 19th- and early 20th-century European and American "orientalism," a fascination with anything that seems *different*, without the ability to put the images in proper context. Marker's film often makes large claims for the banal activities he explores. For example, his observation of Japanese horror movies—"Japanese horror movies have the cunning beauty of certain corpses"—may be an absolutely legitimate conclusion, but one would like to know how he has come to this conclusion and where it leads. Time and again, Marker's narrator settles on such seemingly profound generalities without explaining their meaning or significance in the whole.

Of course, this also creates a kind of poetic quality to the work which brings it, at times, an evocative power. And perhaps the focus on the small acts and odd components of a society may better help to make us remember, bringing us closer to the filmmaker's goal of creating a "loss of forgetting." But at times *Sunless* is so dark and vague that it becomes hard to even know where we have been, let alone to remember the place.

LOS ANGELES, AUGUST 25, 2012
Reprinted from *World Cinema Review* (August 2012).

Natural History

DON SUGGS **THERMAL POOL PAINTINGS AND PARADISE PRINTS**, LA LOUVER, MAY 24–JUNE 30, 2012

IN HIS NEWEST SHOW, *Thermal Pool Paintings and Paradise Prints*, at LA Louver gallery in Venice, artist Don Suggs again shows work that, at first sight, appear to be brightly colored geometric abstractions in the shape of targets. Upstairs in the gallery, however, he has branched out into large black-and-white photographic prints of famed natural sites from national parks such as Zion and Cathedral Rock in Sedona, Arizona, along with scenes, vaguely reminiscent of photographer Ansel Adams, of clouds, California beaches, and other natural wonders—within which he has again inserted images of his brightly colored target-like paintings, produced by ink-jet.

What becomes apparent in this show, particularly through the seemingly oppositional images of nature and his colored wheels, is that Suggs' works are not

what they first appear to be. Rather than simply being highly colored geometric shapes, the paintings are associative images of various thermal pools in Yellowstone National Park, and relate most specifically to the photographic prints.

Suggs explained that his choice of colors depends on various combinations of the time of day, the slant of the sun, and other natural phenomena surrounding the pools, including, perhaps, his own emotional responses to the natural sites.

"Pod," for example, is a picture of a mountain peak, where below a group of Korean sightseers are gathered, small figures in the foreground looking up at the towering natural wonder. The colors of the circular image imposed just above their heads—golden yellows and olive greens—was determined, he told me, by their nearby tourist bus, sporting those very hues.

The couple peering through an optical viewer of "Sight" do, in fact, seem to be "taking a shot" at the looming tower of rock, reflected again in the colors of the circular "target" hovering over their heads.

"Zion Rose," a photograph of "Angel's Landing" in Zion National Park, is illuminated with a circular form that features pinks, greens, and reds, suggesting the colors of that flowering plant.

The target below the beach palms of "di Suvero," a reference to the sculptor Mark di Suvero, whose art is embedded within the palms, has all the hot pinks and coral colors that one associates with the Venice beach of Los Angeles, a block away from the gallery.

In this context Suggs' paintings take on new meanings; their abstractions give way to more associative and even private combinations of intense color, helping one to understand why, as Suggs puts it, "I see these pools differently every time I observe them."

This new show, accordingly, reveals that, while his work still clearly has connections with abstraction and conceptual art, Suggs is perhaps more of a natural historian, an artist who connects the moment of creation not only to nature but to what was happening at those natural sites at the very moment of his witnessing of them, thus balancing the sense of their permanence with the very human moments in time through which we glimpse their significance.

LOS ANGELES, MAY 29, 2012
Reprinted from *Green Integer Blog* (June 2012).

Rock of Ages

MICHAEL HEIZER **LEVITATED MASS**, LOS ANGELES
COUNTY MUSEUM OF ART, 2012

WITH OUT-OF-TOWN FRIENDS, we visited Michael
Heizer's "Levitated Mass," a work of art that is famous
in Los Angeles for its long, complicated journey—given
local road constrictions throughout the region and the
impossibly large machine it took to carry the rock to its
location—from quarry to museum. Along the way, in
its many daytime pauses (the machine could only travel
on late-night empty streets), numerous communities
came out to greet the oversized manifestation of expensive "art," celebrating its street journey, and further pro-
moting this over-the-top art manifestation. Although
the Los Angeles County Museum of Art and its dynamic director, Michael Govan, insisted that no public
money had gone into the support of this multi-million
dollar project, some people could only wonder, was it
worth the hype? Govan insisted it was, declaring the

work a piece that would last centuries and represent the museum into a kind of artistic eternity, like, perhaps, the very popular Chris Burden piece, "Urban Light," which greets the visitor to LACMA. "Urban Light" is now backed, in the opposite museum entry, by the "Heizer" rock.

The publicity aroused so much public interest that the museum gracefully invited people from all those neighborhoods through which the "rock" had traveled to the opening, which Howard—a former curator at the museum—attended; I had another event on that day. The crowd was so intense that Howard did not even walk "under" the monumental natural force— which is what the whole experience of this earthworks-based piece is all about.

I'm delighted, actually, that the "rock" is so appealing to audiences since the installation exists across the street from our condominium. One hopes for the museum's success. It defines our neighborhood. But there are some doubts. My intelligent typesetter, Pablo Capra, visited it with great consternation: "I didn't want to walk under it, and it seemed just like a cold concrete tunnel." Others had had similar responses.

445

Indeed, the tunnel, under which one needs to pass to experience the "intense" feeling of the size and power of natural forces, *is* rather cold, certainly not endearing to the exploration of nature: even if well-designed, it puts one in an intense opposition to nature itself. The rock stolidly sits on two struts imposed upon the concrete bunker, but one feels, in the process of the long trek through the "tunnel," that at any moment, the "rock" might crumble into its historical inevitability. On the day we entered, I muttered, "God forbid that a major earthquake were to occur as we walked below." The next day temblors shook throughout nearby Orange County.

Yet, it wasn't the fear that made this impossibly large project so memorable: I was much more awed by the two (now one) Richard Serra (*Band*, 2006) sculptures embedded in the basement of the Eli Broad Gallery nearby. This large "rock," which can never be properly perceived as immense as it truly is, seemed like a place to simply "duck and dodge," a massive natural impediment that didn't quite belong to the space upon which it was impaled. It may be, as director Michael Govan has stated, that it is an art piece that will survive for a very long time, but one can only wonder at the poised rock: will the major earthquake we certainly will suffer in the next several years crack that natural symbol in half? And, if that rock were to survive, we can only

 ask what it might tell us about its own natural existence, now so carefully positioned into a museum installation. Can nature truly be expressed in such a constructed situation? What does it mean to be poised there? And, most importantly, we must ask, why has a significant force of nature been brought and installed there for millions of dollars? The question is not whether it is art, but whether it is a strong enough expression to capture our pagan need to worship natural images? Can one absurdly transferred rock compare to the millenniums of constructed stone pyramids? The comparison is, of course, ridiculous. As wonderful as Heizer's rock may be, it is clearly not a rock of ages.

LOS ANGELES, AUGUST 8, 2012
Reprinted from *Green Integer Blog* (August 2012).

Euclid's First Axiom

TONY KUSHNER (SCREENPLAY, BASED, IN PART, ON
DORIS KEARNS GOODWIN'S *TEAM OF RIVALS*), STEVEN
SPIELBERG (DIRECTOR) **LINCOLN** / 2012

STEVEN SPIELBERG's film *Lincoln* is so much more am-
bitious and intelligent than any other American movie
of the year that one would have to be a cynic to deny
its worth. True, there are numerous sentimental moments, particularly when Lincoln (the brilliant Daniel
Day-Lewis) nears the presence of his beloved son, Tad
(Gulliver McGrath), and there are numerous scenes of
clumsy exposition early in the film, such as three black
soldiers' recitation of Lincoln's "Gettysburg Address"
to his face, and Lincoln and his wife's (Sally Field) reiteration of their son's death and her near insanity. However, these are necessary to provide us with information
we need to evaluate the president and his situation.
Tony Kushner, our best epic and political playwright,
has done a remarkable job in creating a literate and ba-

sically focused script that, in turn, has encouraged the director to tamp down his often unbridled sentiments—which have  tended to turn most of his works into behemoth pop cultural icons—and fully reveal his considerable filmmaking talents.

Spielberg's and Kushner's determination, moreover, to concentrate their story upon the final four months of Lincoln's life as he attempted to end the Civil War and pass the Emancipation Act, freeing the slaves, transforms the film from a lumbering biopic into a stunning reenactment of American politics. That the political scene of the day was even more entrenched and far more contentious and bawdier than it is now, makes this film, accordingly, a timely statement that clearly demonstrates, as Doris Kearns Goodwin had in her book *Team of Rivals*, just how brilliant a political force Lincoln was. Unlike most depictions of Lincoln, finally, this film—while reasserting the man's monumentality—does not portray the president as a saint; Day-Lewis' Lincoln is a flawed man, a gawky giant of a being, who could be contentious, insistent, and particularly moody, caught up as he was in the bloody slaughter of so many of his countrymen. If he was a wit,

 so too was his humor often so homespun that it bordered on the corny. His numerous maxims at times seem vague and pointless. Even he described himself, at moments, as a preacher who was too lazy to stop his sermon. In short, this Lincoln is very much a human being, a man, although determined to bring equality into law, who was not always sure he was comfortable with the black culture for which he was battling. As he tells the ex-slave Elizabeth Keckley, a White House dressmaker and confidant of Mary, after she questions whether he will accept her and her people as equals, "I don't know you"— although tempering his reply with a phrase from *King Lear*, suggesting that since blacks appear to be, like himself, "bare, forked animals," presumably he will become used to them. Spielberg's and Kushner's Lincoln is a man not above selling political positions in return for votes, through the film's three comic figures, with William N. Bilbo (James Spader) at the center.

The most morally outspoken voice of the work, Thaddeus Stevens (Tommy Lee Jones), an absolute abolitionist, who we discover near the end of the film sleeps with his black housekeeper, describes Lincoln as a "dawdler" and fears Lincoln will "turn his back on emancipation." Lincoln and his Republican supporters must draw in Stevens' "compass point" morality—as Lincoln explains, the compass always points due north but it does not tell you what chasms, swamps and other natural phenomena lie between—while demanding that Stevens endorse the amendment does not assure blacks equality in social and voting rights, but simply assures equality before the law. The painful scene in which Stevens backs away from his belief in universal equality brought tears to my eyes as righteousness necessarily gave way to political expediency. Attacked by a fellow radical abolitionist for his changes in position, the nearly destroyed Stevens can only admit that his goal is simply to get the bill passed; when asked if there was anything he might not say for that purpose, his only answer is a grim admission: "Seems not."

The dilemma at the heart of this remarkable drama is that, although he wants the bill passed, Lincoln is even more impassioned to end the war. When Confederacy leaders send a delegation to discuss peace, he—particularly given Republican Party founder Francis Preston Blair's pressures—cannot simply dismiss talking with the rebels. If the war ends, however, there is little chance that emancipation will be granted, and blacks will inevitably return to their roles as slaves. When the Democrats get wind of a possible truce, the House demands a postponement on the very day of the vote. Playing

 with partial truths, Lincoln assures the legislative body that no such delegates are in Washington. And we recognize in this half-truth just how far Lincoln has come in his determination to see emancipation happen.

Part of the reason this movie is so excellent is its superlative actors who totally embody their roles. Daniel Day-Lewis, in particular, not only creates an utterly believable Abraham Lincoln, but seems to have almost transmogrified himself into the historical figure. In his long, deep silences particularly—moments in which it seems that Lincoln has gone into speculative hibernation—the actor is so convincing that we cannot even imagine the President himself enacting his life better. At a point when Lincoln is almost ready to choose peace over freedom, to sacrifice his moral position to the desirable social and political expediencies, his casual conversation with his two Morse code operators changes everything. Are we fitted to our times or simply living our time out are the issues which underlie his questions. One man, responding that he is, by education, an engineer, triggers a memory in Lincoln of when he first read Euclid's axiom: "Things which are equal to the same thing are also equal to one another." The implications of that statement, in the context, are suddenly immense. If people, black and white, are both "Bare, forked animals," as he has told Elizabeth Keckley, then they are axiomatically "equal to one another." The pondering leader suddenly changes his message: the Southern delegates are to be delayed in their voyage. The 13th Amendment to the US Constitution passes the House of Representatives, moving on to become national law.

As we know from history, Wilmington and Richmond were vanquished, thousands more soldiers died, but the war did finally come to a close. Lincoln's tour of the South with his son Tad, as he himself notes, is indescribable as he encounters so many corpses of young men: "I have seen nothing like it." Lee surrenders to Grant. We all know what happened next, but this restrained film does not show it. Rather, the young Tad, attending an operatic production, is forced to hear the news from a slightly hysterical theater manager, who announces that at another theater the President has been shot. The boy clings to the edge of his balcony booth in horror, until finally an adult pulls him away. Although writer and director repeat yet another of Lincoln's speeches, truly nothing else need be said.

LOS ANGELES, NOVEMBER 20, 2012
Reprinted from *Nth Position* (December 2012).

The Beauty of Her Own Beast

PIERRE BOILEAU, THOMAS NARCEJAC, JEAN REDON,
AND CLAUDE SAUTET (ADAPTATION, BASED ON A FIC-
TION BY JEAN REDON), PIERRE GASCAR (DIALOGUE),
GEORGES FRANJU (DIRECTOR) **LES YEUX SANS VISAGE**
(**EYES WITHOUT A FACE**) / 1960, USA 1962

I SAW THIS classic "horror/science fiction" film at the AFI Fest in November 2011, selected by the Guest Artistic Director of that year, Pedro Almodóvar, who also introduced the four films he had chosen. The Franju film had obviously been one source for his *The Skin I Live In*, playing in the theaters at the time.

Almodóvar even complimented the audience (a bit sparse for the large Egyptian Ringler Theatre) for its taste, speaking of the film's formal qualities. "There's only one scene that is a bit gory," he declared. "But generally the film is elegant and understated."

Basically, I agree with Almodóvar, and would rather release the film from its horror and science fiction

genres—my least favorite of film genres in any event—
and speak of it more, as did its director, as a film of "anguish," much quieter in its mood and more penetrating
than any horror film. The fact that *Les yeux sans visage*
was dubbed into English and retitled *The Horror Cham-
ber of Dr. Faustus*, shown in a double feature with *The
Manster*, certainly did not help the film move beyond
the attacks made by some UK audiences. In Scotland,
so it is said, seven audience members swooned during
the famed heterografting scene (Franju's witty answer:
"Now I know why Scotsmen wear skirts"). British critic
Isabel Quigly labeled it "the sickest film since I started
film criticism." Americans were not far behind in their
howls.

Today with gore and violence so graphically pre-

sented in all films it
is hard to understand
the outrage. Or, let
us say, given Franju's
dramatically poetic
presentation of hor-
rific events, events of
"anguish," perhaps we can easily comprehend the out-
rage. This is not some silly conception of a Hollywood
B-film studio, but a tightly-structured and quite beautifully filmed work which suggests far more than it actually portrays.

Indeed, its "hero"—if the Frankenstein-like doctor
can be described as such—is very much a creature of
anguish. He is, after all, responsible for an accident in
which his daughter's face was evidently so burned and
scarred that little skin has remained; only her eyes have
been saved. Living in a large villa near the mental clinic
which he runs, Doctor Génessier (Pierre Brasseur) has
somewhat secretly been experimenting with skin grafts
(something, as Almodóvar points out, we take for
granted today), attempting to find a way to graft them
upon his patients without having the tissue rejected.
Mostly he experiments on large dogs stored away in the
basement near his laboratory, but he must also find human subjects so that he can restore his daughter's face.
He has already succeeded on his assistant, Louise (the

stunning Aida Valli), upon whom he is more dependent than we might imagine, and who, we discover, is strangely willing to meet all his demands, including sharing his lie that his daughter, Christine (Edith Scob), is missing.

The film begins with intense music by composer Maurice Jarre, as Louise drives down a country lane lined by trees, whose silhouettes puncture the nighttime sky. She seems terrified by something: perhaps the rain or just the occasional truck whose bright lights nearly fracture the car's back window. For a few moments we might even fear that she herself will go hurling off the road. Gradually, however, we discover that there is another passenger in the back seat: a man, it appears, who seems to be sleeping. As the journey progresses, however, we begin to perceive that something far worse is occurring; and, as she approaches a river with a small falls, we watch her drag the man from the car and toss him into the water.

A public lecture by the doctor about the very subject of his experiments titillates and intrigues his audience, but the doctor has no time after to chat. As one elderly admirer speaks to him of the future, he interrupts, "The future, Madame, is something we should have started on a long time ago," disappearing into the night. He has been called by the police, who believe they have found his missing daughter or perhaps another missing girl, Mlle. Tessot, whose father they have called in as well. The doctor expediently identifies the body as being that of his daughter, in-creasing the anguish of the waiting Mr. Tessot, whose daughter is still missing.

We soon discover the truth. Christine remains locked away in the villa, forced to wear a mask over what is left of her face, while the girl buried in the Génessier vault is the missing Tessot girl, whose face was clearly removed in another failed experiment by the doctor.

The most horrifying of events follows, as Louise, wearing always a pearl choker around her neck to hide the scars of her surgery (Almodóvar suggested that the necklace itself had become almost grafted to her neck), stalks a young girl she has seen on the street, who has a face not unlike Christine's former milk-white skin. Little by little, Louise insinuates herself into this stranger's life, inviting Edna to a performance (she has an extra ticket), and finally meeting her over lunch, declaring that she has found an apartment, for which Edna has been searching.

The "apartment," of course, is in the villa. Edna,

disliking the long trip from the city and sensing that something is amiss, attempts to leave, but is quickly anesthetized by the doctor. He is eager to attempt the grafting once again.

That scene is the gory cutting and pasting of the entire face against which the critics so railed. But even here, more is implied than shown, as pencil and forceps (called for again and again) become the focus of the scene, more than the skin-raising result. This time, however, the doctor and Louise are convinced of their success. They even allow Edna sustenance, and, possibly, some more time to live; but she, recognizing the horror of their acts upon her, escapes, jumping to her suicide from a high window. Together, both doctor and assistant take her body into the family vault, dropping it with a heavy thump upon the others buried within.

Christine's scars seem to heal. The transplant appears to have been a success, and the haunted doctor and Louise, aware of their horrible deeds, wonder even if they might now be cleansed of the past. While examining his daughter's face soon after, however, the doctor detects signs of a slight rosiness in the cheeks, suggesting that the new face has been rejected by the patient. Within weeks, Christine's beautiful face begins to darken and wither away. She must return to her ghostly mask. Obviously, another woman will have to be found.

This time, the plot is a bit more complicated, entailing the doctor's clinic, Christine's former lover Jacques Vernon who works in the clinic, the police, and a young shoplifter whose blue eyes and blond hair fit the bill of the next victim.

I will spare the reader all the details, except to say the new girl, Paulette, is released from the clinic unharmed, suggesting to Jacques and the police that the doctor has not been involved. Louise, however, picks up the young girl on her way back to Paris, delivering

her, like the others, to the laboratory.

Yet the interruption of the police visit to the clinic, as they wonder why Paulette has not yet returned home, gives time for the anesthesia to wear off, and Paulette awakens tied to the operating table. Her struggles arouse pity in Christine, waiting upon another table, for a new face. Christine, who is torn between her desire for a new possibility for life or accepting death, has long been horrified by the events surrounding her, and determines to free Paulette, just as Louise returns to the operating room. With the same knife Louise uses to break Paulette's bonds, Christine stabs Louise in her pearl-encircled neck, and in a mad trance enters the kennel, one by one freeing the wild dogs on which the doctor has experimented.

At that very moment, the doctor, returning home and wondering at the excited barking of his dogs, opens the door to the kennel, the beasts leaping out upon him. When they have finished, we get a glimpse of the doctor lying dead, his own face having been torn to bits, his eyes staring out in disbelief and wonderment.

Christine frees the birds the doctor had also caged, some of them gathering around her, sitting upon her shoulders, reminding us very much of the painting of a young girl hanging in the villa hallway. If nothing else, the girl without a face has finally turned into the image of her imagined self, becoming the beauty of her own beast.

LOS ANGELES, NOVEMBER 6, 2011
Reprinted from *World Cinema Review* (November 2011).

Facing In

KŌBŌ ABE (SCREENPLAY, BASED ON HIS NOVEL), HI-
ROSHI TESHIGAHARA (DIRECTOR) **TANIN NO KAO (THE
FACE OF ANOTHER)** / 1966, USA 1967

IN POSTWAR JAPAN a formerly wealthy businessman,
Okuyama (Tatsuya Nakadai), has been disfigured with
burns to his face during an industrial accident. His head
completely wrapped in bandages, not unlike the hero of
the James Whale 1933 classic horror film, *The Invisible
Man*, he lives with his wife in a now-cynical relationship, where he feels tortured by her supportive comments but obviously distracted behavior and her refusal
to cease motion while around him. She, in turn, understandably feels as if she too were a victim in this horrible
accident, as he poses impossible-to-answer questions
and muses on philosophical issues, such as the conten-
tion that the face is the door to the soul. "Does he still
have a soul?" he ponders. And who is this being who
he was before his identity disappeared to those around

him? His partner's secretary greets him as if his face were not hidden behind bandages, while others who encounter him turn away in horror and disgust.

But the true theme of Teshigahara's and Abe's collaboration is concerned less with "invisibility"—although it remains a subtext of this work—than with defining a human being through his face; or to put it another way, the film asks the question, who is the person *behind* his or her face? Okuyama's wife attempts to explore that issue through a discussion of why women wear makeup. It is not, she declares, to present an appealing look to the outsider, but, in the manner of ancient cultures and the remnants of those values in Arab culture, it is rather an attempt to hide behind the face, to build up a kind of mask to keep the true being protected within out of a sense of humility, a reverence for the inner self.

Okuyama gets an opportunity to test that idea out when his psychiatrist, Dr. Hira (Mikijiro Hira), suggests that he can fashion a mask that, will fit to Okuyama's face—not only the facial contours, but the sweat glands, the various pores of the individual facial makeup. Encountering by accident a man in a small cafe (Hisashi Igawa), the two offer him money to borrow his face, recreating it to match the dimensions of Okuyama's facial structure.

Unlike Abe's original fiction, Teshigahara creates a double tale—indeed his entire story is based on a series of doublings—by taking us, bit by bit, through the relationship of a Nagasaki-born woman, whose beautiful face has been horribly disfigured on one side by the results of the atomic bomb, and her supportive brother (Kakuya Saeki). The beautiful woman, who hides her scars behind her long hair, works in a home for World War II veterans, most of whom have lost their sanity to their wartime experiences; and she, herself, is haunted and terrorized by the possibility of a new war breaking out, fears which she and her brother discuss. Unfortunately, he suggests, one only recognizes that a war exists after it has started.

Dr. Hira, meanwhile, has grown fearful of the possible effects of the mask he and his nurse are concocting, and demands assurances from his increasingly bitter friend, Okuyama, that he will keep the doctor abreast of all of his emotional responses to the mask. The relationship between the two—wherein the doctor suddenly takes the role of a kind of brother, father, advisor, guide, and policeman to the now-dangerous Okuyama—links Teshigahara's film with Georges Franju's *Les yeux sans visage* (*Eyes without a Face*), where Doctor Génessier plays a kind of anguished creator/confidant to his own Frankenstein-like daughter, Christine. The doctor and his patient's first outing after the creation of the mask takes place in a Japanese-German pub, where a chanteuse sings German songs of the loss of love and points out the strange wartime pairing of the two countries and the horrific results it has had upon the culture as a whole, linking the mask of Okuyama even more closely to the unmasked girl whose face has been scarred by the bomb triggered to end the war.

Although we might have feared that Okuyama was intent, once the "face of another" had become his own, on doing violence to his own wife, we soon discover that his "plot" does not involve physical assault as much as it does a psychological revenge, entailing a plan to seduce his own spouse.

Dr. Hira, meanwhile, has developed even more general concerns regarding the results of such a facial

transformation, fears that a man might, under the influence of the face, become someone else or, that, able to live without an identifiable past, one might be led to commit unspeakable acts or crimes not previously thought of. In a sense, all of this occurs in *The Face of Another*, as Okuyama,  having obtained two nearly identical apartments in another building—one for his bandaged self, another for the new man-in-the-mask—sets out, as a stranger, to test his wife's faithfulness. His seduction is all too easy, as within a few hours after following her, she not only accepts his sexual insinuations, but readily joins him in his second apartment for a sexual rendezvous. Disgusted by his apparent success, he confronts his wife, who quickly counters that she knew all along, and thought only that it was an attempt at game-playing, a kind of sexual masquerade which might bring them back into a loving relationship. The fact that he actually meant to deceive her, she declares, disgusts her, drawing an end to their already fraught relationship.

Okuyama's attempts to later return to their house, where she sits, refusing his entry, reveals that as the new "man with the mole," he can never go "home" again. He is now a new being who must act out the inner behavior of that beast.

For, of course, with a new, seemingly unrecognizable face, he must look to who he was perhaps all along within: not at all the socialized industrialist of old, but a horribly destroyed and psychologically altered being, a man capable of even more perverse acts.

So too has the young woman with a scar, on vacation with her brother, come to realize that within she is not at all the beautifully demure woman hoping to hide her facial blemish, but a passionate, lusting animal, who demands that her brother kiss her, resulting in an intense incestuous coupling. It quickly becomes clear that her brother loves not her apparent beauty as much as he does her hidden scars, which symbolizes the woman calling him from within. Their illicit encounter demands a kind of expiation, which she accomplishes by walking into the surrounding sea to drown, while her brother calls out to her, unable to prevent the results of his acts.

Similarly, Okuyama, now rejected by his seemingly faithful lover, looks within, resulting in an attempt to rape an unsuspecting woman. Arrested, he is saved by his psychiatrist, who lies to the police, claiming that Okuyama is an escaped mental patient.

Throughout the film, the director has presented the viewer with strange images and events. The many scenes in the psychiatrist's clinic in which body-parts float in diagramed positions mid-air, the bizarre behavior of the superintendent's yo-yo-loving daughter, the ever-present Western-loving affectations of the entire populace, the several near-repetitions of events (such as Okuyama's two visits to obtain an apartment, the attempted rape of the woman with a scar and the  later attempted rape by Okuyama), and Teshigahara's several cinematic devices—blurred, stopped, tilted and sped-up images)—now coalescence into a kind of surrealist film, as Okuyama's mad inner self is projected onto the society at large, the busy streets filled with men and women with masks instead of faces. Finally, as in the Franju work and the later Almodóvar tribute to Franju, *La piel que habito* (*The Skin I Live In*), the victim, as Okuyama has always declared himself to be, must exact his revenge: he unflinchingly plunges a knife into his former friend's body, abandoning his identity to the self he has discovered by facing in.

LOS ANGELES, MAY 13, 2012
Reprinted from *World Cinema Review* (May 2012).

The I Who Still Breathes

PEDRO ALMODÓVAR (SCREENPLAY, BASED ON A
FICTION BY THIERRY JONQUET), PEDRO ALMODÓVAR
(DIRECTOR) **LA PIEL QUE HABITO (THE SKIN I LIVE IN)**
/ 2011

INFLUENCED to a certain degree by Georges Franju's
elegant horror film, *Les yeux sans visage,* Almodóvar's
languorous study of control over another takes us into
the secret world of a tortured Dr. Frankenstein who,
with the advances of today's science, can completely
transform the human body. Much like Franju's Dr. Génessier, Robert Ledgard, heading an isolated clinic and
operating out of his house, has suffered the horror of
seeing his wife severely burned in an automobile accident, evidently caused by his half-brother, the brutal
and bestial Zeca, with whom she was having an affair.
Through patient nursing and the attentions of her doc-
tor-husband, the wife survives, but upon witnessing the
burned shell of her body in the glass of a window, she

leaps to her death.

Robert (Antonio Banderas) is left with a daughter, Norma, who never quite recovers from the shock of her mother's death, and is unable to deal publicly with other people. As Robert and Zeca's mother relays the news early on in the movie, Norma followed the route of her mother, falling from a high window of the institute where she had been committed.

Although this information is summarized early on, we don't actually see the events play out until after the director has introduced us to another, more mysterious figure, Vera Cruz (Elena Anaya), a beautiful woman kept locked up in Robert's home. We see little evidence of any outward operations—and certainly none of the masks and late-night activities of Franju's film. But we do know that, like the doctor of that work, Robert has experimented on skin transplants, and we can only suspect that Vera has been at the center of his attention.

He has, so it is hinted, made over the imprisoned girl somewhat in the image of his dead wife, a fact for which his mother, serving as the head of the house and cook, despairs. Now that he has finished with her, she suggests, he should destroy her instead of keeping her locked away in a room where she reads, exercises, and, occasionally, writes upon the walls. She is a dangerous being.

We recognize some of that potential danger when Zeca shows up at the house on carnival night, dressed, absurdly, as a tiger, demanding that his mother hide him for a few days since he has just been involved in a heist. The mother, Marilia (Marisa Paredes), is outraged and quickly rejects any such suggestion, and, accordingly, is tied up and gagged by her son. Glimpsing the young wife lookalike of Robert on a television monitor, Zeca—a bestial figure if there ever was one—frantically searches the house for the girl, and finding the room, rapes her, Vera, strangely enough, both accepting the brutal action and crying out in terrible pain.

Robert, returning home mid-rape, rushes to the room to shoot his half-brother dead, while his mother below screams out that he should kill Zeca and Vera both.

What follows is even stranger, as a sexual relationship suddenly develops between Robert and Vera. After he has destroyed Zeca's body, he returns to her bed. The implications are frightening: if she indeed looks like his wife, has Vera been created merely for his sexual gratification? We are never given an answer, but we sense something grandly amiss.

Almodóvar—as the director of *Women on the Verge of a Nervous Breakdown* and other comedies—has often been described as creating a frenetic or, at least, hectic pace in his works. But here he almost lugubriously takes us back in time, retelling some of his tale, and, in so doing, revealing new truths that are even more frightening than those we already suspect.

Although she has had a difficult time with social relationships, Robert's daughter accompanies him to a pre-wedding party, where the young Norma seems to be acclimating herself well to other young women her age. Suddenly, however, many of the younger generation seem to be missing, and following their tracks, Robert finds a group of them, boy and girls, in the middle of the woods, engaging in group sex. His daughter is nowhere in sight.

We have already been introduced to a young man, Vicente, who works as a window dresser in his mother's second-hand dress shop. He asks the young shop assistant to go with him to the party, but she turns him down, evidently being more interested in women than in men. When he suggests she put on a dress he is displaying, she disparagingly suggests he wear it himself. The suggestion is that he may be gay, but he scoffs at her suggestion.

When he shows up at the party, he has already ingested—as have the other young people—a substantial amount of drugs. Meeting the young Norma, he lures her outdoors, asking her what drugs she has taken. Innocently, she reports the numerous drugs she is being prescribed for her psychological condition, while he interprets it in his own way:

VICENTE: You are different. I am different as well.
NORMA: Are you in therapy, too?

She, he is convinced, will be a willing participant in his experiment. As he takes off into the woods to have sex, she grows frightened, screaming out, to which he responds by trying to silence her, slapping her as he attempts to rape her. She passes out, and he, horrified, quickly re-dresses her and disappears from the event. Robert comes upon her at that very moment, observing the boy on a motorcycle speeding away.

After the attack, Norma's condition worsens. Locked away in a sanatorium, she appears to grow sicker, hiding from her father upon each of his visits. She, at least, has associated the young rapist with her own

father, and we must wonder if Robert has also sexually abused his daughter. He is asked to no longer visit her, and soon after, as Marilia has already told us, she jumps to her death.

Only a few frames later, the young handsome Vicente is kidnapped and chained in a dark space for several days, fed only water and a little rice. We comprehend Robert's sense of revenge, but why is he torturing the youth? What might possibly be gained?

Perhaps his mother said it best when she observed: "The things for love a madman can do!"

One of the most eerie scenes of the film occurs when we observe Robert spraying a hose over the filthy Vicente, the boy convinced he is about to be murdered.

 Gently and patiently, however, the handsome Robert almost lovingly shaves the young man, who, we soon discover, is about to undergo an operation. We can only suspect the worst, but when the boy awakens from the surgery, we discover something even beyond the expected castration. Robert has replaced the boy's genitals with a vagina, producing various sizes of dildos with which the boy is ordered to practice in order to help heal the crevice.

Within a few months, Robert has completed the sex change, as we witness the young beauty, now Vera, after the transformation. Against his will, he has been made over from a man into a woman. At first, the patient lashes out in rebellion filling the walls with words and numbers, dates of changes on his body and the statement, over and over: "I breathe. I breathe. I breathe. I know I breathe," as if his very respiration, a the sign of his survival, were a reiteration of the Cartesian principle, "I think, therefore, I am."

We've already seen what happens, but its meaning haunts us in a new way. Was Vicente truly gay all along, unknowingly seeking the very transformation that has been forced upon him? What kind of man is Robert, who must transform a boy into the woman of his desires? The implications, although Almodóvar does not explore them, are immense. Who are these men or women, including Robert's terrifyingly collaborationist mother? Perhaps she has no other choice, but Vera now agrees to never run away. It is like a vow of marriage, which the strangely naïve Robert readily accepts.

Vera-Vicente even makes a trip with Marilia into town, but when Robert and she attempt sex after her return, she insists that she has bought a lotion, which she briefly leaves the room to retrieve. Upon her return she has brought his gun, shooting him at close range near the heart. His almost poignant shock at the turn of events reveals his insanity:

ROBERT LEDGARD: You promised not to run away.
VERA: I lied.

As Marilia climbs the stairs, gun in hand, to check out the situation, she too is shot by the victim.

If in the final scene Vera-Vicente's return to his mother's dress shop seems almost banal, it is simultaneously an expression of immense courage and resilience, as the young woman proclaims to his mother his true identity: "Soy Vincente."*

*It appears that there may be a strong need for those who have undergone such major transformations to still be recognized or remembered, at least, in their former identity. Next door to my office was a small printing and copy shop run by a born-again Korean-American. Among his shop assistants was a very young, lean Thai boy whom I seldom spoke to, but occasionally greeted. I suspect that I was talked of, by this highly conservative businessman, as the neighborhood "queer."

The reason I imagine this is that one day I noticed the wan, Thai boy was missing. "What happened to Teo?" I asked.

Another assistant responded, "Oh, you didn't hear? He borrowed money from Richard and then ran off—for a sex operation!" he giggled.

"What?"

"A sex change," he scoffed.

About a half year later, a young, quite beautiful, and well-dressed Asian woman appeared in my Sun & Moon Press shop. After a few moments, I went forward to ask if she needed any help. The only thing I found unusual about her was that she was wearing high heels in the middle of the day. But in Los Angeles, of course, such things can happen.

"Do you remember me?" she asked.

I looked more intensely into her face. I paused. "I think I might."

"I am Teo," she reported, not without some pride.

"You are quite lovely," I lamely responded.

She blushed. "Thank you," she said simply, "thank you." And turning, she left.

LOS ANGELES, NOVEMBER 16, 2011
Reprinted from *N*th *Position* [England] (December 2011).

Survivors

LORRAINE HANSBERY **A RAISIN IN THE SUN** / CUL-
VER CITY, CALIFORNIA, THE KIRK DOUGLAS THEATRE /
THE PERFORMANCE I SAW WAS ON FEBRUARY 18, 2012

I HAD NOT previously seen a stage performance of the
original Lorraine Hansbery play, *A Raisin in the Sun*,
although I had long ago seen the film version with
Sidney Poitier and Ruby Dee, and I had read the play
some time in college, as well as seeing the sentimental-
ized musical version in its premiere on May 30, 1973,
my 26th birthday, at Washington, D.C.'s Arena Stage.
So I thought it only fitting that I check out a new stage
production at the Kirk Douglas Theatre in Culver City,
just a short drive from my Los Angeles home.

Although the well-made play of political and social
concerns is not generally my kind of theater, I thought
it might be interesting to see how the play has stood, to
use a tired cliché, "the test of time." And the fact that
my previous physician, with the strangely appropriate

478

 name of Dr. Redcross, was married to a niece of Hansbery's, who was very involved in her aunt's estate and interested in theater, made the visit an even more family-related event.

When I mentioned my attendance of this play to an intelligent and highly esteemed friend, her response was: "I couldn't possibly ever see anything so sweet. If that makes an elitist, so be it."

Although at times *A Raisin in the Sun* may be bittersweet, I would never characterize anything in this gritty story of the Younger family as "sweet." Even the mother, Lena (Kim Staunton), played to type as the sort of reaffirming, religious center of family life, is rarely joyful. And the rest of the family, Walter Lee (Kevin T. Carroll) and Beneatha (Kenya Alexander) particularly, battle it out in a Chicago ghetto world that has little room for anyone but survivors. The youngest of the Younger family, Travis, is forced to sleep on the couch, and is sent out of the house to play whenever there is a serious family discussion or argument—both of which occur at regular intervals throughout the play.

Walter Lee's wife, Ruth (Deidrie Henry), is again pregnant and, given the condition of their apartment and the family squabbles, is considering having an abortion. Her husband, an incompetent dreamer, is so belittled by his chauffeur job that he is near the level of despair suggested by the title, a quote from the Langston Hughes poem "A Dream Deferred."

The family's major battle is over money, the insurance left by the death of the father. For Lena, the decision is an obvious one: a part of it will go for Beneatha's education to become a doctor, the rest for a new home in Clybourne Park. But her son's loss of manhood and despair forces her to hand over some of the money so that he may play the role of the family head. Without even depositing the amount, he invests it in a shoddy deal with a friend to open a bar, only to find that the crook has absconded with the whole sum.

What struck me as particularly interesting in this play was the fact that the issues it raises are still current. The most interesting character of the drama is Beneatha, a strong young woman determined to make a success through education, an opinionated being who is also fascinated by her lost African roots. When her education money goes missing, she is still determined to travel with her friend, Joseph Asagi (Amad Jackson), to his homeland in Nigeria in order to experience new worlds and sights.

The final straw that breaks this family is the racist reaction of the "welcoming" committee to their new home, represented by the white Mr. Karl Linder (Scott Mosenson), who tries to skirt the issue of racism by describing a sense of community difference from the Youngers. This community is even willing to buy the house at a higher price than they have paid! At first, all family members join in their disdain of the proposal, quickly showing him the door. But the saddest moment of the play comes when, having lost the remaining money, Walter Lee, completely giving up their dreams, decides to capitulate, agreeing the Clybourne community's offer.

No sweetness in these choices, I can assure you. That these troubling issues were spoken of in a 1959 play by a black woman, moreover, is startling. Hansbery may not be an adventuresome writer, but she is certainly a forceful voice and a strong social conscience.

The only problem with the version, directed by Phylicia Rashad, that I attended was some of the characters attempts to play to the obviously sympathetic audience. The character of Walter Lee, in particular, was often played for humor. There is indeed irony, if not outright humor, in many of Hansbery's lines,

 but to milk that in a role centered upon despair defeats the playwright's purpose. Since Beneatha, in her more sophisticated thinking, is almost an outsider to her own family, she was saved from these winking asides, and was the stronger figure for it.

Yet overall and over all these years, Hansbery's *A Raisin in the Sun* remains a strong American statement of faith and strength against the daily travails of inner city life. If that means these characters or this play are somehow "sweet," then call me a populist—something no one has ever described me as being before.

LOS ANGELES, MARCH 14, 2012
Reprinted from *US Theater, Opera, and Performance* (March 2012).

Something to be Touched

RUSSELL BANKS **LOST MEMORY OF SKIN** (NEW YORK: HARPERCOLLINS, 2011)

IN WHAT I BELIEVE is his 17th work of fiction to date—two works of which, *Relation of My Imprisonment* and *Family Life*, I originally published—US novelist Russell Banks has created a long humanist-based investigation into our society's attitudes toward sexuality and its often-hypocritical views of what we define or perceive as sexual predators. Yet the work extends into far more complex metaphysical issues concerning questions of what is truth and what is a person's life story.

By focusing on a young man in his early 20s called simply The Kid, who loves animals (first an iguana, and then an old dog and an eccentric speaking parrot), Banks is able to remove much of his audiences' innate fear and detestation of child molesters, and consider the issue far more rationally than he might otherwise have been able to, particularly given Americans almost rabid attitudes toward such offenders. For The Kid, strangely enough, is still a virgin and has technically "done" nothing; his crime is perhaps that he has also done  nothing with his life. A lonely, almost abandoned child in his sexually-active mother's home, The Kid, coming of age, does little but sit in front of the internet, obsessed with heterosexual porn sites. His entire understanding of the world comes creeping in from the edges of these sites and maternal influences, none of which provides a true perspective on adult experience. Even serving in the military gives him little comprehension of the larger world; a loner even in communal military life, The Kid tries to gain popularity by buying up a large number of sex tapes of his favorite performer, Willow, handing them out to his fellow soldiers, an act which gets him kicked out of the service.

Now even more confused and lonely, The Kid begins to participate in a chat room with a young girl going by the code name of *brandi18*, who admits she is 14, but who chats in a seemingly far more experienced and knowledgeable sexual language than The Kid, creating a disbelief in the reader that she is real. Stupidly, The

Kid arranges to visit her at her house, loading himself up with a bag of beer, dildos, and Vaseline for what may potentially be his first actual sexual encounter. What he encounters instead is the girl's father, who, having followed their chat-room conversations, confronts The Kid with the facts, turning him over to the police.

The inevitable occurs, with The Kid serving prison time and, throughout most of the novel, serving probation with numerous other sex offenders, who are forced to live under the Calusa Bay, Florida causeway since they cannot find places sufficiently distant from schools, libraries, and other locations which children frequent.

These sorry and unforgiven individuals live in a kind of unspoken harmony as they attempt simply to survive the police attacks—a result of the locals complaints about their very existence—and the ravages of hurricanes. The men, although hardly speaking to one another and seldom discussing their crimes, still function as a kind of dissociated social community, which allows them to survive—at least until they are too tired and worn out to want to continue to exist.

Banks' portrayal of these men alone is worth the read. And, although Banks does not condone or simplify the villainy of their actions, his portrayal of these men with nowhere else to go, weekly revving up their ankle bracelets so that they can continually be tracked by a society that no longer wants them, is sympathetic and moving.

Into this lower-depths world comes a larger-than-life figure, The Professor, determined to check out the under-the-causeway society for his social and psychological studies. Coming upon the encampment at the very moment when most of the men have been temporarily dispersed, The Professor discovers The Kid, following him as he shifts location to a seedy outpost named Benbows and back again to the causeway, questioning, challenging, and even helping The Kid to financially survive in return for his answers.

This "Haystack" of a man, as The Kid dubs the large proportions of his body, is a genius with a wife and two children, but with a past that even he can't explain. If The Kid's past is all too familiar, The Professor's past, we gradually discover, is a compartmentalized world of contradictions as the author reveals his involvement with leftist groups, and his role as an informant for various government and even international agencies. The Professor's world is that of 1960s and 1970s politics, interminably complex and rationalized, like something—as The Kid says time and again—out of a novel or a movie. Indeed, at times, Banks' imagination of this man's past is so glib it almost seems that he has cribbed from *The Spy Who Came in from the Cold* and other such fictions. But then one doesn't have to be a conspiracy theorist to know that such individuals *did* and, perhaps, still do exist.

Slowly, as the two, an odd couple—the boy a skinny outcast who attempts to dissociate himself from his body, and the highly obese man whose life is clearly centered in his heft—develop a kind of relationship, playing out a kind of 21st-century version of Huckleberry Finn and Jim—wherein the scrappy, uneducated Kid weathers all kinds of adventures with the help of the wiser slave to his own body and past.

As The Kid's true self—if he has a "true" self—is gradually revealed, so does the balance between the two shift, The Professor ultimately insisting the boy interview him on camera, so that he can leave a testimony to his wife. Fearing that elements from his past have gradually come back to haunt him, the Professor, with cold recognition, insists that some scandal from his past will be created and that, eventually, he will be found dead, apparently of suicide, after which the accuser—individual, media, or police—will disappear, the case dropped. The CD that The Kid produces through the interview is to be given, after his death, to the Professor's wife, so that she and his children can know "the truth" as opposed to the rumors and lies reported.

Indeed the Professor is found dead, in the very canal which he has pointed out as a likely place to The Kid. But "the truth" of what the Professor has "professed" comes under even greater scrutiny as The Kid and a new accomplice—a kind of Hemingway-like stand-in for the author himself—enter the scene, The Kid, coincidentally, finding evidence in papers of one of his fellow sex-offenders that the Professor, under the name Dr. Hoo, may have been deeply involved in child rapes.

Having been paid for his services with a substantial amount of money, The Kid now reveals a deeper aspect of his being, having to face the moral dilemma of returning the money—wanting no gains from a man who might have participated in these horrendous acts—or accepting the $10,000 cash, which would allow him to continue to feed his old dog, his eccentric parrot, and himself for an indefinite period of time. Finally, it depends on what The Kid wants to believe, whether he can make a leap of faith or will return to the cynicism of his self-protective past.

When The Kid finally discovers that the Dr. Hoo of the emails committed suicide by gunpoint years earlier, he accepts the Professor's own depiction of reality, which, in turn, permits him finally to begin to perceive himself as a real human being with a third dimension, a moral conscience which has a reality and a standing in the world. Returning to the causeway, The Kid now perceives himself as "guilty," as a man who has made wrong choices, and he is determined to create a different, more substantial self, while the authorial stand-in moves in with Banks' warmest character, the Professor's librarian wife, Gloria.

Banks' issues are profound moral American dilemmas that have no easy answers. At times, for my taste, the author moves too closely to correct thinking, arguing simplistically for the psychological motivations of his figures related to their lack of self-worth and other societal deficiencies. In his disapproval of the internet addiction of too many children and adults, Banks even goes so far as to suggest that our society, in its endless fascination with the internet and pornography, is being transformed into a world of two-dimensional beings— to my thinking a kind of clichéd vision, a presumption that "pornography" is necessarily at the center of a horrific cultural transformation. In truth, pornography, in one form or another, has always been there. The issues Banks brings forward, however, are important ones, worthy of being thought about with the greatest of subtlety, without religious and moral prejudice. And overall, Banks has gone further than most writers in helping US readers to begin to recognize these important issues concerning what to do with people who sexually and socially "cross the line," Banks suggesting that there may be a way to bring them back into society instead of pretending to exterminate them by continued imprisonment or damning them to outcast, leper-like colonies.

Despite his recognition of "guilt," The Kid is still more innocent at fiction's end than most of us, and is also one of us. Instead of being cast out of our midst, perhaps he should be carefully embraced, something that might have made him years earlier come to understand that he had a body, that his skin was something not only to be pulled upon, but to be warmly and lovingly touched.

ST. COLLEGE, PENNSYLVANIA, APRIL 2, 2012
Reprinted [in a different version] from *Rain Taxi* (Summer 2012).

An Overwhelming Desire

NOËL COWARD, ANTHONY HAVELOCK-ALLAN, DA-
VID LEAN, AND RONALD NEAME (UNCREDITED, BASED
ON A PLAY BY NOËL COWARD), DAVID LEAN (DIRECTOR)
BRIEF ENCOUNTER / 1945, USA 1946

FLIP THROUGH ALMOST any standard video guide and you will read of the high praises for David Lean's romantic melodrama, *Brief Encounter*—so much so that, at times, one might almost think of the film as a British classic. *Halliwell's Film Guide* (a volume intolerant to most movies) declares of the film, for example, "An outstanding example of good middle-class cinema turned by sheer professional craft into a masterpiece." On the other hand, as my favorite quick guide, *Time Out*, argues: "Much beloved, but still exemplary in demonstrating what is wrong with so much of British cinema."

The work has a story, even though it is hard to say the film has real "events." A suburban woman of Milford, England, Laura (Celia Johnson) once a week

travels to the city where, after shopping, she takes in a movie, returning by the evening train to her conventional marriage and two children. Much of the story centers around the small tearoom, and its mostly comical patrons, near the train's waiting platform, wherein travelers sip tea and munch on pastries.

On one such visit, Laura stands on the platform when another train, not stopping there, passes, throwing a small cinder into her eye. Inside the tearoom she asks for a glass a water to wash her eye free of the painful bit of grit, whereupon a man, Alec Harvey (Trevor Howard), stands up to help, noting that he is a doctor.

This simple event is almost forgotten until the following week when the two run into each other again, this time at a busy restaurant where almost every table is taken. Accordingly, the two share a table and, later, an afternoon at the movie house. Charmed by the idealistic doctor, Laura also intrigues the married Alec with her strong sense of self and her easy laugh (as he later puts it: "I love you. I love your wide eyes, the way you smile, your shyness, and the way you laugh at my jokes"). Feeling a bit guilty, the couple furtively make plans to repeat their outing the next week, but this time the doctor, who fills in once a week at the local hospital for a friend, does not show up until Laura is at the tearoom, where he hurriedly explains his absence as his train, traveling in the opposite direction as hers, arrives. The two again plan an outing the next week.

Their next venture together, a comical boating trip downstream, quickly develops into a furtive relationship, in which they both admit their love for one another. When they take a drive into the country on this penultimate meeting, however, he purposely misses his train, intending to stay at his doctor-friend's flat, into

which he invites her. She refuses, returning to the station and her voyage back to Milford, but, at the very last moment, rushes from her train, running through the rain to the flat in which she has left Alec. At almost the same instant she arrives, however, the friend returns early, so that she is forced to rush out the back entrance, ashamed for what has almost occurred.

Realizing the impossibility of their relationship, and the dark consequences arising in both their relationships with their spouses, he announces upon their final meeting that he will be traveling with his family to Africa, and will never see her again. Painfully, they sit together in the tearoom—which, in fact, has been the very first scene of the film—awaiting perhaps a tender goodbye, until one of Laura's chattering, suburban friends enters, and the two are unable to say anything. When Alec's train arrives, he has no option but to gently squeeze her shoulder before disappearing forever, Laura rushing out of the tearoom as another train passes, possibly intending suicide to squelch what she describes as:

> I had no thoughts at all, only an overwhelming desire not to feel anything ever again.

She returns, however, to the tearoom, riding home with her incessantly chatting friend to suffer out the night, while she mentally repeats the events to her seemingly unaware husband, as he studies a crossword puzzle. When they are about to go up to bed, he approaches her.

> FRED JESSON: You've been a long way away.
> LAURA JESSON: Yes.
> FRED JESSON: Thank you for coming back to me.

So this tale of guilt for an imaginative, if not actual, sexual digression ends.

Perhaps in the immediate postwar context of

English and American life, wherein returning soldiers might have wondered about the faithfulness of their wives during their absence, this all meant something. Lean seems to focus on the chastity of Laura despite her duplicity and her would-be faithlessness. The lure of illicit sex seems perfectly balanced with the draws of home and hearth.

Yet the dramatization of these events, accompanied by the lush romanticism of Sergei Rachmaninoff's Piano Concerto No. 2, seems almost goofy, as if some high drama where being played throughout perfectly ordinary events. As Laura herself describes her condition, she is almost hysterical about feelings that "can't last."

> This misery can't last. I must remember that and try to control myself. Nothing lasts really. Neither happiness nor despair. Not even life lasts very long. There'll come a time in the future when I shan't mind about this anymore, when I can look back and say quite peacefully and cheerfully how silly I was.

Yet she does not want to forget, but to remember, for Alec is clearly the superior of the two men in her life, just as we suspect (without ever being allowed to see Alec's wife) that Laura is a better choice for his love. At

 least Alec is allowed to have an adventure: he is on his way, after all, to Africa, while Laura must remain in the little community of Milford with no real excitement the passion she has inwardly felt. One almost feels she has been a bit betrayed by her creators, who have asked her to express such intense emotions for no sensual rewards. What is there even that she might be allowed to remember?

The film, accordingly, has riled up (for both its central character and its audience) feelings that are never fulfilled, transforming it from being a true romance or even a melodrama into merely a symbol of one. It's so hard to get excited, I am afraid, over a symbol. One has to ask, what is all the fuss about? Although Laura may have temporarily been caught up in an "overwhelming desire," this viewer, at least, is thoroughly underwhelmed.

LOS ANGELES, MARCH 23, 2012
Reprinted from *World Cinema Review* (March 2012).

Pleasure, Passion, Lust

TERENCE DAVIES (SCREENPLAY, BASED ON THE
PLAY BY TERENCE RATTIGAN), TERENCE DAVIES (DIREC-
TOR) **THE DEEP BLUE SEA** / 2011, USA 2012

ALTHOUGH DIRECTOR Terence Davies admits to some
admiration for David Lean's *Brief Encounter*, with nods
to it in his new film, *The Deep Blue Sea*, I would argue
that the two are utterly different in their approaches
and impacts. Certainly both films are stories of illicit
love affairs in postwar England, a time when such behavior was not only—to use the language of the day—
"frowned upon," but was actually scandalous, particularly for the upper class, to which the heroine of Davies'
work belongs. And both films end with their couples
parting company, leaving them, especially their wom-
en, lonely and romantically "devastated." But whereas
Lean's heroine does not engage in sex and has little to
show for her "romantic slip," Lady Hester Collyer (the
radiant Rachel Weisz) of *The Deep Blue Sea* is a woman

of passion whose only link with her lover, Freddie Page (Tom Hiddleston), is sex. While the suburban housewife of *Brief Encounter* is a meek and shy lover, Hester, as her *Scarlet Letter*-first name implies, is not only sexually active, but is a passionate woman determined, despite the mores of the day, to engage her whole being in sexuality. Like D. H. Lawrence's male figures or the exceptional Lady Chatterly, Hester—as opposed to the advice of her dreadful mother-in-law—is willing commit herself wholeheartedly to passion, or, as her husband, Sir William Collyer describes it, lust. At the end of the day (and the movie), unlike the regretful Laura of Lean's work, Hester is fully aware of what she has had and what she will now miss. Finally, Davies' work, unlike Lean's tepid black-and-white tea-shop drama, is a richly dark, color rendering of the cheap rooming house and backstreet bar which Hester has  chosen over her beautiful but deadly boring manor house life.

That is not to say she is any happier than Laura at film's end. If anything, Laura will go on living as a faithful wife and mother, while Laura will face, perhaps, poverty and sexual deprivation. But at least Hester knows who she is. Her only real failure in life is her attempted suicide at the film's beginning, an event which catapults her into the haunting loneliness she must face at the end.

As opposed to Rattigan's chatty and somewhat musty melodrama, Davies (with the expressed permission of the Rattigan estate) plunges the audience into the midst of Hester's inner life through its presentation of a woman so unhappy with her lot that she is determined to die. Not only does she feed herself her numerous barbiturates, Hester turns on the gas full blast as she sits patiently down to face her end. Her busybody landlady, Mrs. Elton (Ann Mitchell), and medically knowledgeable neighbor, however, come to the rescue, saving her life. But it is the aftermath and her retrieval of a suicide note to her lover, which he later discovers, that do her in.

Having long ago left her libido-less husband, the boring Judge Collyer (played by the excellent actor Simon Russell Beale), Hester has taken up with a dashing former pilot, Freddie, who, as she herself later explains, has no life beyond 1940, the dark days of the war in which he and friends lived out daring adventures. Like millions of World War II men, Freddie never got "over" the war, not because of its horrors, but because of the deep bonding between men that the war encouraged. Although Freddie is clearly a handsomely potent heterosexual on the outside and, apparently, an excellent lover, he has no "feeling" for women, no emotional way to truly relate to Hester, something that she has recognized from the very beginning of their relationship, and yet is at the heart of her sorrow: he can never reach the depths of her emotional commitment.

Far more sensitive, if almost asexual, is her wealthy husband. He would never go off golfing and forget his wife's birthday, which Freddie has. He would never brutally scream at her for seeking out culture, for desiring to engage her mind as well as her body. But then, William would prefer sleeping—as his mother and father clearly did—in separate beds. He is the kind of man, the son of the kind of woman, who, as Davies re-

cently comically described in a *Los Angeles Times* interview, knows exactly how to spoon up soup: employing the spoon in the direction away from the diner, into the center of the bowl, instead of from the center toward oneself (as a Cambridge attendee of Davies' movies explained to him). The action of the disavowal of self is symbolic, one might argue, and is at the heart of their loveless relationship: Sir Collyer has no self from which to love, while Hester would devour life—certainly a dangerous position to be in after the self-sacrifice and destruction of war-torn London, an image of which Davies leaves the viewer with at film's close.

The problem with Hester is that she is a sensualist at a time when the society as a whole has been diminished, individuals transformed from living, breathing humans into somewhat frightened prescribers of the principles of life. Passion, as Hester's mother-in-law has proclaimed, is a dangerous thing. Even her flowers, which Hester is passionate about, give her only pleasure, as if that were the best one might expect from life. As the Pages' landlady puts it, "Love is about wiping your lover's ass," about being there day after day, and not worth killing oneself over!

In his own way, Hester's Freddie is also willing to take chances, determined as he is to return to work as a test pilot as soon as he becomes sober again. Yet his adventure is one that excludes others except those of his same sex. And in that sense, although he may be a wonderful lover in bed, he is almost as sexless in life as Sir Collyer! Here, unlike Lean's hysterically loyal Laura, Hester has—again as Lawrence might have put it—"come through" in the penultimate scene of Davies' beautiful film, boldly pulling open the curtains as she stands determinedly looking out to the street, facing forward to the future.

LOS ANGELES, MARCH 26, 2012
Reprinted from N^{th} Position (April 2012).

Breaking Up is Hard to Do

IRA SACHS AND MAURICIO ZACHARIAS (SCREEN-
PLAY), IRA SACHS (DIRECTOR) **KEEP THE LIGHTS ON** /
2012

THE FIRST FEATURE FILM of documentary filmmaker Ira Sachs still seems, in its unremitting linear
structure—portraying 10 years of a complex and difficult relationship between two young gay men in New
York—very much like a documentary film. Although
Sachs has made clear that a great deal of this film is fictional, it is based on his past relationship with a closeted literary agent, Bill Clegg (Zachary Booth in the
film, who works as a publishing-house lawyer), and he
and his co-writer created many of the films memorable
scenes by perusing his journal of the 10 years of his own
fraught relationship, also recounted in a book by Sachs'
ex-lover.

Like many documentaries, the film begins with a
defining event and expresses its story through a series

of revealing scenes that convey the vagaries of the story and point up the inevitable outcome—in this case, the end of their relationship. And, in that sense, this film lacks the substantive richness that might have been achieved by occasionally focusing on characters other than the director's stand-in himself (in the movie a Danish documentary filmmaker, Erik [Thure Lindhardt]) and Paul. Although, by the end of the movie, we do have some idea of the problems facing both these young men, it would have helped, moreover, if the filmmaker and his co-author had somehow given us a few clues, without over-psychologizing the work, as to how these two had developed into the ciphers who, through a casual sexual hookup, suddenly fall in love.

Part of the difficulties facing them has simply to do with the time of their encounter, beginning in 1998 and moving over a span of 10 years, when the quick sex of bar life, having been replaced with furtive cell-phone hookups, turned into a kind of hyper-kinetic speed-dating converted into speed-dialing. The dark specter of death, in the form of AIDS, has now spread over everything. When you add to this Paul's closeted sexuality and drug addiction, doom is in the air from the very beginning. Finally, there is the charming Erik's own addiction to casual sex and his failure to express his life fully to others, and we suddenly realize that theirs is clearly a world of quick fixes instead of coherent social behavior.

 In some senses, despite its deep honesty about the behavior of gays which still may shock some heterosexuals—who often pretend their own aberrations are "normal"—Sachs' film is not so much a "gay" film as it is, like Andrew Haigh's *Weekend* of last year, a film about a relationship and the problems those involved encounter.

Despite the fact that the film is so plot-heavy, the characters, particularly Erik, are absolutely charming. Both Erik—who underneath his sexual addiction truly seeks a monogamous relationship and, as the director reveals again and again, to use the cliché, is "head-over-heels" in love with the attractive Paul—and his companion seem immediately right for one another, despite Paul's inability to totally commit. Paul is, nonetheless, a hard worker and, evidently, makes a decent salary. At several points in the story, Erik is needled (in one instance by his sister, in another by Paul himself) for not having "a job," as if working as a documentary artist were less a profession than a hobby. It is little wonder that, later in the film, Erik is attracted—both physically and psychologically—by a young gay man, Igor, who is studying to be an "artist." The wage-earners of this

world, perhaps justifiably, but always mistakenly, are dismissive of those who create as opposed to those who work by the clock. Throughout *Keep the Lights On*, Paul insists he must work the next morning and, when morning arrives, that he is afraid he will be late. Such a mantra, in fact, becomes, at times, another ruse not to discuss the real issues at hand.

What we also discern early on is that it not only takes a great deal of time (four years, at least, for the film that Erik is working on) to accomplish his art, but it takes an enormous outpouring of money (I had earlier in the day watched Godard's *Tout va bien*, which begins with a satirical look at how much money a film takes to get made by showing check after check being torn away from a checkbook). Fortuitously, Erik appears to have been born into a fairly wealthy family, and his father has bankrolled his first film, a fact his well-off sister—who evidently feels she has more entitlement to the inheritance than her more-independent brother—somewhat maliciously reminds him of. Obviously, we must put Erik's fairly affluent upbringing and his ability to see the world both from a European and an American point of view (Paul is his first American boyfriend) into the brew of their bubbling relationship.

For the first several "scenes" of this film, love seems to dominate, as, despite occasional instances—for example, when the two male lovers encounter Paul's girlfriend visiting the same gallery in which they are strolling—they seem truly to discover and enjoy one another. Erik's few friends, mostly straight co-workers, are enchanted by his new love interest, and the couple seem on their way—despite the dreadful times—to some sense of permanence. Paul is both beautiful and intelligent; Erik almost boyishly hopeful and creative. It is a couple everyone who loves happiness might envy.

Yet Erik's travels for his work breed difficulties, deep-lined resentments, and simple temptations for his mate. Telephoning home, he is met increasingly with unanswered calls, long silences, and, upon returning, with equally unexplained absences. When Paul sees Erik even talking with a young man on the street, he goes into a quiet frenzy, determined to spend the night on the couch, Erik equally determined to force him back into bed. Erik's increasing attempts to save Paul from himself further send Paul into the drugged-out corners of his life. The very night Erik wins a "Teddy" in Berlin (an award for documentary film, which, co-incidentally, the director has since won), Paul is not to be found, and upon Erik's return to New York he discovers that his lover has been missing—clearly on a drug binge—for several days. With Erik's insistence and caring, Paul suffers a several-month rehabilitation program, but as part of the program, must keep away sexually for a period from the very man who has saved him. Erik's loving tribute to Paul and his courageousness at a Christmas dinner party only exacerbates Paul's sensitivity.

Life goes on. But when Erik is given the possibility of working in a writers' colony, Paul again goes missing. Erik's return to reclaim him is the most powerful and perverse scene in the movie, as he discovers the missing Paul in a hotel room, after days of crack-cocaine, awaiting the services of a hustler whom he has hired to fuck him brutally, obviously as self-punishment and also in a desperate attempt to reclaim his own being. He insists Erik leave, that he not be witness to his drugs and self-immolation, but Erik, almost saintly but also clearly out of intense love, remains—at first painfully separated in the other room, but when his name is called, coming into the bedroom to hold his lover's hand at the very moment he is being roughly screwed. I know there are millions of Americans who will not understand this scene as one of the deepest expressions of love and compassion, but they are, quite simply, mistaken. Yet Erik's great sacrifice can only come with further expectations and disappointments. It is followed with a subterfuge visit—in Erik's own enactment of self-hatred—to one of his earlier sexual partners, an exhibitionist, slob of a human being who represents Erik's polar opposite.

Paul returns to therapy, joining his friend again on a night where they lie next to one another naked without—through his insistence, evidently part of the therapy—their being able to have sex. Erik is so delighted just for Paul's presence that he will not allow the lights to go out; Erik wants to see, to "witness" the embodiment of his love.

It is at that very moment that we realize there has been a deep toll to pay. The couple, spending a few days at a country retreat, might as well be on different planets, Erik, perhaps because of his lover's continued abstinence of sex (which is, after all, for both men, another kind of drug), quietly masturbating in the woods before demanding a discussion with Paul about their future. For once, Paul turns the tables, demanding Erik express his own feelings rather than passively relying on

him, insisting that Erik take responsibility for his own emotions. But even here, Erik bases his responses on his lover's. "What do *you* want?"

To our surprise, Paul suggests that they return to living together. But this time, he gives no room for equivocation. He demands Erik make his decision in three hours. As Erik drives Paul to the train station, intending himself to return to New York the next day, Paul demands his decision. Erik agrees to continue the relationship.

We all may hope for that. Certainly my companion, Howard—with whom I have lived through mostly good times, but many difficult periods as well, for almost 43 years—desired the happy ending. Yet such an ending might have required these two to go on living in their own very different realities, lying to themselves about their own natures, despite the deep love that they obviously hold for one another. Upon Erik's return to New York, Paul again asks the question. For once, Erik is completely honest with himself, despite his need to see things the way they "should be," instead of the way they are. He has decided to abandon what for a decade he has worked to maintain.

That is the way most relationships end; and most relationships, unfortunately, do end these days. At least here, both men end in a hug instead of hatred, and move on with their lives. Perhaps that happens only in movies, but I'd like to think that at least the ending of Sachs' moving and honest film was closer to a documentation of the facts than a fiction.

LOS ANGELES, SEPTEMBER 14, 2012
Reprinted from *N^th Position* [England] (October 2012).

Something Rotten in Denmark

NIKOLAJ ARCEL AND RASMUS HEISTERBERG
(SCREENPLAY, BASED ON A BOOK BY BODIL STEENSEN-
LETH), NIKOLAJ ARCEL (DIRECTOR) **EN KONGELIG
AFFÆRE (A ROYAL AFFAIR)** / 2012

IN 2009, in a conversation with Polish writer-director
Zbigniew Kaminski, I was asked if I knew of any good
new books which he might adapt for film production in
Poland. Having just read Per Olav Enquist's historical
fiction, *The Royal Physician's Visit* (see *My Year 2001*),
I suggested that title and, if I remember correctly, even
loaned him my copy of the book.

He felt, evidently, since the film would have to be
shot in Denmark, it would be too expensive for his
company. However, some film company did ultimately
buy those rights, planning to make an English-language
movie, but they evidently had difficulty in getting
funding.

Meanwhile Zentropa Entertainments, Danmarks

Radio, and a consortium of other producers sold the same story, this time based on a work by Bodil Steensen-Leth, *Prinsesse af blodet*. Knowing of the other project, the scriptwriters, Nikolaj Arcel (also its director) and Rasmus Heisterberg, worked hard with Enquist to discover what was documented and what were the fictional scenes that he had added in order to avoid any question of rights.

The result, *A Royal Affair* (2012), is a resplendent tale of the beautiful Caroline Matilda of Great Britain (Alicia Vikander), her mad young husband Christian VII of Denmark (Mikkel Følsgaard), and Johann Friedrich Struensee (Mads Mikkelsen), the royal physician with whom Matilda has an affair.

With the royal court as its setting, the film is breathtakingly lovely to look at, and the plot is filled with court intrigue, particularly with the plotting of Ove Høegh-Guldberg (David Dencik) and the queen dowager, Juliana Maria of Brunswick-Wolfenbüttel (Trinen Dyrholm). Yet Struensee is himself involved in an attempted takeover of the government, working with two former courtiers, Enevold Brandt (Cyron Bjørn Melville) and Schack Carl Rantzau (Thomas W. Gabrielsson).

But the real center of this film is revealed early on in the quick transformation from the medievally-run country of 18th Denmark into an enlightened nation, the fact of which led Voltaire himself to pen a letter to the King. To bring this about, Struensee, a reader of enlightenment writers such as Jean-Jacques Rousseau and Voltaire, manipulates his young royal charge to oppose of privy council—who actually rule the country while Christian VII merely adds his signature—and to pass radical changes for the good of the Danish people, including universal inoculation against smallpox, a clean-up of Copenhagen's filthy streets, and other important changes...some 1,069 decrees in all.

In Enquist's version of the tale, Christian—whose major passions appear to be theater and whores—is perceived as quite literally mad; but in the film we are more uncertain about his mental instability, having to wonder, as the wise physician seems to suggest, if it isn't simply a pose to free himself from the responsibilities of state. As he says early on in his battles with the privy council:

> Who is more disturbed, the King or someone who believes the Earth was created in six days?

Struensee, who quickly befriends Christian, does free the young king from his passive role by reciting Christian's daily new proposals and, ultimately, after doing away with the privy council, taking over the bill-signing himself.

Although Matilda does have a son with Christian, Frederick, mostly she is deserted, kept apart in an unfriendly world where even several of the books she has brought with her from England are taken away, having been banned in Denmark.

Is it any wonder that, as the physician and she come together to discuss ideas, she falls passionately in love with Struensee, becoming pregnant with his daughter, who later would be related to many of Europe's royal families? Her daughter, Caroline Amalie, for example, would become Queen of Denmark.

In a sense Matilda, whom Christian continually refers to as "mother," and Struensee, who clearly plays the role of a loving and doting father, are almost des-

tined to have their own spousal-like relationship, the latter joining her in bed every night. And at moments, particularly when the troubled Christian falls into the arms of the genial and clearly loving physician, it almost seems that the relationship between this trio is a kind of perverse *ménage-a-trois*, particularly when, discovering that she is pregnant with Struensee's daughter, Matilda is forced to encourage Christian to return to her bed as a ruse to hide the fact that her child is a bastard.

When the queen dowager actually does perceive that Matilda and Struensee are in love, however, there is little hope for Struensee's life, even though Christian is quite ready to forgive him and stay his execution. But the privy council has returned to power, and the evil Høegh-Guldberg ignores Christian's reprieve, beheading one of the few men of the country who had a truly good mind and caring constitution.

Matilda is sent away, but her son Frederick eventually comes to power, an afternote letting us know that he later restored many of the reformations previously ordered by his father, and imagined by his physician.

Although many of the incidents presented in the movie are fictions, most of them did occur. And the only truly unbelievable aspect of this film is that the scenes we are witnessing come from a long epistle Matilda is writing to explain  her actions to her children. As several critics noted, had she actually written such a letter, it would surely have gotten into the hands of enemies, and would probably have resulted in the death of her daughter. In reality, this unhappy young queen kept her silence in painful isolation, returning to England to become involved with charities.

In the end, we might almost see this film as a presaging of the liberal, open-minded, and economically successful country that Denmark is today. Perhaps the royalty, after years of inbreeding, needed a good dose of German peasant stock from a country doctor. If nothing else, Matilda, brought an aura of what Christian describes as "the dramatic" into the oppressive Danish court. It's too bad that this film did not incorporate the fact that Matilda, far from being the fragile beauty as she is here represented, often appeared in men's clothing and appeared at formal occasions in riding breeches.

LOS ANGELES, DECEMBER 23, 2012
Reprinted from *World Cinema Review* (December 2012).

The Conscience of a King

NICOLA FRANCESCO HAYM (LIBRETTO, BASED ON A LIBRETTO BY ANTONIO SALVI), GEORGE FRIDERIC HANDEL (COMPOSER) **RODELINDA** / THE PERFORMANCE I SAW WAS A LIVE HD BROADCAST FROM THE METROPOLITAN OPERA OF NEW YORK ON DECEMBER 3, 2011

ON THE SURFACE *Rodelinda* seems like a somewhat confusing story about a King, Bertarido (Andreas Scholl), who has just been defeated, and presumably killed, by Grimoaldo (Joseph Kaiser). The former queen, Rodelinda (Renée Fleming), and her son Flavio are immediately arrested and put into chains, sequestered away—at least in the Met production—in what seems like an abandoned bedroom somewhere in the bowels of the castle.

Before Grimoaldo's usurpation of the throne, he had been offered the hand of Bertarido's sister, Eduige (Stephanie Blythe), which would have made him the

 heir apparent to the throne, but she had several times denied him; and now that he has illegally taken over, he lusts for Bertarido's widow, Rodelinda. When he approaches her with his desires, however, she is outraged and insists upon her devotion to her former husband and the protection of his child.

Meanwhile Grimoaldo's advisor Garibaldo (Shenyang) prods his master on to more evil deeds, insisting that only the forceful, even the brutal, are fit to rule. He has his own plans, moreover, to take the throne for himself by marrying Eduige and becoming the rightful ruler.

Only the court advisor Unulfo (Iestyn Davies) knows that Bertarido is still alive, pretending death in order to evaluate the situation and retrieve Rodelinda and his son from harm's way.

Through her lovely arias we know that Rodelinda is loyal to her husband, denying the approaches of Grimoaldo. But when Bertarido is hidden away in a nearby horse barn by his friend Unulfo, he overhears yet another encounter between Rodelinda and Grimoaldo in which she first insists of her love for her dead husband, but then suddenly seems to change heart, accepting Grimoaldo's proposal of marriage. What the two men hiding in the barn do not see is that Garibaldo has threatened to kill her son if she does not give in, putting a knife to the son's neck.

Suddenly Bertarido's world collapses around him as he believes that his wife has not been able to remain faithful. Unulfo attempts to cheer him with an aria that relays the underlying theme of Handel's work: what seems unbearable today will look different in the future. Performed as it is between the two countertenors, there is a slightly homoerotic suggestion in the plea that Bertarido should try to forget his wife's faithlessness.

Unulfo suggests that Bertarido tell his wife that he is still living, an idea which, at first, Bertarido rejects, but then perceives it will help to torture her for her deeds. It soon becomes apparent, however, that Rodelinda has no intentions of becoming Grimoaldo's wife, insisting that if she is to marry him he must personally kill her young son, that she cannot be a mother to the boy who would have been king and wife of the throne's usurper both. The ploy works, as Grimoaldo backs down, and Rodelinda is freed, temporarily at least, from any vows.

Meanwhile, Eduige discovers that her brother is still alive, meeting him upon a pathway in the night, reassuring Bertarido of his wife's constancy. Unulfo brings Rodelinda to him, and the two are lovingly reunited, joyful to be in each other's company again. At that very moment, however, they are discovered by Grimoaldo, who orders Bertarido's arrest and death.

In collaboration, Eduige and Unulfo plan Bertarido's rescue, she secretly passing him a sword, Unulfo determined to lead him through a secret garden passage to his son so he can escape. However, when Unulfo comes to guide Bertarido to safety, in the dark room where he lies Bertarido mistakes the intruder for  one of Grimoaldo's henchmen come to kill him, and he stabs Unulfo, who, although badly wounded, still pulls Bertarido to safety.

Grimoaldo, meanwhile, is in deep torment. All that he has sought has slipped through his fingers. His first love Eduige has rejected him and Rodelinda has declared him a monster. Power has not fulfilled him, and he is tormented by his conscience. Finding him in such despair, Garibaldo is disgusted with his lack of will and determines to put a sword through his heart. At that very moment Bertarido and his family are passing. The former king leaps into action, killing Garibaldo and, in so doing, saving Grimoaldo's life.

Recognizing his position, Grimoaldo is only too happy to give up the throne to its rightful king. Eduige finally accepts his apologies, and the happy survivors sing in celebration of the future.

Just recounting this breathless plot nearly exhausts me. One by one, each of the major performers sing marvelous arias, revealing their feelings and situations. This production was particularly blessed with the glorious soprano of Renée Fleming who premiered as Rodelinda at the Met in 2004. Both countertenors were splendid, while Stephanie Blythe performed with her usual high artistry. The surprise of the opera, to me, was the tenor Joseph Kaiser, who as the opera proceeded changed in both costume and voice from a seemingly pompous and puffed-up murderer into a handsome man of sorrow and conscience. It was a remarkably revealing performance, both in its musical expression and acting abilities.

In all, this was a marvelous opera. If only the director, Stephen Wadsworth—who the singers all highly praised—had not felt it necessary to keep everything in motion by bringing in and out ancillary individuals during each aria, and arming his singers with flowerpots, books, even toys, which at some point were often flung or crashed into the set. We understand that Handel's arias are structured with a beginning theme

that is elaborated on and repeated several times before returning us to the original theme, but that does not mean that we need to be continually distracted. If the singers are good enough actors—as all of these were—to revitalize and slightly revise each repeated phrase, the music enwraps us in a kind of trance that works against this production's realist interruptions.

Although he is a powerful storyteller and a masterful dramatist, Handel is not Verdi.

Nonetheless, with such great singers I would love to see the Met look into yet more Handel and other Baroque operas. *Rodelinda* was a joy.

LOS ANGELES, DECEMBER 9, 2011
Reprinted from *Green Integer Blog* (December 2011).

Index

GREEN INTEGER
Pataphysics and Pedantry
Douglas Messerli, *Publisher*

Essays, Manifestos, Statements, Speeches, Maxims,
Epistles, Diaristic Notes, Narrative, Natural Histories,
Poems, Plays, Performances, Ramblings, Revelations and
all such ephemera as may appear necessary to bring society
into a slight tremolo of confusion and fright at least.

Individuals may order through www.greeninteger.com
Bookstores and libraries should order through our distributor
Consortium Book Sales & Distribution / Ingram Books
(800) 283-3572 / www.cbsd.com

*

SELECTED NEW TITLES

Paul Celan *Lightduress* [1-931243-75-1] $19.95 [REPRINT]
Maria Irene Fornes *Abingdon Square* [1-892295-64-4] $19.95 [REPRINT]
Jean Grenier *Islands: Lyrical Essays* [1-892295-95-4] $19.95 [REPRINT]
Atilla Jozsef *A Transparent Lion* [978-1-933382-50-0] $19.95 [REPRINT]
Ko Un *Songs for Tomorrow: A Collection of Poems 1960-2002* [978-1-933382-70-8] $19.95 [REPRINT]
  Ten Thousand Lives [1-933382-06-6] $19.95 [REPRINT]
Vladimir Mayakovsky *Vladimir Mayakovsky: A Tragedy* [978-1-55713-444-8] $19.95
Douglas Messerli *My Year 2000: Leaving Something Behind* [978-1-55713-443-1] $15.95
  My Year 2011: No One's Home [978-1-55713-442-4] $15.95
  Stay [978-1-55713-447-9] $12.95
Steven Moore *My Back Pages* [978-1557134387] $23.00
Toby Olson *The Life of Jesus: An Apocryphal Novel* [978-1-55713-441-7] $19.95
Gertrude Stein *Tender Buttons* [1-931243-42-5] $19.95 [REPRINT]
  Three Lives [1-892295-33-4] $19.95 [REPRINT]
Paul Verlaine *The Cursed Poets* [1-931243-15-8] $19.95 [REPRINT]